P9-EJI-354

Axis Sally

Axis Sally

THE AMERICAN VOICE OF NAZI GERMANY

By
RICHARD LUCAS

CASEMATE

Philadelphia & Newbury

Published in the United States of America and Great Britain in 2010 by
CASEMATE
908 Darby Road, Havertown, PA 19083
and
17 Cheap Street, Newbury, Berkshire, RG14 5DD

Copyright 2010 © Richard Lucas

ISBN 978-1-935149-43-9

Cataloging-in-publication data is available from the Library of Congress
and the British Library.

All rights reserved. No part of this book may be reproduced or transmitted in
any form or by any means, electronic or mechanical including photocopying,
recording or by any information storage and retrieval system, without
permission from the Publisher in writing.

10 9 8 7 6 5 4 3 2 1

Printed and bound in the United States of America.

For a complete list of Casemate titles please contact:

CASEMATE PUBLISHERS (US)
Telephone (610) 853-9131, Fax (610) 853-9146
E-mail: casemate@casematepublishing.com

CASEMATE PUBLISHERS (UK)
Telephone (01635) 231091, Fax (01635) 41619
E-mail: casemate-uk@casematepublishing.co.uk

Mixed Sources
Product group from well-managed
forests and other controlled sources
www.fsc.org Cert no. SW-COC-002283
© 1996 Forest Stewardship Council
FSC

Contents

For Jordan and Taylor

Preface

While browsing through a website devoted to rare and historic audio clips in 2003, I first heard the voice of Axis Sally. This woman (Mildred Gillars) was the notorious Nazi propagandist whose theme song *Lili Marlene* became an international favorite during and after the war. Despite her undeniable skills as a broadcaster, the recording also featured a vile anti-Semitism rant. Insinuating that Franklin Roosevelt was a homosexual surrounded by Jewish "boyfriends," her words were jarring and repulsive. Yet I wondered how Mildred Gillars, who described herself as a "100% American girl," became a willing mouthpiece for a genocidal regime. How did this woman with middle-class Ohio roots end up on the wrong side of history, convicted of aiding the Nazi regime and betraying her country? I looked for a biography that answered the question, but none existed. Books on the subject of treason mentioned her in passing and tended to focus on her illicit relationship with a former Hunter College professor who served as her "Svengali." Her *New York Times* obituary in November 1988 focused on the *"frisson"* her somewhat scandalous testimony caused at her 1949 trial.

As I listened to the Axis Sally audio clips that first day, I noticed that one of the recordings featured another woman with an American accent. Her on-air sidekick addressed her as "Sally" but the voice was clearly not that of Mildred Gillars. Aware of the circumstances that led to the conviction of Iva Toguri d'Aquino as the one and only Tokyo Rose (in fact, there had been several other women employed by

Japanese radio who broadcast under the moniker "Orphan Ann"), I wondered how many other Axis Sallies there might have been, and whether any of those women were punished as Gillars and d'Aquino were.

A visit to the National Archives in College Park, Maryland to look at the Department of Justice's "Notorious Offenders" case files on Axis Sally, as well as a telephone conversation with John Carver Edwards (the author of the excellent 1991 book *Berlin Calling*, about Americans who broadcast for the Third Reich) convinced me to write a factual, documented biography of Axis Sally. Over the next seven years of research and writing, I discovered a deeply flawed but fascinating woman whose thirst for fame led her to the heart of Hitler's Germany; whose hope for love and marriage convinced her to remain; and whose inner strength compelled her to survive in the death-strewn shelters and cellars of defeated Berlin.

In my younger years, I was a devoted listener to shortwave radio. The radio waves were a battleground of the Cold War in those days. Radio Moscow, Radio Peking, Radio Liberty and Radio Free Europe were propaganda powerhouses that fought for the hearts and minds of countless millions for whom radio was their only link to the developed world. In the darkest and farthest reaches of the earth, the signal from the shortwave transmitters represented nations and peoples and political ideologies. It was Joseph Goebbels who envisioned the power of the medium long before the advent of the Second World War. By 1940, Berlin's foreign radio service sang the praises of Adolf Hitler and the new Germany twenty-four hours a day in twelve languages. An unemployed American named Mildred Gillars stepped into that burgeoning radio empire and became, along with William Joyce ("Lord Haw Haw"), one of the regime's most effective propagandists.

Today, radio is arguably one of the most pervasive means of political persuasion. One wonders how a woman with the innate talents of Mildred Gillars would have fared in her native land in a more forgiving time.

Richard Lucas
September 2010

Acknowledgments

I wish to thank the many people whose dedicated assistance made this book a reality. First and foremost is Rita Rosenkranz of Rita Rosenkranz Literary Agency, whose faith in this project has been nothing short of heroic. Martin Noble of AESOP, Oxford, UK provide proofreading, editing and became a friend over the course of five years. Kay Schlichting and Emily Haddaway of the Ohio Wesleyan University Historical Archives were extremely helpful in the process of researching Mildred Gillars' college years. Gail Connors of the Conneaut Public Library in Conneaut, Ohio provided a wonderful selection of contemporaneous newspaper accounts and items from high school yearbooks of long ago. Faye Haskins and Jason R. Moore of the Washingtoniania Collection of the District of Columbia Public Library located photographs from the defunct Washington Evening Star collection. These and so many other photographs would be lost to history without their dedicated care and maintenance. Mr. John Taylor and the staff at Archives II in College Park, Maryland deserve much thanks; as well as the very helpful staff of the Manuscript Division of the Library of Congress.

Paul Beekman Taylor and Walter Driscoll were extremely gracious as I traced the connection between Mildred Gillars, Bernard Metz and the Gurdjieff movement. I also owe a debt of gratitude to the journalists who tracked the story of Axis Sally. First, the late Ambassador John Bartlow Martin, whose papers possessed the only (albeit abridged) copy of the original trial transcript. Helene Anne Spicer generously shared her memories of interviewing Axis Sally. I am most grateful to Iris Wiley, Jim Dury and James Sauer who took the time to speak to me and remember Mildred Gillars' final years.

Most importantly, I thank my wife Sachi for her love and understanding throughout this experience; our two sons, Jordan and Taylor, who no longer have to ask "When will your book be finished?" Jordan, especially, deserves thanks for patiently spending many hours in libraries and archives near and far. Thank you to my parents, Richard and Gail Lucas, for their love and support.

Also, I would like to express my appreciation to:
Alexander Library, Rutgers University, New Brunswick, New Jersey; Archives II, National Archives and Records Administration, College Park Maryland; Beinecke Library at Yale University, New Haven, Connecticut; Bentley Historical Library, University of Michigan, Ann Arbor Michigan; Bishop Watterson High School Alumni Office, Columbus Ohio; Bishop Watterson High School, Columbus Ohio; Camden Historical Society, Camden New Jersey; Christine Witzmann, translator; Conneaut Public Library, Conneaut Ohio; District of Columbia Public Library, Washingtoniana Division, Washington DC; Harry S. Truman Presidential Library, Independence, Missouri; Hunter College Archives, New York, New York; John Carver Edwards; Molly E Tully; Jennifer Stepp of *Stars and Stripes;* Dr. Joachim Kundler; Library of Congress Manuscript Collection, Washington DC; Lyndon Baines Johnson Presidential Library, Austin Texas; Maine State Archives, Portland Maine; National Archives, Washington DC; Newspaper Archives; New York Public Library, New York, New York; Ohio Historical Society, Columbus Ohio; Paul Robeson Library, Rutgers University, Camden, New Jersey; Spike Lee; The late Stephen Bach for his encouragement; University of Delaware, Newark, Delaware; Guy Aceto, Weider History Group; Bill Horne, Karen Jensen and Caitlin Newman of *World War II* magazine.

Axis Sally

Prologue

January 1949: The US District Court in Washington, DC is teeming with reporters, photographers and curious onlookers. At the center of the mass of popping flashbulbs and shouting newsmen is a silver-haired former showgirl named Mildred Gillars, better known to thousands of GIs as "Axis Sally." Facing a possible death sentence for treason, the only crime specified in the United States Constitution, she is on trial for broadcasting radio propaganda aimed at demoralizing American troops in their struggle against Nazi Germany.

The world had changed since Axis Sally made her last broadcast in a besieged Berlin radio studio. Deteriorating relations between the victorious Allies preoccupied the postwar world. Communism and subversion from within was the latest threat to the American way of life. The trial of Axis Sally was front-page news, but it was a front page shared with headlines of the entry of Mao Tse Tung's forces into Peking and the continuing Cold War crisis over Berlin. Internal scandals had rocked the nation, including former Communist Party member Whittaker Chambers' revelation that Soviet agents, including senior State Department official Alger Hiss, had infiltrated the United States government and sabotaged foreign policy. President Harry S. Truman barely survived Governor Thomas Dewey's bid to unseat him and end sixteen straight years of Democratic rule. Faced with an uphill electoral battle, the Truman Administration needed to show that the President knew how to deal with America's enemies.

Two months before the November 1948 election, two infamous figures of World War II returned to the United States to face trial. One

1

was the Japanese-American Iva Toguri d'Aquino, one of several women who worked for Tokyo radio during the war and called herself "Orphan Ann." The soldiers and sailors in the Pacific theatre called her "Tokyo Rose." The other woman was a lesser-known but equally reviled American radio broadcaster who worked for Berlin's *Reichsradio*. Since March 1946 she had languished in an Allied internment camp without charges or the aid of counsel. On the radio, she went by the name Midge, but to the soldier in the field she was "Axis Sally." Her signature theme song, "Lili Marlene," was a worldwide hit, and she captured the imagination of the foot soldier with her seductive, lilting voice. Accompanied by a live orchestra playing the GIs' favorite jazz and swing music, Axis Sally had an audience of literally millions, despite the vile anti-Semitic propaganda she often offered on the side.

What drove the woman who proudly called herself "a 100% American girl" to collaborate with a genocidal regime? What forces made her cut the final tie to her native land and betray an entire nation? Mildred Gillars' story is one of poverty and hunger—a woman who, like the Führer she served, wished to accomplish great artistic feats but instead thrust herself into infamy. An ambitious female coping with the realities of her time, she was an attractive young woman who said "no" to marriage and instead relied on the good graces of a series of questionable men to achieve her dreams of independence and notoriety.

How that reliance played a central role in her descent into the ranks of traitor will become evident as this book examines the circumstances that led her to represent the Third Reich on radio. For the first time, the facts of Axis Sally's life will supplant the speculation and false claims that have worked their way into her life story over the decades. The myth of Axis Sally—the all-knowing, hate-filled disseminator of military and logistical information—needs to be reconsidered in light of declassified documents from the files of the FBI, the Department of Justice, the Office of Alien Property and the Army Counter-Intelligence Corps, as well as wartime records of the German Foreign Office.

Like Iva Toguri d'Aquino, who bore the punishment for several Tokyo Roses, there was more than one Axis Sally. Infantrymen in the deserts of North Africa and later in northern Europe heard one woman speak from Berlin, while another "Sally"—a native New Yorker—welcomed American troops to Italy from a studio in Rome. The book examines the deeds of Berlin's Axis Sally and the uneven justice meted out in the immediate aftermath of the Second World War. Not intended to be an *apologia* for a convicted traitor, this book aims to portray a life lived on the "wrong side of history" with compassion and insight.

CHAPTER 1

An Unwelcome Child

On a cold morning in October 1928 a slim, attractive woman walked into the Camden, New Jersey offices of the *The Evening Courier* newspaper. Teary-eyed, she approached the front desk and asked to place an advertisement for that day's edition. She identified herself as Mrs. Barbara Elliott and told the clerk that she was searching for her missing husband Charles, whom she had married only six weeks before. Her husband had left their New York apartment and never returned. A few days after his departure, Barbara discovered that she was expecting a child. A friend told her that he had spotted Charles in Camden, and the distraught mother-to-be had come to New Jersey in search of the man who had abandoned her.

The desk clerk knew a good human interest story when he heard one and called upstairs for a reporter to take down the woman's story. *The Evening Courier* regularly printed melodramatic stories about lucky Ziegfeld Follies dancers marrying wealthy heirs, lonely and lovesick women driven to suicide, and couples finding love against all odds. Because Camden is only a few miles across the river from Philadelphia, some of the stories printed in the local paper found their way to the wire services and the big New York newspapers. In a weary voice, Barbara Elliott told the newsman her sad story in detail.

It all began when a girlfriend invited her on a double date where she was introduced to a "dark, slender, ascetic-looking" man of thirty—a linguist and world traveler who regaled her with tales of his visits to Morocco, Singapore and Baghdad. Barbara was enthralled with the handsome, urbane stranger named Charles Elliott. The two couples danced the night away at a roadhouse in Greenwich, Connecticut. There, Barbara and Charles held hands under the table and were swept away with happiness.

Within twenty-four hours, the two lovers agreed to an "ultra-modern" marriage, with the understanding that if either party grew tired of the other—the marriage would end. Barbara explained their pact:

"It's the bonds that kill love. People must be free, untrammeled. Love must not be forced or shackled. . . . It was a mad thing to do, but to us it seemed so right. We were so much in love. And we agreed never to hold each other back. I would continue my work as interior decorator; he, his as a tour director and linguist. 'When love dies we will part,' we told each other. And so by leaving love free we hoped to keep it always."[1]

Two weeks later, it all fell apart. Charles promised to meet his wife for dinner but never returned. Heartache turned to panic when Barbara found out that she was pregnant: "I was frantic when I discovered a few days later that I would become a mother. Then a friend said he had seen Charles in Camden, at least he thought it was he and I came down here to search for him."[2] That evening, pressed in between articles about the political battle between Herbert Hoover and Governor Alfred E. Smith of New York for the White House, *The Evening Courier* told the shocking tale and launched a citywide search for the missing husband:

MISSING MATE SOUGHT BY COMPANIONATE BRIDE
Six Weeks of Marriage Was Unmarred by Rites or Contracts
CHILD NOW COMING WITH FATHER GONE
Not for Self, But for Baby She Says, She Hunts "Pal" Husband[3]

Anyone knowing the whereabouts of Charles Elliott, last heard of in Camden, will please inform him that he is about to become a father. His wife, Barbara, who is now registered at the Hotel Walt Whitman, pleads with him to forget the circumstances surrounding their marriage and the immediate separation, and believes that for the sake of all concerned reconciliation should be effected.[4]

The next morning Barbara telephoned the *Courier* reporter to thank him for his sympathy and kindness. In a voice choked with emotion and portent, she told him that the money for her hotel bill had been left on the nightstand. "They will understand," she said and abruptly hung up.[5] Barbara then called the Hotel Walt Whitman and told the front desk clerk to go upstairs to her room, where he would find something. He did—a suicide note written on hotel stationery:

> *To Whom It May Concern,*
>
> *It is not humanly possible to continue any longer this bitter agony of bringing into this poor, deluded world another unwelcome child. The few who may give my sorry act any thought at all will probably think only in a conventional way, saying "What a weak thing she must have been." Who will ever have the perception to realize that I am taking this step because I have an intelligence and soul that are sensitized to the nth degree?*
>
> *It is the greatest maternal tenderness I can bestow upon my dear child that I end my life with his that he may not be numbered among the hosts of unwelcome children.*
>
> *Barbara Elliott*[6]

Published in full on the front page of the *Courier*, the suicide note thrust Barbara Elliott into the spotlight. (See Appendix I for its full text.) Camden police were placed on alert and county detectives were told to be on the lookout for the deserted bride. A photograph of Barbara Elliott sitting on a wooden chair wearing a full-length fur coat and a hat popular among the flappers of the time was emblazoned on page one under the banner "Suicide." Although the *Courier* noted that the authorities considered "the possibility that Mrs. Elliott's unusual actions might be in the nature of a publicity stunt for a motion picture, play or book, etc.,"[7] the police decided to err on the side of caution. Dubbed the "companionate bride," her story spread to the New York newspapers and the wire services. The International Wire Service and

United Press sent representatives to Camden to cover the impending tragedy.

At this point, the hard-bitten city journalists stepped in to verify Barbara Elliott's story. The *New York World* attempted to confirm Barbara's stated address but had no success. Other New York papers could not confirm details of the story. Nevertheless, the dramatic story took on a life of its own, transcending mere details, and the "companionate" bride's command of the front page was not yet over.

At 7:30 a.m. on the morning of October 19, Officer William Basier of the Camden police department was patrolling the great bridge that spans the Delaware River, connecting Camden with Philadelphia. In the morning mist, the young policeman saw the figure of a woman on the bridge's walkway. Within seconds, Basier saw her remove her coat and dangle her foot over the side rail. The bridge was a popular site for suicides, and the patrolman snapped into action.

By then the woman was straddling the rail and Basier grabbed her as she swung 135 feet above the icy river. Pulling her back from the rail, he soon realized that the disturbed girl did not want to be saved. Lashing out at her rescuer, she fought him off vigorously. Several other officers arrived to assist Basier and they soon had control of the flailing woman who screamed, "This is a free country and one ought to be able to do as one wants ... If I am not allowed to jump off this bridge, I'll jump off another!"[8]

The officers carried the distraught woman into the bridge's security office. The policemen asked if she was Mrs. Barbara Elliott, the "companionate bride" of the newspaper. She denied it, but after further questioning finally admitted that she was the woman for whom all Camden had been searching. She moaned, "Oh, why didn't you let me carry out my plans?"[9]

Barbara was taken to police headquarters for her own protection where she was met by an inquisitive press. Greeted by popping flashbulbs and peppered with questions, she and her background came under increasing scrutiny. She said she was an interior decorator by profession, and that she had attended the Art Students League and Ohio Wesleyan College. She had lived in a number of cities and claimed to have a number of "influential" relatives in Philadelphia and New York whom she didn't wish to bother with her troubles.

Soon the pressure of the press inquisition in the court hallway began to affect her demeanor. She alternately sobbed and laughed hysterically when confronted with the speculation that her story was nothing more than a publicity stunt. When a *Courier* reporter asked her to comment on the allegation, Barbara was indignant: "You have no right to suggest such a thing to me. I am on the level. I admit I am in great trouble and I tried to take the easiest way out but I guess I've caused trouble for everyone."[10]

Ushered into police court, Barbara beseeched the judge for mercy: "It doesn't much matter what happens. I didn't know I was committing an offense. I thought I could do as I wanted to. You have any promise that I won't take my life here—I won't say it won't happen again however."[11]

Crying, she told the judge that she had no money and nothing to live for, and insisted, "I refuse to bring an unwanted child into this world, and I was taking the easy way out."[12] It was Friday morning and the judge decided to put her in protective custody over the weekend. She would remain in jail until she was composed enough to guarantee that there would be no more suicide attempts.

That night, the story of Barbara Elliott was again front-page news. As she sat in a holding cell in the Camden jail, the photograph of heroic Officer William Basier appeared on the *Courier*'s front page:

HE SPOILED HER SUICIDE
Deserted Bride, Foiled in Leap into Delaware
Cop Grabs Barbara Elliott As
She Climbs Over Span Rail
Sobs Out Her Story in Public Hearing
Begs to Die and Insists That She'll Leap Off Some Other Bridge[13]

As the story of the seemingly well-bred woman with the cultivated accent spread on the news wires, the press demanded answers about her background and sought verification of her story. That same morning, a wire service reporter received word from his New York headquarters that she should be asked if she worked for a "moving picture producer known to be ready to release a film on companionate marriage."[14] Mrs. Elliott was unmoved, replying that she had never heard of the company. She stood her ground, "What I have told you and other newspapermen and the police here in Camden is the truth."[15] Despite the allegations, Barbara received several proposals from chivalrous men willing to marry the distressed mother-to-be.

On Saturday morning, Camden police investigators became even more suspicious of Barbara Elliott's story when a young man walked into the offices of the *Courier* claiming that he was Charles Elliott. Questioned about his whirlwind courtship and marriage, the police soon discovered that his version of events did not correspond with Barbara's. Accompanied by several newspapermen eager to witness the ecstatic reunion of two lovers, Captain John Golden, the Chief of Detectives, took Charles down to the detention area. The police captain quietly waited to gauge Barbara Elliott's response to the obvious fraud. *The Evening Courier* described what happened next:

> There, "Barbara Elliott" staged her last bit of realistic acting; she flung herself at "the long lost husband" the moment he loomed up in the corridor. She staged a faint almost equal in intensity to Sarah Bernhardt's.
>
> "Pretty good, little girl," commented Captain Golden and newspapermen.
>
> Revived, without the slightest need for first aid methods, she and her "companionate husband" were told plainly how their story had failed of verification in nearly every check-up.[16]

"Charles" quickly confessed that his real identity was John Ramsey, a New York writer. After some hesitation, "Barbara" admitted that she was a struggling New York actress named Mildred Gillars. Ramsey and Gillars had been college friends, both members of the dramatic arts fraternity Theta Alpha Phi at Ohio Wesleyan University. The now-impoverished pair had been offered $75 each to impersonate an abandoned mother-to-be and her caddish husband by a motion picture producer. The whole incident was a hoax designed to promote a new silent film entitled *Unwelcome Children*.

The phony couple was brought before the court of Judge Bernard Bertman who immediately sentenced them to three months in jail for contempt of court. Dozens of supporters gathered in court to observe the conclusion of the story. Some were "so touched that they had come to court prepared to offer her a home if the judge let her off."[17]

With a dramatic flourish, Mildred Gillars tearfully apologized to the judge. The out-of-work actress said she had taken the job in financial desperation and told the court that neither she nor Ramsey had been paid the $75 promised to them by the movie company. Judge Bertram suspended their sentences, placing blame squarely on the film's producers and pronouncing that "the movie men who are back of this ought to be before me."[18] The relieved 27-year-old rushed to the bench and grabbed the judge exclaiming, "You sweet thing!" Police restrained the defendant from kissing the surprised judge. Ordered by the judge to leave town, Mildred Gillars and John Ramsey did not have even the car fare to get home. Several newspaper reporters pooled their funds to finance their return trip. One of the contributing reporters told the hoaxers, "You did your best to put it over. It was worth $12.75—car fare back to New York."[19]

After this close brush with the law, Mildred Gillars could not possibly know that one day, far from America, she would assume a name and perform a role far more infamous than that of the "deserted bride"—it would be a name synonymous with treachery and anti-Semitism: Axis Sally.

As Mildred Gillars sat with the producers of *Unwelcome Children* to plan her portrayal of Mrs. Barbara Elliott, she built its foundation on memories of her own unhappy childhood and her desperate need for acceptance and acclaim. It was that same reckless search for fame and notoriety that led a star-struck Ohio teenager to wander far from home, abandon family and friends, and ultimately cast her lot with a murderous and tyrannical regime.

I know so bitterly the awful loneliness of a life without parental love. I have visualized completely the arrival of this baby of ours. I have seen myself watching it through the years. I know the agony I would suffer every time I would catch that wistful gleam in his eye when he saw another child happy in his father's love.

Mildred Gillars, 1928

* * *

She was born Mildred Elizabeth Sisk, the daughter of Vincent Sisk, a Canadian, and Mary (Mae) Hewitson, a 23-year-old seamstress from Fredericton, New Brunswick. Born on November 29, 1900 in Portland, Maine, Mildred was raised with the fierce pride of an Irish nationalist and the anti-British prejudice that came with it.

A strikingly lovely girl with porcelain white skin, dark eyes and raven hair, her early childhood was marred by her father's alcoholism. Vincent and Mae were married on February 21, 1900, slightly more than nine months before their daughter's birth, so it is likely that Mae's pregnancy was the deciding factor in the pair's union.

From the beginning of the marriage Sisk drank heavily, and his recreational pursuits included smoking opium. Mae was a strict Episcopalian from a middle-class Canadian home (her father was a magistrate in Fredericton) and her husband's drinking and drug abuse were unbearable. Sisk was the tough son of a stonemason from rural Bathurst, New Brunswick—a mining and shipbuilding community on the province's northeastern coast. The strapping blacksmith could deliver a punishing beating, and his wife was regularly the victim of his drunken rages.

After almost seven years of misery, Mae took six-year-old Mildred away from their Portland home. It would be the last time Mildred would ever see her natural father. Although Mae would return briefly three weeks later, the marriage was doomed and she would file for divorce in April 1907. Accusing Vincent Sisk of "cruel and abusive treatment," the court awarded full custody of the child to Mae on October 31, 1907.[20] While the divorce decree did not mention abuse directed at the child, the terrifying atmosphere in the home must have had a serious effect on the little girl, who was witnessing the effects of alcoholism and drug abuse firsthand in her most formative years. It would also cement a bond between mother and daughter that would be difficult to break.

Throughout Mildred's childhood, Mae was close-mouthed about her ex-husband. As an adult, Mildred claimed to know "nothing about my father except his name."[21] Mae was likely shamed by her status as a divorced woman with a child, and never discussed the dark stain on her past. That she was willing to endure the gossip and stigma that followed a divorced woman in those days is testament to the severity of the abuse. She instilled that same strength and self-reliance in her daughter. Years later, Mildred's stepsister Edna Mae marveled that her mother was "successful in keeping her feeling of a marriage failure from both of us, since neither of us knew this man Sisk was alive..."[22] In the face of such an embarrassing family secret, Mae went on to raise Mildred as though her biological father never existed.

As her marriage collapsed, Mae became acquainted with a Portland couple named Dr. and Mrs. Twitchell. The Twitchells introduced her to an itinerant dentist from Pottsville, Pennsylvania named Robert Bruce Gillars. Gillars, also divorced, began courting Mae in earnest. Less than ten months after the finalization of her divorce from Vincent Sisk, Mae married Gillars in Woodstock, Ontario on July 8, 1908.[23] Dr. Gillars was a markedly improved prospect for the young divorced mother. Educated at the Philadelphia College of Dentistry, he was a hardworking, traveling professional who was in the process of applying for a license to practice in the state of Maine. Three months after the wedding, Mae was pregnant again and on July 21, 1909, Edna Mae Gillars was born.[24] Although the dentist never formally adopted Mae's daughter, Gillars took the seven-year-old as his own. From that point on, she took the name Mildred Gillars.

Despite his boast to state officials that he had "pulled teeth from coast to coast," Dr. Gillars was denied a license to practice in Maine.[25] This reversal forced the dentist to move his family from town to town with breathtaking speed. Mildred attended schools in St. Johns, New Brunswick in 1910, then moved on to Halifax, Nova Scotia and Pittsburgh, Pennsylvania. By 1914, she was enrolled in the Bellevue, Ohio school district. Many of Dr. Gillars' patients were railroad workers and laborers who moved wherever their occupation demanded.

For a short time, Mae and Edna Mae returned to Maine while Mildred, a teenager of growing beauty, was inexplicably sent to a convent. Her stepsister remembered that, "Mildred entered a convent as a child, despite the fact that her mother was not a Catholic. When the family left Maine for their new home in Conneaut, Ohio, she had to leave."[26] By 1916, Gillars had a large ten-room house built at 145 Grant Street in the small town of Conneaut. The town was a central point for Dr. Gillars to attend to his many regular and potential patients. Conneaut sits at the junction of several railroad lines where the Norfolk Southern, Norfolk & Western, Conrail and Bessemer & Lake Erie lines run today.

Dr. Gillars' stepdaughter was a lonely, withdrawn and solitary youngster. A former neighbor recalled the little girl as "a very quiet, overdressed child who was never allowed to play with other children and who had the most beautiful black curls that I have ever seen on a child."[27] Although her younger stepsister idolized the cultured and pretty girl with porcelain skin, Mildred was emotionally distant. Edna Mae sadly recalled shortly before her death in 2002: "When we were kids, I would be downstairs making a racket and Mildred would be upstairs. Our lives never crossed."[28] The two girls were of completely different temperaments, with Mildred leading an almost separate existence from her stepsister. Edna Mae was a tomboy while Mildred was a delicate "little lady." The younger girl was in awe of her older, more sophisticated sister, fearing even to interrupt her when she spoke. She also recalled that Mildred was so obedient and submissive that, if told to do so, she would sit in one place day and night.

The rootless nature of her childhood shaped Mildred's restless and headstrong personality. It also intensified her need to stand out and gain acceptance, especially with the opposite sex. Nicknamed "Ronnie," she arrived at Conneaut High School on November 28, 1916 and immediately made an impression on her fellow students by wearing brightly colored, stylish outfits that few of her peers could afford. The high school newspaper noted in 1917 that Mildred's favorite song was "Won't You Come and Love Me?" a title remarkably similar to the inviting selections she would play for American troops more than twenty years later.[29] A mediocre student, she performed best in English and Domestic Science. Although she would later become a fluent German speaker who could read Goethe in his native tongue, she earned a D in German in her last semester. It was in high school that she developed her interest in the theater and perhaps her unhappiness at home propelled her toward the stage. At the end of her senior year, the high school publication *The Tattler* listed the features that each student was most known for. Mildred Gillars was noted not for her great love of theater or literature, but her hair.[30]

After graduation, Mildred briefly studied to become a dental assistant at Western Reserve University, but her love for the dramatic arts led her to abandon that path. Her mother had been assisting her stepfather in the dental office for years, but Mildred had no interest in the family business. In September 1918, she enrolled at Ohio Wesleyan University in Delaware, Ohio.

"I chose Ohio Wesleyan because of the excellent dramatic department, and I wished to study under Professor Charles M. Newcomb whose reputation I had already heard of," she recalled. "I took every course that was possible to take and joined the dramatic club besides, and played the lead in practically every college production that we had."[31] The first of a series of intellectual older men whose influence shaped her fate, Newcomb was a charismatic married professor, who had a reputation as an engaging lecturer and drama coach. He grew to be a mentor, and more, to the young, impressionable girl with an absent father.

The Painless Dentist

While Mildred had no relationship with and little knowledge of her biological father, the activities and influence of her stepfather raise disturbing questions. Mildred's stepsister Edna Mae described her father to John Bartlow Martin of *McCall's* magazine in 1948 as an "exceptionally brilliant man, but he had a weakness...." Ironically, it was the same weakness that plagued Vincent Sisk—alcoholism.[32] Gillars worked extremely long hours, nights and weekends, visiting patients at their homes as was the custom in those days. She described the dentist with an unwieldy moustache and long beard as a doctor "who worked for the working man" and served railroad families of limited means. Charging 50 cents for a tooth extraction, Gillars was financially successful but not necessarily "an ethical man."[33] Although Edna Mae considered him a "wizard" at dentistry with an extensive knowledge of medicine, she told a troubling story about his practices.

A woman came to Dr. Gillars demanding that all of her teeth be extracted, claiming that her medical doctor recommended it. Despite the danger of infection in a time before antibiotics, Gillars obliged. The woman soon fell ill and died.[34] By the standards of the early

1900s, Dr. Gillars had a thriving business, averaging, at times, $1,000 per week.[35] In 1919, with Mildred at college, the dentist had opened another office in Elyria approximately one hundred miles away from the family home. Upon his arrival in town, he advertised heavily in the local newspaper as:

DR. GILLARS PAINLESS DENTIST
Why don't you have those old decayed teeth removed?
You say you haven't got the nerve. Well, let me tell you,
I have the nerve already corked up in a bottle here in my office
and it is NOT COCAINE.

You can have them removed without the least particle of pain.
I do all branches of up-to-date first class dentistry and at prices to
suit all.

Twenty-five years experience. All work guaranteed.
By coming in the morning you can have your work done
the same day.
Examinations and Consultations Free[36]

The dark side of Dr. Gillars extended beyond his love of liquor and money. John Bartlow Martin wrote a letter to his editor at *McCall's* for his proposed article on the Axis Sally trial. In the letter, he described Mildred to his editor as "the wilful [*sic*] daughter of an indulgent mother; *she grew up in the unhappy home of a drunken, incestuous father*"[37] (author's italics). As the outline was written after his interview with Edna Mae, it raises disturbing questions about Mildred's relationship with her stepfather.

Martin suspected that all had not been well in the household. In the published article, he euphemistically described the dentist's relationship with Mildred as "obscure," claiming that while the younger Edna Mae defied her father, Mildred was "hurt by him."[38] She described her sister as "a little china doll" with "a beautiful disposition and her obedience was the bain of my existence. I used to wish she wouldn't set such a high standard for me to be judged by."[39] That "beautiful disposition" would erode into a flirtatious arrogance and a thirst for attention and worldly acclaim as the years wore on. Dr. Gillars' behavior may also explain her mother's sudden unexplained decision to put Mildred in a Roman Catholic convent school in Maine prior to moving to Ohio in 1916. The good doctor was vigilant in making sure that boys from the high school were not pursuing his stepdaughter. But his controlling behavior only humiliated the comely teenager. Edna Mae did not understand her father's concern: "For some reason, Father was so strict with Mildred in regards to dates, embarrassing her on several occasions [so] that she didn't make many dates until after she went to college."[40] Now a young woman, Mildred longed to be independent from a stepfather she despised.

CHAPTER 2

In Front of the Footlights

College provided some freedom from the shadow of Dr. Gillars and life in Conneaut. During her freshman year at Ohio Wesleyan in 1918, Mildred proved to be a popular girl but a poor student. Although she longed to be among the intelligentsia, she did not welcome the rigors of actual study. "Millie" wore a thick veneer of what passed for sophistication and worldliness in the days of the silent film star. In 1966, a fellow student summed up how her female classmates viewed her:

> Suffice it to say that she was not very bright, though she made a great pretense of being an intellectual; she loved to read poetry of what was then considered a far-out type; she was always using words of which she had only the vaguest idea of the meaning, but if they were unusual or highbrow, they were for her. "Esoteric" is one word, in particular, I remember her using incorrectly a good many times. She was really funny; she tried to be what she wasn't. She was always posing or acting ... she didn't go to class if she didn't feel like it. In fact, we all wondered how she got by with a lot of things she did.[41]

Mildred Gillars was well known for being the most stylish and expensively dressed girl at the university. A trendsetter, she was the first to wear four-buckle galoshes. While the other girls looked down on the clunky shoes as something they "wouldn't be caught dead in," the

18

galoshes became all the rage on campus a year later.[42] Her stepfather's financial success enabled her to be one of only two girls at the college with a fur coat. In 1919, she caused a sensation, strolling through campus in the luxurious fur. Three years later, fur was a common sight on campus. She wore her hair long and shoulder-length at a time when the average college girl wore her hair in a bun—long before the "bobbed" style became popular. Although she had striking black curly hair and a pristine complexion, Mildred's face was symmetrical above the nose but spoiled by what one faculty member at Ohio Wesleyan uncharitably called "a simian jaw"— one that "spoiled the symmetry or beauty of her features."[43]

Her flirty manner and coquettish ways unnerved the other girls at Ohio Wesleyan. One fellow student remembered:

> She had almost no female friends among the women students; she was completely indifferent to girls, concentrating her attention upon members of the opposite sex. Yet with almost all the men on campus she soon became a subject of ridicule rather than of admiration; she was so evidently exerting her charm all the time. Those were the days of the movie "vamps" and Mildred tried to act like the exaggerated sirens of the screen at that time—Theda Bara, for instance…. Mildred even went so far as to adopt some of the more advertised poses of Theda—like resting her chin upon intertwined fingers, both elbows upon the table, and gazing with lower lids upon the male she was trying to seduce at the time…. Not that Milly was a real seducer; girls just didn't go that far in those days! We never thought of Milly as immoral—just silly, affected. The men interlarded their conversations with malarkey—and she was so convinced of her irresistibility that she didn't suspect that they were laughing behind her back.[44]

One young freshman was not laughing. Calvin Gladding ("Kelly") Elliott was immediately attracted to the young "vamp" with the affected manner. A dashing youth, Kelly was known as the bohemian of the class. An artistic "free spirit," he caused a stir among the students when he became the first boy to grow a beard. He was so taken with Mildred that his friends justly feared that he was ruining his college career. One of Kelly's fraternity brothers was Allen C. Long, whose wife also attended the university at the time and in 1966 recalled the romance:

> The men in the fraternity did everything possible to stop Kelly's infatuation, as they recognized the fact that it was ruining his life; he could have been a brilliant student, but he spent so much time with Mildred, or day-dreaming about her, that his studies suffered and he, like Mildred, was unable to earn a degree.... Together Kelly and Mildred would sit in a booth at the college hangout for hours over a couple of nickel cokes, and read poetry to each other, cutting classes to do it; they would gaze into each other's eyes and be lost to the crass world around them.[45]

Mrs. Long remembered an incident that took place in those carefree college days. In the early hours of a spring evening, Kelly Elliott approached his love's dormitory in the dark of night to serenade her. Breaking out in song, he awakened Mildred and the rest of the girls in the house. An annoyed, "old-maidish" type of girl who lived on the floor above Mildred decided to act. "I'll cool his ardor," she shouted and proceeded to dump a pitcher of cold water on his head.

The young lovers were inseparable on campus, and Kelly Elliott gave Mildred his fraternity pin as a token of his affection. A few months later, he proposed marriage and she accepted. Despite Dr. Gillars' resistance to boys courting his stepdaughter, the handsome young man became a regular guest at Thanksgiving and Christmas dinners. During summer and school breaks, Mildred returned to Conneaut whenever she could to visit her mother. With her stepfather working out of town, she would sit up until the small hours of the morning visiting with her closest friend, her mother Mae.[46]

Laughing Gas

The distance between Dr. Gillars and his family grew even further, when in 1922 he combined his practice with that of another dentist in

Piqua, Ohio. The advances in dental science that brought "painless dentistry" to northern Ohio had a disastrous effect on the Gillars family. Mae remained in Conneaut with Edna Mae while Dr. Gillars plied his trade almost three hundred miles away. The couple was, for all intents and purposes, separated. His partner, Dr. Richard Shipley, described Gillars at that time as "a very unstable person addicted to the use of anesthesia and liquor."[47] Shipley recalled "the reason that the business dissolved is that Dr. Gillars went on an extended drunken spree and drew numerous checks on the firm's bank account."[48] On July 5, 1923, Mae and Robert Gillars were divorced after fifteen years of marriage. It fell to Mae Gillars to go to Piqua and dissolve the failed business of her second ex-husband.

Dr. Gillars lived only a few more years, relocating his office for a final time to Mansfield, Ohio in January 1927. An advanced alcoholic, he became gravely ill on March 30 and was diagnosed with appendicitis. Rushed to Mansfield General Hospital, the dentist underwent emergency surgery. Over the next five days, his condition worsened and he died on April 4, 1927.[49] The body was sent to his native Pottsville, Pennsylvania for burial. Gillars' sad last days in Mansfield were remembered by the local newspaper in 1949: "While several Mansfield professional men remember Axis Sally's father during his short residence in Mansfield, none recalled either his wife or daughters visiting him here. As far as could be learned, his family maintained their residence in Pennsylvania, while the eldest daughter Edna Mae lived in Piqua, Ohio."[50]

Robert Bruce Gillars died alone and destitute at the age of fifty. His brother, who paid for his dental school education in 1897, also paid for his burial.

As her mother's second marriage crumbled, so did Mildred's academic career at Ohio Wesleyan. Although she had received steady Bs and Cs in the previous three years, even excelling at times with As in her favorite subject, Oratory, in 1921 there was a drastic downturn in her academic performance. She became immersed in the college theater and equally entranced by the charismatic Professor Charles M. Newcomb, who persuaded Mildred to abandon her studies and pursue a career in theater. At college, she had a series of lead and supporting roles in the Histrionic Club's productions, *Mrs. Dane's*

Defense in December 1920 and *The Truth* in November 1921, and she capped off her college acting career playing the role of Rosalind in an open air production of Shakespeare's *As You Like It* in June of 1922.[51] Filled with dreams of success and stardom, Mildred returned home to Conneaut to tell her mother of her plans:

"I told her that Professor Newcomb felt that I should pursue a dramatic career. My mother objected very, very strenuously, and I told her that Professor Newcomb had plans for me to attend the Chronicle House in Cleveland and there further preparation for the professional stage."[52] One can imagine Mae Gillars' shock and dismay when her educated daughter, poised to graduate from a fine university, announced that she would not return to finish her final courses. Even more unnerving was that this foolish and reckless step was at the behest of a married man. Newcomb was leaving Ohio Wesleyan for a job in Cleveland, telling young Mildred that his salary was so poor that he was unable to send his own children to college.[53] He encouraged his young protégée to abandon her university studies and claimed to know just the place to pursue her dreams of stardom.

Chronicle House was a for-profit school that gave young actors the opportunity to play bit parts (and at times, lead roles) opposite the leading thespians of the New York and European stage. Newcomb was a friend of the owners, and Mildred was immediately accepted upon his recommendation. It was an exciting time for Chronicle House. The respected husband and wife team Julia Marlowe and E.H. Southern starred in Shakespeare's *The Taming of the Shrew* in 1923. In May of that year, the Charter Chroniclers of Chronicle House presented Ibsen's *Hedda Gabler* with several professional Scandinavian actors.

At Newcomb's urging, Mildred withdrew from Ohio Wesleyan in her senior year on June 19, 1922 without completing her degree. She had neither the blessing of her mother nor her financial assistance. With only $20 in her pocket and no means to pay for her schooling fees at Chronicle House, she went to Newcomb for help. The former professor introduced her to Samuel Halle, the owner of Halle Brothers, a leading department store in downtown Cleveland. Mr. Halle, the owner, gave her a job as a sales girl at $15 per week and allowed her to work on commission to assist her in her living expenses and fees. Ten dollars a week went to Chronicle House for her tuition while two dollars went to her rent. She lived in what she described as a "little room ... it was really a closet, without any windows in it; just a kind of trap door which allowed a little air to come in, and there was just a cot."[54] Virtually penniless, she survived on a meager diet of apples and crackers.

The shadow of her mother's failed marriage hung heavily over Mildred and she was determined not to make the same mistakes. In June 1922 she broke off her engagement to Kelly Elliott. Her stepsister Edna Mae reflected that although Mildred was capable of love, she was afraid of marriage: "Seeing the many heartaches Mother experienced with her marriages, with none of them due to Mother's fault, I believe gave Mildred a shocking picture of marriage. Sort of the idea Love wouldn't last after the altar."[55]

It was only after Newcomb convinced his star student to pursue a life in the theater that she broke up with Kelly—a decision that Edna Mae attributed to the fact that her "stage ambitions were stronger than becoming a wife."[56] The end of her engagement coincided with the crisis in her mother's marriage and the increasing influence of Professor Newcomb. Witnessing her mother's pain had a decisive influence on her decision not to marry. Her relationship with Mae grew even stronger, and Edna Mae recalled that the two were so close that they were often taken for sisters.[57]

Calvin (Kelly) Gladding Elliott, who spent his college career devoted to a woman who ultimately abandoned him, never graduated from Ohio Wesleyan. He withdrew from OWU the same year as Mildred and moved to New York City. He wandered Greenwich Village in the hope of becoming an artist. After a succession of jobs in New York, he became an interior decorator and married a woman who closely resembled his former fiancé. Never fully recovered from the failed romance of his college days, Kelly turned to drinking and reportedly committed suicide before the age of forty.[58]

In Cleveland, Halle assigned Mildred to the costume jewelry counter where she proved to be a successful saleswoman. During the Christmas season of 1922, she earned a large $89 commission check, and the owner offered to promote her to buyer. Mildred refused:

"I finally received something like $89, only in commissions, and

Mr. Halle was speechless. He said it never happened before and he sent for me, and asked me to report to his office, which was a very unusual procedure, and told me that in the whole history of his store that a beginner had ever received such a gigantic commission check. He said he was very pleased with my work and hoped in a short time that I would become a buyer, or at least, an assistant buyer. I informed him that with the $89 I intended to leave his store after Christmas because I wanted to devote my entire time to studies at Chronicle House.[59]

Before going to work at Halle's store, Mildred worked by day and rehearsed at night. The windfall of that Christmas led her to impetuously quit her job so that she could devote all her time to acting, but it was not long before she was again in dire need of funds. When she needed to economize, Mildred cut back on food. One night, she passed out from hunger in the middle of a rehearsal:

"I fainted one night during the rehearsal. Afterwards, when I regained consciousness, everyone asked how that happened, and for the first time I explained the great sacrifice this has been for me, and so Mrs. Brown [the director of Chronicle House] reduced my tuition from $10 to five."[60]

As Mildred approached the end of her year at Chronicle House, she planned to move to New York City. Broadway was the place for young actors to make their mark and she could hardly wait to complete her studies and leave Cleveland. She needed a job to save up enough money for her move to New York. Mildred noticed that some of the female students were coming and going at very strange hours for young, unmarried women of that era. She approached Mrs. Brown and asked if these girls had some kind of employment. Mrs. Brown told her that she could not divulge the girls' secret, so Mildred asked them.

The young actresses were working as waitresses at diners and restaurants around the Cleveland area. She applied for a job at a restaurant on the outskirts of the city where she thought she would not be recognized. The other girls advised Mildred to tell prospective employers that she had prior experience as a waitress, but it became apparent on her first night on the job that she had exaggerated her qualifications when she dropped and shattered an armful of plates.

Fortunately, the owner kept the hardworking student on the payroll and she was able to complete her studies.

With her year at Chronicle House at an end, Mildred bade farewell to Cleveland and to Charles Newcomb. Armed with a series of bit roles on her resume and having worked with acting notables like Julia Marlowe, her expectations were high as she boarded a train east in the autumn of 1923 to conquer the Great White Way.

On the Circuit

The Broadway of 1923 was a thrilling, bustling place for a young actor or actress in love with the footlights. Although Mildred longed to perform the works of Shakespeare and Ibsen on the New York stage, she arrived that summer to find a theater scene dominated by musical comedies with plot lines ranging from fantasy to farce. The most popular shows of the year were lighthearted fare such as George M. Cohan's *Adrienne, Little Jessie James* and *Little Miss Bluebeard*. By 1927, a record 264 shows and musicals were being presented on New York stages, an increase that led to an explosion of theater construction. Over the next ten years, twenty new houses were built in the area between West 40th and West 50th Streets alone.[61]

In addition to "legitimate" theater, approximately half the New York houses were filled with the popular entertainment known as vaudeville. Singers, dancers, actors, musicians, magicians, ventriloquists, wirewalkers and showgirls all faced keen competition for places in the two to three shows per day variety revues. The *Ziegfeld Follies, Music Box Revue, Artists and Models* and *Earl Carroll's Vanities* lit up the stage with beautiful showgirls revealing just the right (i.e. legal) amount of skin. Tightly controlled by owner/impresarios such as Marcus Loew, E.F. Albee, B.F. Keith, and the Shubert Brothers, performers honed their skills on the "circuit" where they traveled to second- and third-tier cities such as Yonkers, Jersey City, Norfolk and Toronto. These touring road shows were often painful experiences for performers who were greeted by primitive living conditions and little pay. A performing artist rarely rose to Broadway's first-class venues without first experiencing the travails of the road.

Freshly arrived from Cleveland, Mildred visited the offices of

Broadway's leading talent agents every morning. These men directed aspiring actors and actresses to "cattle call" auditions and recommended performers for upcoming productions. Turned away by agents and their secretaries, she doggedly attempted to get auditions. The rejection was frustrating for a young woman accustomed to the support and encouragement of teachers and friends. Mildred had lost contact with Charles Newcomb, the man who set her on her path. Although she would run into her former mentor on Broadway "quite by chance" (as she described it), she floundered without a strong or influential man to illuminate her way. Cut off from her mother and stepfather's financial help, she soon found herself without friends, funds or a job.

With little more than youth and a thin Midwestern resume, Mildred sat in the waiting room of casting agents day after day only to hear the same disappointing refrain. After one particularly fruitless day of audition seeking, she saw a familiar face. Walking through the office of the prominent casting agent Max Hart, Florence Pendleton was one of the professional actresses whose work Mildred had seen in Cleveland. Seeing an opportunity, she greeted the successful character actress as though she were a gift from heaven: "I felt that that was just fate finally giving me a break, and I approached her and told her I liked her work at home in Cleveland."[62] Pouring out her troubles to the older woman, Florence was persuaded to take Mildred under her wing. It was an exceptionally busy and successful year for Pendleton. She was starring on Broadway in the show *Tweedles* and was able to offer the struggling 23-year-old an empty room in her Greenwich Village apartment. Mildred accepted and moved into the tiny bedroom while she looked for work. Florence would also offer guidance, contacts and advice in the coming years.

Florence Pendleton was an old hand in the world of stage and film. In 1916, she appeared in the silent film *The Lurking Peril*—the thirteenth installment of a cliffhanger serial. A year later, she debuted on Broadway in *The Pipes of Pan*, a comedy well received by critics, including the *New York Times*.[63] For more than a decade, Florence performed in a string of successful plays and musical comedies on Broadway including *Her Honor, The Mayor* (1918), *The Goose Hangs High* (1924), *Magda* (1926), *The Pearl of Great Price* (1926),

Veils (1928), *Penal Law 2010* (1930), and *Grand Hotel* (1931).[64]

With the help and advice of her more experienced roommate, Mildred won her first role in 1924. She was cast in a Canadian road show of the play *Little Lord Fauntleroy*. *Fauntleroy*, first produced in 1888, did not have an especially illustrious history on the stage. It was briefly revived in 1903 and lasted for only twelve performances. In the winter of 1923 it found an audience again when Mary Pickford starred in a wildly successful silent 1922 film version of the story.[65] Mildred joined a small theater group presenting the play in small towns throughout Ontario and Quebec. Receiving fifty dollars a week, she moved from town to town on one-night stands in the brutal Canadian winter.

By the tour's end in the spring of 1925, Mildred returned to New York where she played bit parts in a stock theater company. Dorothy Long, her classmate at Ohio Wesleyan, recalled an unverified story about that time:

> In 1926 or 1927 a former classmate from Cleveland ... told me of seeing Mildred a short while before that and hearing about her troubles. Mildred told her that she had joined a stock company playing through the Canadian provinces; she had married the director-manager, and later divorced him on the grounds of mental cruelty because he gave the feminine leads to a blonde in the company and she got only minor parts.[66]

This story reveals the beginning of a pattern that Mildred Gillars repeated throughout her adult life. She habitually conducted romantic relationships with and sought marriage to powerful men who could further her career aspirations. In this instance, she "married" the director of the stock company production but left him when her career did not benefit from being his wife. When the director favored a blonde and possibly more attractive or talented actress, she left him. She demanded star turns but was relegated to frustratingly small roles as a stock player.

After returning to New York, she quickly won a role in a tour of *My Girl*, the hit musical comedy running at the now-defunct

Vanderbilt Theater. The show was a major success that ran for 291 performances until August 1925. Written by Harlan Thompson, the author and lyricist of the hit *Little Jessie James*, *My Girl* played to full houses as it passed through the small and medium cities of Ohio, Indiana and Illinois. Mildred was featured in "The Wonder Chorus," described by the show's press as "a bevy of chorus beauties."[67] Opening in Akron in the fall of 1925, the cast played a string of dates throughout her home state and the Midwest. Despite the success of the tour, Mildred was impatient and dissatisfied with the role:

"I was getting nowhere playing this sort of innocuous musical comedy, and I went to the manager and said I felt very unhappy. I didn't feel my career was being helped by playing this sort of part month in and month out. And he said 'You are too young in the theater and you don't realize it is a great mistake, but I can't keep you, if you insist on going.'"[68]

She gave the show's manager two weeks' notice and left the production. Her fellow cast members were dumbfounded by her decision to leave a successful tour to return to joblessness in New York. Following the same pattern that she exhibited after her financial success at Halle's department store, Mildred took the money she had saved from the tour and returned to New York in search of more serious dramatic opportunities. Such roles were few and far between in a Broadway built on light entertainment. Before long, her savings from *My Girl* were gone. Once again, she was penniless and hungry. She paid her rent by giving pieces from her wardrobe to her landlady:

"Finally with no more money left," she remembered, "I had been giving a dress a week to my landlady, and I had moved from uptown to save car fare, to save every cent I could and so I moved in on 48th or 49th Street, to one of those awful theatrical boarding houses."[69] At that time, single-sex boarding houses for young actresses were common in the theater district. For many artistic aspirants these houses were the only affordable living arrangements while they sought work.

Poverty began to take its toll—she was starting to look haggard and worn from malnourishment and exhaustion. Casting agents looking for fresh, young faces rejected her out of hand. Mildred had barely eaten for eight days when she walked into the Old Heidelberg restaurant on 49th Street and asked for work. She offered to do anything in return for lunch. The owner took pity on the hungry young lady and hired her to type menus. He also allowed her to eat dinner on credit. It was Christmas week and Mildred was touched by the kindness of the German owners: "I remember sitting in the restaurant, how sweet everyone was to me, and the waiter taking out a little package of cigarettes on Christmas Day and saying 'Merry Christmas' to me..."[70] The memory of the owner's warmth and hospitality when she was hungry and cold would affect her regard for the German people for the rest of her life.

On December 30, 1925, Mildred received another Yuletide surprise. A wire arrived from her colleagues in the *My Girl* troupe. The cast and crew were extremely unhappy with her replacement and asked if she would consider returning to the show. The musical was to open at the Tulane Theater in New Orleans on January 1. She accepted and the tour manager wired the funds for her ticket to Louisiana. Thrilled and relieved, Mildred was grateful for the opportunity to return to *My Girl*. The play was given rave reviews by both the *New Orleans Item* and the *Times-Picayune*.[71] She remained with the tour as it traveled through the South, moving from Louisiana to Texas, Mississippi, Missouri, Maryland and finally New York. At the end of her first week of employment, she kept her promise to the owners of the Old Heidelberg and sent a money order to New York to reimburse them for her dinners.

The *My Girl* tour ended in the spring of 1927 and a chastened Mildred Gillars was again looking for a job. The bitter days of hunger taught her a lesson that she would not forget: never to walk away from a paycheck again. "Serious" actors tended to look down on vaudeville, but despite its lowbrow nature, it paid the bills. Before long, Mildred had joined the ranks of those performers who worked two and three shows a day to earn their daily bread. One of these immensely popular musical revues was *George White's Scandals,* which was the first major challenge to the type of revue originated by the legendary Florenz Ziegfeld, and was later joined by other imitators. His *Follies* featured long-legged showgirls showing just the right amount of leg without intruding into the realm of burlesque.

George White was not an impresario but a dancer who had once worked for Flo Ziegfeld, and he employed the likes of George

Gershwin to compose music for his shows. By the time Mildred had joined the cast to perform in sketches, the *Scandals* were touring the Loews circuit—a series of theaters owned and operated by Marcus Loew in several states. The revue opened at the Loews State in New York City and moved on to Brooklyn, Newark, Yonkers, Philadelphia and other cities. Despite the high quality of the production and venues, Mildred nonetheless was frustrated with the sketches that she was reduced to performing for an uncultured audience. "I felt that there was no future at that time ... I was always torn between the need for funds and the desire to do something worthwhile in the American theater."[72]

The introverted, friendless little girl who kept to her room had evolved into an attention-seeking chorus girl with a taste for the fast life. She dyed her black hair platinum blonde and was relentless in her quest for a good time. The syndicated columnist Inez Robb recalled a party in Ohio with Mildred in attendance. Bored with the festivities, the chorus girl took it upon herself to get things moving. Robb remembered:

> Her idea of livening up a party was to go downstairs and throw a heavy garbage can thru [sic] the plate glass window of a little grocery store about four doors down the street. No one knew what she'd done until the cops began banging on the door of [the host's] apartment. It seems they were in the next block when Mildred heaved the can ... and when Mildred saw the cops; she dived into the bedroom and under the bed.[73]

The police followed the trail of the fleeing vandal to the host's apartment. He vehemently denied that any of his upstanding guests could have broken the shop window. The policemen were then invited in for a drink of illegal "bathtub gin." At the height of Prohibition, inexpensive alcohol and water was combined with fruit juice or the oil of juniper berries to cover the dreadful taste. The officers "lapped up enough gin and canned grapefruit juice ... to soothe a cage of lions. They never did get around to searching the apartment but Mildred had to stay under the bed for two or three hours because the cops liked the party and decided to stay."[74]

Mildred's recklessness would bring her into far greater trouble with the law a few years later when she went to an audition at the Hotel Empire in New York City. The producers of a new film depicting the plight of fatherless children were searching for an actress to portray a pregnant woman abandoned by the father of her unborn child. Mildred had not worked for several weeks and needed the $75 plus expenses that the producers promised. She agreed to place an advertisement in a New Jersey newspaper, threaten suicide and then dramatically "attempt" to end her life. John Ramsey, her classmate and friend from Ohio Wesleyan, would play the cad who would reunite with the woman he abandoned. The hoax would thrust the issues presented in the film's plot onto the front page and win the film *Unwelcome Children* welcome publicity.

The next day, Mildred Gillars boarded a bus for Camden, New Jersey to play the most notable role of her disappointing acting career—Barbara Elliott, the deserted bride.*

---

*Interestingly, Mildred took the surname of her real-life former fiancé (Calvin Elliott) for her fictional bride.

CHAPTER 3

Expatriate

MAY 1929–AUGUST 1939

Although the fame of "Barbara Elliot" reached far and wide, the career of Mildred Gillars fared less well. She returned from Camden to New York without a dime. Throughout the 1920s, Mildred took occasional jobs as an artist's model. By 1929, she was posing regularly for the sculptor Mario Korbel. The endless cycle of audition and rejection overwhelmed the ambitious 28-year-old and she began to look for hope abroad. Mildred asked her employer if she could borrow money for a ticket to France so she could find work as a model or dancer.[75] Korbel agreed, and although she later insisted that the money was merely a loan which she subsequently repaid, the two rendezvoused in Paris. The French capital was a haven for American expatriate artists and writers—the locus of activity in the world of arts and letters. The magnetic pull of Paris for young, bright Americans was given a name—the "French Disease." Parisian cafés and salons were filled with the leading writers and philosophers of a generation: Ernest Hemingway, Gertrude Stein, John Dos Passos, Scott and Zelda Fitzgerald, e.e. cummings, James Joyce and, ironically, the poet who would later be indicted for treason against the United States—Ezra Pound.

By the time Mildred arrived in Paris in 1929, the American colony in France numbered over 60,000. One of the reasons for the city's popularity among the artistic set was the strength of the American dollar against the post-World War I French franc. Hemingway famously described the city as "anything you want ... and cheap."[76] The inexpensive cost of living allowed American artists and intellectuals to pursue their craft while maintaining part-time or modestly salaried employment. It was a scene tailor-made for Mildred Gillars. Café society, so reminiscent of her days at Ohio Wesleyan reading poetry with Kelly Elliott over nickel cokes, was a welcome respite from hand-to-mouth survival in New York.

After six months savoring the exciting life of a single woman on the Left Bank, Mildred returned to New York on the SS *Majestic* on October 22, 1929.[77] Ready to return to the stage, her arrival was met by the disaster of the stock market crash and the ensuing economic downturn. She was only able to scrape together a bare existence performing small roles in a stock company.

After almost two more years of bitter struggle and financial hardship, Mildred was ready to abandon her hopes of Broadway fame. Acutely aware of her fading chances of stardom, she was now 31 and no longer an ingénue. Even those unsatisfying parts that characterized her theatrical career to date were difficult to come by. America was in the depths of the Great Depression, and approximately one in four Americans was out of work.[78] Vaudeville was facing a slow but certain death. The economic crisis, the rising popularity of radio, and the advent of the sound motion picture led to falling attendance at live shows. Vaudevillians such as Fred Allen, George Burns, Gracie Allen and Eddie Cantor successfully made the transition to radio, but many more performers were left to struggle for roles at fewer and fewer venues. Mildred had no inclination to forge a career in the new medium. Despite her failure to be cast in dramatic roles, she still held out some hope that she might work in "serious" dramatic theater.

The seeds of anti-Semitism and resentment toward the upper class might well have been planted during those bitter, hungry days in New York. In a July 1943 broadcast, she told listeners that "in a weathered shanty you will never find a Jew. No sir, the Jews are all in the marble palaces along Park Avenue and Fifth Avenue, New York City."[79]

Despairing of success in America and fondly remembering her days in Paris, she looked again to Europe. It was at about this time that she came into contact with a British-born secretary of a well-known philosopher, and developed a friendship with the young man that would lead her fatefully away from the country of her birth. Once again, a man would motivate her to sacrifice a frustrating present to pursue an uncertain and questionable future.

A thin, professorial man with tousled, curly brown hair, Bernard Metz was an unlikely match for the former showgirl with an Irish-bred dislike for all things British. In London, he was a student of the Russian mathematician and novelist Peter D. Ouspensky (1878–1947). Paul Beekman Taylor who, as a child, knew Metz, called him "a small, slim man with a furtive look, someone intense and curious, even nervous about everything going on about him."[80] Taylor's mother, Edith, described Metz as "a slight, smiling perky Jew."[81] Metz's teacher and mentor Ouspensky had, for several years, sought to find a philosophical bridge between Western Rationalism and Eastern Mysticism. After a trip to India that had left him unfulfilled and searching, Ouspensky journeyed back to Russia in 1915 where he encountered the Greek-Armenian philosopher George Ivanovich Gurdjieff (1866–1949).

Gurdjieff and his fellow "seekers of truth" traveled across Central Asia, Persia, India, Tibet and Mongolia where they observed the ancient rituals, dances and behavior-modification techniques of Eastern religious traditions and cults. Gurdjieff put this collected knowledge to use in a philosophy and discipline of his own. After witnessing the habits of monks and shamans, he sought to achieve a perfect balance between man's physical, mental and spiritual centers. As the "fakirs" of India and early Christians had mastered their physical bodies through asceticism, as the monks of Tibet espoused monasticism to gain control over their emotional or fantasy life, and as the Yogis of India demonstrated control over the mind—Gurdjieff maintained that all three could be achieved through harmony and balance.[82]

This approach became known as the *Fourth Way*—in which each man or woman achieves the balance of his or her intellectual, physical and spiritual faculties. Dances and rituals originating from the pre-Islamic cult of Sufism were combined with mental exercises appropriated from Buddhist monasteries to enhance the modern life of Western man—a life deemed "mechanical" and unthinking. "The Work," as it was known, was aimed at overthrowing the unsatisfying and dreamlike mechanical life and replacing it with self-observation, self-awareness and self-consciousness.

In Moscow, Gurdjieff began to teach the sacred exercises to a growing coterie of followers, but the violence and unrest of the Bolshevik Revolution pushed him westward. Eventually, Gurdjieff and his followers settled in France where he established the "Institute for the Harmonious Development of Man" (known as "Le Prieuré") in 1922. Located 70 kilometers south of Paris at Fontainebleau, Le Prieuré drew a stream of eager and curious followers from Europe and America, including notables such as the artist Man Ray (Eugene Radnitzsky), novelist Thornton Wilder, and the poets Edna St. Vincent Millay and Ezra Pound.[83] Gurdjieff sought to expand his following through traveling exhibitions featuring the costumed dances learned at Fontainebleau.

In 1923, a dancing troupe traveled to Paris and London; and on January 13, 1924, the charismatic, hypnotic mystic with balding head and piercing eyes arrived in New York. Young Bernard Metz and a group of twenty dancers traveled with their "master" to demonstrate the Fourth Way in action. The strange display of rituals and dances captured the attention of New York's "smart set." *The New York Tribune* announced the arrival of a "New Cult Hero Here to Water Acid Emotions" and the *Syracuse Herald* declared that the mysterious European had come "To Teach America to Dance Its Troubles Away," promising "Novel Methods by Which a Modern Mystic Expects to Make All Our Difficulties over Taxes, Prohibition and the High Cost of Living Quickly Vanish."[84]

After his wildly successful visit to America, Gurdjieff returned to France. A novice driver, he was nearly killed when he drove his car into a tree. During his convalescence at the Prieuré, Bernard Metz tended to his temporarily crippled master and carried his chair. During the next two years (1925–26), Metz became a notable figure in the movement, not only serving as one of Gurdjieff's personal secretaries but also helping to translate his first book, *Beelzebub's Tales to His Grandson*, into the English language.

In later years, Mildred was circumspect and vague about her association with Metz and the Gurdjieff movement. She would claim that her relationship with Metz was "fleeting"—but it is evident that the dashing Briton had made quite an impression on her. She recalled Metz many years later:

> He was a very serious person whom I had known in New York, London and Paris. He had been secretary to a well-known philosopher.... We had both been more or less students with the philosopher, and he knew all my ideas on life and ideals, he realized that it was a very grave step which I had made, that of leaving the United States, and leaving the theater behind me—which I loved above everything else.[85]

Mildred's claim that she and Metz were "more or less students" of Gurdjieff points to at least a flirtation with the charismatic leader's teaching. It is clear that she wished to continue her relationship with Bernard Metz even after he was assigned as a diplomat at the British Consulate in Algiers. In December 1932 she made the fateful decision to leave the United States. Many years later, thoroughly imbued with the National Socialist mindset, Mildred was not eager to admit the depth of her involvement with Metz. It was likely embarrassing for Axis Sally, whose diatribes against the British Empire and International Jewry were legend, to admit that it was her interest in an English Jew that led her across the sea to North Africa.

After sailing to Cherbourg on the *SS Champlain*, she visited Paris for a few days and then traveled to Marseilles. From Marseilles, she sailed on to Algiers and landed at the end of January 1933. Metz was busy in the winter months of 1932–33 as one of the last remaining followers of Gurdjieff to remain at the Prieuré—closing up the Institute as it fell into receivership. The two were reunited in the exotic port city when Metz was appointed pro-consul in August 1933. She decided to remain in Algiers and seek employment in the colony. Years later, Mildred would not elaborate about her reasons for staying, explaining in 1949: "[I was] feeling very unhappy about my failure in the American theater, and felt that [she] would like to get close to nature and have a chance to seek a lot of sunshine, á la Rousseau, back to nature...." She neglected to mention that Algiers was the destination of Britain's newest recruit to the diplomatic corps.

The Algiers that Mildred Gillars and Bernard Metz encountered in 1933 was a popular winter vacation spot and a profitable port for Europeans, but for the native Arabs it was a hopelessly impoverished backwater of Colonial France. The Muslim population were a subjected people who could not gain French citizenship as long as they adhered to Islam. These French subjects were forbidden to assemble in large groups, bear arms or leave their villages and homes to travel without permission. Large, tree-lined boulevards where European businesses thrived contrasted with the crooked, narrow alleys and streets four to six feet wide on which the locals trod. Correspondent Charles K. McClatchy described the sights, sounds and smells of the city to American newspaper readers after he returned from a February 1929 voyage:

> In Algiers the most alluring charms are blended with the filthiest stains. As probably nowhere else has God created a more beautiful picture, probably nowhere has man—and woman— more brutally, more beastly, defaced his handiwork.... [We walked] through the most noisome and filthy alleys ... amid scenes of human degradation that would shame even the pen of Zola ...[86]

Upon her arrival, Mildred consulted a consular official named Touchette about the possibility of obtaining employment in the colony. Although he told her that it would be very difficult to get work in North Africa, Touchette eventually found her a job as a tutor to the son of an American family. Within weeks she was fired, blaming the loss of her job on the recalcitrance of the little boy.[87] She met with considerably more success as a model and salesgirl for an Algiers dressmaker named Madame Zegue. Her French improved greatly over the ensuing months, and she earned the modest sum of a thousand French francs. Meanwhile, Bernard Metz moved quickly up the diplomatic ladder and was promoted to vice-consul on January 22, 1934, but his relationship with Mildred cooled.[88] His rise in the diplomatic service continued long after she left the city when he was promoted again to run the Algiers consulate until the outbreak of war in 1939.

In the spring of 1934, Mildred received a letter from her mother. Mae Gillars was coming to Europe, and asked her daughter to meet her in Hungary that summer. After a year and a half in Algiers, Mildred said goodbye to Bernard Metz and sailed to Italy to begin the trek to Budapest. Briefly passing through Naples, Florence, Rome and Venice, she met her mother in the Hungarian capital after a three and a half year separation. The happy reunion lasted over a month when they received a cable from a family friend who happened to be vacationing in Hamburg. Mae Gillars remembered in 1946: "While we were there [in Budapest], a friend who was on a Cook's tour sent us a telegram saying she would be in Hamburg for five or six days and asked us to join her there. We went, and then when she left, Mildred and I decided to visit Berlin. We were just touring around."[89]

On to Berlin

Adolf Hitler had been Chancellor of Germany for over a year and a half when Mildred and Mae Gillars arrived in Berlin on September 4, 1934. The regime was in the process of consolidating power and removing the last vestiges of Weimar democracy from the political arena. The systematic repression of Germany's Jews was not yet fully implemented. The first concentration camp, Dachau, had opened in June 1934 to intern Communists, Social Democrats and other political opponents.

Even at that early date, though, laws were already in place to remove Jews from key sectors of German society. In April 1933 legislation was enacted to remove "non-Aryans" from the civil service, to exclude Jews from the legal profession, and to limit Jewish access to German schools. The German population was being slowly conditioned to accept the gradual elimination of Jews from the political, economic and social landscape.

Three months before Mildred and Mae entered Berlin, Hitler eliminated the greatest threat to his leadership when he ordered the execution of Ernst Röhm, the leader of the *SA* (*Sturm Abteilung* or Storm Troopers) as well as hundreds of storm troopers on the evening of June 30 in the purge known as the Night of the Long Knives (*Nacht der langen Messer*). When the elderly president Paul von Hindenburg died on August 2, Hitler's power became absolute. Now the unquestioned leader of the Reich, with the sworn allegiance of the armed forces to the Führer alone, Hitler and his ministers turned their attention to the elimination of Jewish influence from German life.

For the average citizen, the disorder and street violence that characterized the Weimar period had been replaced by an uneasy calm and a noticeably improving economy. By September 1934, Nazi economic policies of increased government spending, abolition of trade unions and nonpayment of war reparations to Germany's former enemies began to bear fruit. Six million Germans were unemployed when Hitler assumed the Chancellorship on January 30, 1933. In 1934 unemployment had been reduced to less than four million. The downward trend would continue in 1935 when universal conscription took thousands of men of working age into the armed forces and off the unemployment rolls. When the regime formally scrapped the provisions of the Versailles Treaty proscribing rearmament, the nation's factories began to function at full productivity.

Newspaper and radio correspondent William L. Shirer arrived in Berlin the very week that Mildred and Mae Gillars came to the city. He described his own feelings as he took in the atmosphere of the New Berlin:

> The constant *Heil Hitlers*, clicking of heels and brown shirted storm troopers or black-coated SS guards marching up and down the street grate me, though the old-timers say there are not nearly so many since the (Röhm) purge. We've had some walks and twice have had to duck into stores to keep from either having to salute the standard of some passing SA or SS battalion or facing the probability of getting beaten up for not doing so.[90]

Mae Gillars was not impressed with the capital of the thousand-year Reich and, within a month, was eager to return to America. Whether it was the improving economy, the contagious spirit of hope or an attraction to the land of Bach, Mozart and Wagner, her daughter decided to remain in Germany. She requested financial help from her widowed mother to pursue a new career:

I told Mother that it had been an age-old dream of mine to study music in Germany, and I should try it for at least a year, and I still felt too depressed about things in America. I loved New York so very much, and felt that advance was impossible, and she told me that she was perfectly willing to supply funds for me to study in Germany if I wanted to continue, and we left it that way, and she returned to America around the end of September.[91]

Despite the fact that Mildred's musical ability was, to say the least, limited, she hoped to study piano:

> I set about to find a room immediately where I could have a piano, because that was of paramount importance, of course, and after I found … a piano teacher, an excellent piano teacher, and practiced diligently eight hours a day, and shortly after my mother returned to America, I got a letter telling me that she regretted very much, but owing to financial reverses, she would not be able to keep her promises…. It was a terrible shock, really, so the next step was to go to the pawnbroker with my jewelry …[92]

Whether Mae actually suffered a financial setback or had second thoughts about subsidizing her 33-year-old daughter's latest artistic endeavor, Mildred was forced to give up her apartment and look for work in Berlin. In a stroke of good fortune reminiscent of her first days in New York with Florence Pendleton, Mildred developed a friendship with the Silesian-born widow of the late American actor and *New York Times* drama correspondent C. Hooper Trask, who wrote a column called "News of the Berlin Scene." Thirty-nine-year-old Trask had died in June 1933 when, on an Italian vacation, the couple's automobile careened off a 45 foot precipice and crashed.[93] A mutual friend in New York advised Mildred to look up Claire Trask and introduce herself.

Mrs. Trask was recovering from the accident that had claimed her husband's life and had left her badly injured. Bereaved and suffering, the 42-year-old widow needed a friend, companion and caretaker. Mildred stepped into the void. Claire Trask assumed her husband's career as a *Times* correspondent, and was well connected to the Berlin drama and film scene. The unemployed music student ingratiated herself with the older woman. In the same manner that she coaxed an invitation to move into Florence Pendleton's apartment, she told Trask that she was on the verge of homelessness:

> She had noticed that my ring was gone, and she said something about it, and I told her that I had pawned it to pay the rent, and she exploded in a very delightful way—she had a way of doing that—and said I should have told her. She said she wasn't going to have any friend of hers going to the pawnshop, and she saw no further reason for me staying with Mrs. Herzfeld, and she would look for me at her place.[94]

Mildred moved into the Trask home in November 1934 and, with her new patron's help, soon found a job as a translator at the Berlitz Language School in Berlin. In January 1935, she began teaching English to German students. Her female manager at Berlitz resented the former showgirl: "You know how women can be with women, sometimes, it is a shame, and it was a rather hard pull for a time because she didn't want any women teachers around." Mildred earned 1 Reich mark, 20 pfennig per lesson but the manager refused to give her a permanent contract and salary. It was only after "certain men in the institution interceded that she weakened" and gave her a contract.[95] Again, Mildred relied on the good graces of men whom she cultivated to further her career or to merely survive.

It was not only the kindness of men that she relied on, for Claire Trask was extremely generous with her new friend. Mrs. Trask gave her a comfortable life at her residence, refusing money for room and board. The maid even served Mildred as though she were a member of the family. Mildred supplemented her teaching income by writing English translations of German books and articles, including the 1937 book *Vivid Portraits, with a Simple Camera* by W.H. Doering (which was published in Boston). It was through Mrs. Trask's connections in the German film industry that Mildred began translating for UFA (*Universum Film AG*), the legendary film studio that had produced such classics as Fritz Lang's *Metropolis* (1927) and Josef von Sternberg's 1930 international hit *The Blue Angel*. Mrs. Trask's late husband often worked on translations and dubbing for the studio during the Weimar years, and in 1931 had hosted a radio program broadcast to the United States with the German stars Emil Jannings, Lilian Harvey and Conrad Veidt.

Claire Trask "knew all the film stars in Germany, and the managers and the directors," she recalled, "and so I began doing a great deal of translating for UFA—doing subtitles for films, and that sort of thing."[96] In essence, Mildred picked up much of the translation work that Hooper Trask had performed before his tragic death. UFA did not fully come under the regime's total control until March 19, 1937 when Goebbels' Ministry of Propaganda and Public Enlightenment assumed responsibilty for every aspect of the studio's output. Mildred's work for UFA would serve as an introduction to working for a propaganda organ of the German government.

Critic or Propagandist?

While living with Claire Trask from 1935 to 1938, Mildred became fluent in the German language, studied interpretive dance, and assisted Mrs. Trask in her job as the *New York Times'* Berlin correspondent. It was a time of growth, opportunity and achievement that towered over anything she had experienced in her own country. Mildred remembered:

> I did quite a lot of writing ... by myself and in conjunction with Mrs. Trask; well, of course, naturally, I never worked on any of her articles—either I did the article or I didn't—but you see, I was responsible for getting the work because I had no friends in Germany and she had good connections with UFA.[97]

Claire Trask walked a fine line as a reviewer of German film and theater in the *Times*. Critical of the political and racially motivated changes that came to the Berlin drama scene with the January 30 revolution, a review of her prodigious output from 1934 to 1938 reveals the progressively heavy hand of the Propaganda Ministry weighing on her ability to write genuine film and theater criticism. Mrs. Trask noted in a December 1934 article that Germany's film industry was in crisis due to the Nazi state's withdrawal of two films from exhibition in the city's theaters. She described the "benign" influence of the Propaganda Minister:

> It has long been evident that Dr. Joseph Goebbels, Minister of Education and Propaganda, is keeping a benign official eye on the celluloid strip.... Dr. Joseph Goebbels himself ... personally stopped the run of the two films. He expressly states that the barring of these two pictures is not due to their running counter to state policy or National Socialistic beliefs but because they are "superficial, tasteless, void of any imagination, misusing their cast, musicians, etc. to turn out dull, stupid film ware."... This controversy had added little to stabilize an already restless, unsure and much hampered industry.[98]

Mrs. Trask tempered her criticism with evenhanded praise for the latest offerings of the major German studios such as UFA and Tobis, and reported on the popularity of American films in Berlin's movie houses. Light Hollywood fare such as *Dancing Lady* starring Joan Crawford and Clark Gable, *Morning Glory* with Katherine Hepburn, and the historical drama *Queen Christina,* starring the immensely popular Greta Garbo, filled the capital's theaters with dubbed German versions.

Clara Trask was even more forceful in describing the plight of the Jewish theater in the new Germany. The *Times* ran two separate Trask-authored columns on the same day—April 8, 1934. The first was an account of the current movie offerings on exhibition in Berlin, pointing out that the British film *Catherine the Great* was pulled from exhibition after only one day because one of it stars, Elisabeth Bergner, was a Jew who had emigrated after the Nazi takeover. The companion article described the achievements of a small Jewish playhouse working in the face of Nazi persecution. Describing the traditional artistry of the Yiddish theater, Trask did not openly criticize government policy but instead revealed telling facts about the conditions under which the theater company performed. She pointedly informed her readers that "non-Jews are not admitted" to the productions presented by the Cultural Association of German Jews (*Kulturbund Deutsche Juden*) at the old Berliner Theater. "It was by an especially stipulated permission obtained from Herr (Hans) Hinkel, Commissary of State at the Prussian Ministry of Science, Art and Education that I was able to attend," she noted.[99]

Mildred's journalistic mentor was less outspoken in her criticism of government meddling in the German film industry after 1934, focusing instead on events such as the farewell appearance of the provincial actress Emmy Sonnemann, the new wife of Reich minister Hermann Goering, telling her readers that Frau Goering was "smothered in flowers and ovations."[100] In the Olympic year of 1936, the Nazi state was eager to showcase itself to the international community as an orderly, happy society brimming with confidence and prosperity. Mildred attended the opening ceremonies of the Olympic games. Subject to a steady diet of Nazi propaganda for over two and a half years and always highly impressionable, her views on "the Jewish Question" went through a change at this time as well. She remembered that happy period in her life in a 1943 broadcast:

> I was up there at the Olympic Stadium, a beautiful bronze, athletic figure running across the field threw the torch into the oil and this marvelous flame flew up into the air. And then the Olympic clock was started with this wonderful call: "I'm calling the youth of the world." ... In 1936, the hands of youth from all the four corners of the world were extended and met here in Germany.... The Germans and the Americans were the best sportsmen in the whole world—got more prizes than anybody else if I'm not mistaken. And at the end of each feat, the victor was crowned by a pretty young German girl with a wreath of laurels.[101]

It became clear to her who was responsible for ending those halcyon days:

And then, all of a sudden, 1939 was there. 1939–1940–1941–
1942–1943 and war drums in America. American youth—
donning their uniforms to come over to Germany and to fight
those people to whom they had given the hand of friendship in
1936. And I realized just how effective had been this Jewish
pestilence which has broken out over the face of the earth,
because in 1936, the hands of youth from all the four corners
of the world were extended and met here in Germany. They
understood each other. They understood that the power and
ability to keep peace once and for all belonged to us, belonged
to the youth. But the Jews didn't want it that way.

The fault all lies with the Jewish influence in the world
today and that this murder which is being committed is not
only a physical murder, but a murder of this understanding—
a murder of this friendship—which in 1936 really was
there.[102]

After the close of the Olympics, Claire Trask discussed the theatrical fare offered during the festivities and the immense popularity
of the American film *Broadway Melody of 1936* in the face of what
she dryly described as "dense as woods German product."[103] Her criticism was tempered with support for the best of Goebbels' stable of
stars—taking pains not to be unduly negative toward performers who
were personal favorites of the Minister. The Minister was a notorious
pursuer of sexual liaisons with actresses who could benefit from his
favor. His two-year relationship with the Czech beauty Lida Baarova
threatened his political career when Magda Goebbels discovered the
affair and barred him entry to their Wannsee home. In the end, Hitler
himself ordered Goebbels to end the relationship. Baarova was forced
to leave Germany and later resumed her acting career in Prague.[104]

Redefining Film Criticism

By late 1936, it was evident that the inferior product produced by a
strictly regulated film industry utterly failed to capture the imagination of theatergoers. The studios were decimated by a massive loss of

talent as Jewish writers, directors and technicians fled Germany. Even before the party's takeover of the studios in 1937, Goebbels had the power to stop a film from being made, controlled the approval of scripts through the office of *Reichsdramaturg*, could grant tax exemptions, and could determine whether or not the finished film would be exhibited in Germany's 5,000-plus theaters.

Reacting to the overwhelming public rejection of his approved films in November 1936, Goebbels issued a decree forbidding art criticism of any kind that did not meet the requirements set by the Reich Chamber of Culture."[105] Angered by the public's lack of interest in the films produced under the auspices of his ministry, he blamed the critics. "To demonstrate the unhalting victory march of our cultural life," the Minister announced, "I have by decree forbidden all criticism and replaced it with *art observation* or *art description*."[106] (Author's italics.) Thereafter, all critics of German film and art were forced to obtain a license from the Propaganda Ministry. Although many professional critics of repute had already gone into exile, it signaled the end of independent art, theater and film criticism in Germany.

The light and breezy tone of Claire Trask's critiques became even more solemn in the following months. As Goebbels and his minions drove the studios into the ground with their meddling, the Nazi Party took advantage of their financial weakness. The party moved in to purchase a controlling interest in all German film studios. UFA was the first to fall under state ownership in March 1937 when the party secretly purchased 72 percent of the company's stock, followed by a takeover of Tobis and the closing of the Bavaria studios. The emigration of the vast majority of the German film industry's Jewish and half-Jewish actors, directors and technicians to the USA and other European nations enabled lesser talents to take their place. Claire Trask's attempt to review the UFA film *Togger* reveals the difficulty that she experienced in finding a way to praise a work she obviously found wanting:

> Scrutinizing closely the picture reveals gaps, halts, inconsistencies, that strain the imagination of the viewer. Besides, it is manifestly a picture of stark propagandistic flavor. But strangely enough, just like this year's UFA film *Verraster*

(Traitors) to which it is congenial in Nazi doctrinary persuasions, *Togger* proves in part a tense bit of entertainment ... The staged burning of a complete building was a fizzle both from the directing and photographic angle. Newsreels would have supplied much more effective material. For once we might have been spared the derogatory nightlife scene of the "debauched" period before the coming of the Third Reich. Yet in spite of its many shortcomings the picture is one of the best the Fatherland has turned out this season.[107]

Limited in what she could report to the *Times* readership, Trask's communiqués became much less frequent during the troubled years of 1937–38. With the regime openly using critics as propaganda tools, and the New York newspaper reader less inclined to care about the Berlin film scene, Claire Trask's output for the *Times* steadily deteriorated. Luckily, she had another outlet that kept her and her eager protégée working through 1937–38.

Mildred volunteered her services to Trask to write film and theater reviews for *Variety*, the American entertainment trade newspaper. Apolitical in nature and overwhelmingly concerned with business prospects in radio, film and legitimate theater, the daily newspaper was interested in upcoming foreign films that would eventually be shown on New York screens. Correspondents from London, Paris, Berlin, Vienna and Budapest dispatched news articles and film, theater and cabaret reviews describing the latest European offerings. Writing without a byline and datelined Berlin, Mildred reviewed several major films, including 1937's *La Habanera*, the last German film of director Detlef Sierck. Sierck's second marriage to a Jewish actress compelled the talented director to flee to Italy in 1937. Like Billy Wilder and Fritz Lang, he eventually went to the United States where he changed his name to Douglas Sirk and directed several classic films for Universal including *Magnificent Obsession* (1954) and *All That Heaven Allows* (1955).

While Claire Trask's prose displayed the restrained elegance of the cultured connoisseur, Mildred's reviews imitated the staccato pulse and lowbrow aim of the gossip column. Brimming with Hollywood slang, the reviews were short in length, punchy in delivery, grammatically clumsy and, at times, incomprehensible. It is hard to imagine that her film reviews would have been published in any newspaper without the intervention of her friend and mentor Trask. Unlike her anti-Nazi patron's urbane and thoughtful assessments, Mildred's pieces were effusive in their praise. Compared with *Variety*'s New York-based reviews of German film at the time, Mildred's "criticism" could only be described as fawning. Reviewing the 1938 film *Gasparone*, Mildred takes on all doubters of one of the regime's favored actresses, Hungarian Marika Rökk:

> If there were any doubts about Marika Rökk, she's put the kibosh on them here, showing that in every department she is stocked with the goods that send folks places where they can do things. As terper, chirper and comedienne, she has finish as she has never shown before.... Sleuthing, smuggling, intrigue, chorines with shapely gambs and a double-headed interest— these are the ingredients—and the dish has been prepared to the king's taste.[108]

A careful review of these anonymous dispatches from Berlin makes the reader wonder if Mildred's film criticism was not "prepared to the king's taste" as well. The Propaganda Minister, with input from Hitler, handpicked those actors and actresses who exemplified the "Aryan" ideal of man and womanhood. Stars like Kristina Sönderbaum, Zarah Leander, Brigitte Horney, Sybille Schmitz and Marika Rökk were placed in the forefront in order to replace great stars such as Greta Garbo and Marlene Dietrich. Mildred left no doubt about her understanding of the critic's role: "trying to give American producers an idea of the kind of material, human material particularly, that was available in Germany."[109] Comfortable with the fact that her role was to promote rather than critique, she was unconcerned or unaware that her role had a political component.

Her breathless review of *Der Gelse Flagge* (The Yellow Flag) is another indication of her early propensity for promoting the interest of the German film industry and its masters in the Propaganda Ministry:

Of all the weird, outlandish concoctions this one takes the blue ribboned pork chops. Based on a Fred Andreas story that got a big reading public via its serial appearance, nothing has been left out in terms of thrills and adventure. As for the masses that are nertz about their [actor Hans] Albers, they've sure got him here, plus variations. Not only does he K.O. a half dozen toughies and prove what a Beau Brummell he is with the ladies, but combats single-handed a whole raft of cannibals in the heart of the jungle. It's a sure wicket spinner in nabe sector, nabe lands, and the sticks.[110]

She sang the praises of the politically sensitive German-Italian co-production *Mutterlied* (Mother Song):

Not a trick has been passed up to make it one of the niftiest turnstile takers within the Hitler–Mussolini confines, plus plenty possibilities beyond these realms.[111]

Because Mrs. Trask refused payment for room and board, Mildred worked for *Variety* without a byline and accepted whatever money Trask offered for her efforts. She claimed that she never knew how much money Claire Trask was being paid by the newspaper. Mildred became so busy that she stopped working for the Berlitz School in 1938 to devote all her time to writing. With the March 1938 *Anschluss* of Austria into the Reich, *Variety*'s editors became increasingly sensitive about publishing anything that could be construed as Nazi propaganda. Almost overnight, the entertainment industry became skittish about accepting content from Berlin. In Canada, a huge outcry erupted over CBC Radio's announcement that it would accept cultural programming from Germany in May 1938.[112] In the United States, NBC's shortwave division fired its newscaster and announcer Ernest Kotz due to charges that he was pro-Nazi. American and Canadian outlets were on guard to ensure that they would not be duped. From March 1938 on, *Variety*'s communiqués from Berlin carried only the name of Claire Trask. Mildred's cheerleading for Nazi film came to an end.

Most likely, Mildred's fevered movie reviews were rewritten with the more sober prose of Claire Trask and published under her byline. When Claire Trask fled Germany for the Netherlands in August 1939 in the face of the imminent declaration of war, eventually making it to the United States, she could maintain that it was her grateful assistant who promoted the virtues of Germany's "human material" for American consumption. The columns bearing her byline carried muted criticisms, while her protégée supplied the enthusiastic praise that ensured that the correspondents would not run afoul of the authorities.

No matter how distasteful the politics or how much her mentor disapproved of the regime, it must have seemed to Mildred that she was finally part of a world she had long dreamed of. She was familiar with the elite of the German film industry, and writing for a leading trade publication aimed at the decision-makers of New York and Hollywood. The "Aryanization" of the German film industry helped her achieve what she found impossible to do in America: build an influential career in the dramatic arts.

As the months passed and the world careened toward conflict over Hitler's territorial demands, exhibition of German films in the United States fell sharply. As the opportunities to publish faded, Mrs. Trask began to look for other employment possibilities for Mildred. One of her favorite actresses was the exotic-looking Brigitte Horney, the stunning, husky-voiced blonde star of several hit films. Horney needed a personal assistant, and Mildred was immediately hired. Brigitte Horney and Mildred Gillars were two independent women from similar backgrounds.

The daughter of the eminent psychotherapist Karen Horney (1885–1952), Brigitte came from a harsh and difficult upbringing. Like Mildred's stepfather, Oskar Horney was a cruel and abusive parent who suffered the collapse of his business. As conditions in the home worsened, Brigitte's mother became suicidal and finally left her husband in 1926. Opportunistic, brilliant and ambitious, Brigitte remained in Nazi Germany after her mother left for the US to benefit from the "Aryanization" of the arts. She became one of Dr. Goebbels' favored actresses; a member of the *Volksböhne* who starred in the cream of Nazi-era films. Groomed as a replacement for the exiled

Marlene Dietrich, Horney starred in the hits *Liebe, Tod und Teufel* (Love, Death and the Devil, 1934), *Savoy-Hotel 217* (1935) and *Das Mädchen von Fanö* (The Girl From the Isle of Fanö, 1941).

The striking actress made four successful films with the popular actor Joachim "Joschy" Gottschalk. Gottschalk's immense popularity temporarily ensured his survival in the German film industry despite his marriage to a Jewish woman and his half-Jewish son. When Gottschalk made the mistake of introducing his wife to prominent Nazis at a social function, Goebbels demanded that the actor end the marriage. Gottschalk refused and the Minister threatened his wife and son with deportation to the Theresienstadt concentration camp. Goebbels arranged for Gottschalk's induction into the army when the actor insisted on going with his family to the camp. In 1941, Gottschalk and his wife sedated their son and turned on the gas. The three perished moments before the arrival of the Gestapo. In open contempt of Goebbels (who wanted to keep news of the actor's death a secret), Brigitte Horney openly attended the funeral of her close friend and colleague.

Despite it all, Brigitte went on working for the Nazi propaganda machine until the end of the war. Her most notable role came in 1943 when she portrayed the Russian empress Cathcrine the Great in the film *The Adventures of Baron Munchausen*. An expensive disaster of epic proportions, *Munchausen* was one of the regime's final productions. She went on to finish the fittingly titled *Am Ende der Welt* (The End of the World, 1944) as Allied bombs fell around her. With her career and country in shambles, Horney fled to Switzerland in 1945 and five years later immigrated to the United States.

Berlin Darkens

While Mildred Gillars was enjoying her patron's connections with Nazi cinema's leading lights, the repression of German Jewry progressed rapidly. It would have been difficult, if not impossible, for the average Berliner not to notice the brutal effects of anti-Jewish legislation. From the inauguration of the Nuremberg Laws in September 1935, when the "Law for the Protection of German Blood and German Honor" forbade intermarriage and sexual relations between

Gentiles and Jews, an unrelenting effort to drive Germany's Jews abroad was underway.

The very definition of German citizenship was changed with the "Reich Citizenship Law" establishing "German or kindred blood" as the sole factor determining citizenship in the Third Reich. The Nuremberg Laws were quickly amended on November 15, 1935, when it was decreed that a Jew could not be a citizen, could not vote, partake in political activities or hold public office. The term "Jew" was defined in law as anyone descended from at least three fully Jewish grandparents. The category *Mischlinge* (half or partially Jewish) was established to denote anyone who was descended from two fully Jewish grandparents, belonged to the Jewish religious community, was married to a Jew, was the offspring of a mixed Gentile–Jewish marriage, or was the offspring of an extramarital sexual relationship with a Jew. This discreet hairsplitting became the foundation for the body of Nazi racial law that would become a niche for pseudo-scientists and barbaric physicians determined to flush out the last drop of Jewish blood from German society.

Despite the lull in street violence and harassment against Jews during the period immediately prior to and during the 1936 Berlin Olympics, 24 laws explicitly discriminating against Jews were instituted that year. An additional 22 followed in 1937.[113] This torrent of exclusionary law ranged from the removal of Jewish children from German schools to the "Aryanization" of Jewish businesses—the brazen expropriation and reassignment of property to party members and their associates. As the world edged toward the conflict that Hitler sought over Czechoslovakia, the race laws were amended again to regulate the naming of Jewish infants. Jewish parents were obligated to adhere to the "Guidelines on the Use of Given Names" issued by the Reich Minister of the Interior. To ensure that Jews were readily identifiable and unable to evade persecution, the decree also announced that as of January 1, 1939, all Jewish males and females must assume an additional given name—Israel for men and boys and Sarah for women and girls.

Those Jews who did not or could not leave faced harassment, arrest and ultimately deportation to concentration camps. On October 18, 1938, Hitler ordered over 12,000 Polish-born Jews deported to the East—4,000 of whom were accepted by the Polish government. The remaining deportees were left on the German–Polish border without a country. The son of one of those wretched and starving families was in Paris when he was notified of his family's plight. Herschel Grynszpan decided to take action and walked into the German Embassy in Paris. Drawing a pistol, he shot and critically injured the German diplomat Ernst vom Rath on November 7, 1938. On the evening of November 9, vom Rath died and Goebbels asked Hitler for permission to unleash the wrath of the German people on the Jews in retaliation for the diplomat's death.

With Hitler's consent, *Kristallnacht* (the Night of Broken Glass) erupted in so-called "spontaneous" outbursts orchestrated by the Gestapo and the SS. Nazis and their followers burned synagogues, beat and humiliated Jews in the streets, looted Jewish-owned businesses, and killed in cold blood. The Gestapo was at least partly responsible for the eleven Berlin synagogues that went up in flames, as well as the destruction of temple books and Torah scrolls. At the end of it all, at least 91 Jews were killed, with hundreds injured and others sent to concentration camps. Foreign journalists, vocal in their disgust and nauseated by the unrestrained orgy of racial hatred, reported on the bloodletting. It was obvious to the Western democracies that Germany was no place for their citizens, and their respective foreign services and embassies counseled their nationals to return home. Mildred, who was riding higher than she had ever been, chose to remain in Berlin.

Mae Gillars made one final attempt in the summer of 1939 to convince her daughter to return to the United States. Mildred traveled to England to meet her mother and brought her back to Germany. Mae remembered her daughter as "very young and happy" that summer. As the two women strolled through the city, they came upon a massive throng of people in a square listening to a speech. Over the loudspeakers came the unmistakable voice of Adolf Hitler.

Mae remembered: "Mildred and I were walking along the street when we came to the square where he was speaking. It was impossible to get by. We slipped into a restaurant and had a cup of coffee. Of course, you couldn't help hearing him. There was a public address system in the restaurant and Mildred translated his speech for me. But she was never interested in politics—never, not even in the U.S."[114]

As Germany's dispute with Poland over Danzig moved Europe toward war, Mae left without her beloved daughter. "I could hardly get out of the country," she recalled. "Trains were almost tied up with troop movements when I left."[115] As Mae Gillars boarded a train crowded with soldiers destined for combat, she embraced her daughter for the very last time.

CHAPTER 4

Wolves at the Door

SEPTEMBER 1939–DECEMBER 1941

When Hitler's armies marched into Poland on September 1, 1939, Mildred had been working for the German actress Brigitte Horney as a personal assistant for over a year. When the film star fell on hard times and could no longer pay a secretary, she was sacked. For the next nine months, she had no regular employment. Attempting to parlay her lifelong interest in antiques into a source of income, she occasionally bought and sold a few pieces, and added to her meager income by teaching a few English lessons and translating documents.[116]

Although the German government sought to minimize the war's economic impact on day-to-day life in the Reich, it nevertheless instituted rationing on clothing, gasoline, soap and other essential goods. Ration coupons were distributed to German citizens, but Mildred as a foreign national was ineligible for such aid. In the spring, when the situation was particularly dire, her luck suddenly changed:

> I received a telephone call one day from a certain art historian whom I had known for many years. He asked me how I was getting along, and I said "horribly" and that the wolves were coming closer and closer to the door.... I was getting along very badly and didn't know what step I could take to keep body and soul together.[117]

The art historian had spoken to Dr. Eugen Kurt Fischer, an acquaintance of Mildred's and a former professor from the University of Königsberg. Although she knew the professor socially, she was unaware of his position in the Nazi government as an official at the European service of Reichsradio (*Reichsrundfunk*). The Reichsradio Corporation, an arm of the Ministry of People's Enlightenment and Propaganda, run jointly with the Foreign Office, was bombarding the British Isles with a steady diet of news and propaganda through its *Sender Bremen* (Station Bremen). The European Service was having considerable success with the broadcasts of one William Joyce, better known as "Lord Haw Haw."

Joyce, an American-born Irish Fascist, was a protégé of Sir Oswald Mosley, the leader of the British Union of Fascists. At the height of his influence, Joyce had a large listening audience—an estimated 6 million regular and 18 million occasional listeners in the United Kingdom alone.[118] He and his wife Margaret Cairns Joyce ("Lady Haw Haw") narrowly escaped arrest and fled England on August 26, 1939. Ingratiating himself with the German Propaganda Ministry and seizing upon his many contacts within the regime, Joyce was hired to anonymously write and record commentaries on British policy, politics and the progress of the war.

Joyce's popularity was not only attributable to his skill as a broadcaster, but also to the lack of forthright news and comment available on the British Broadcasting Corporation. The BBC had suspended entertainment programming the day war was declared and heavily censored all news. The censorship was so indiscriminate that many English listeners immediately turned to Joyce's commentaries after the 9 p.m. BBC news to hear the details their government had been holding back. Making matters worse, the BBC had also unknowingly reported fictitious reports of successes on the front only to report later that the Allied forces were, in fact, retreating.[119] Entertainment programming was limited to theater organ music and records. Inevitably, listeners looked elsewhere on the dial. The BBC had been slow to respond to the German propaganda onslaught. In fact, the programming staff had fled to "undisclosed locations" when war was declared in anticipation of a massive blitzkrieg on London.[120]

As Holland, Luxembourg, Denmark, Belgium and Norway fell in

April and May 1940, those popular commercial stations on the Continent that the British public listened to daily were expropriated by the Germans for pro-Nazi broadcasts.[121] In a matter of months, Reichsradio had the facilities and high-powered transmitters to cover the entire European Continent. Combined with the huge 100 kilowatt transmitters and antennas that the regime established in the Berlin suburb of Zeesen, German shortwave radio covered the world twenty-four hours a day in twelve languages on both medium wave (AM radio) and shortwave bands.

As German forces racked up success after success in Western Europe, Joyce was brutal in his evaluation of the conduct of the British war effort, and singled out Winston Churchill, the man selected as Prime Minister in the face of these reversals, for special contempt. During the withdrawal of British forces from Narvik, and later Dunkirk, "Lord Haw Haw" underlined the differences between the British radio's depiction of events and the reality on the ground:

> This unprecedented slaughter is not called in England by its true name.... As you listened to the British radio a week ago did you get the impression that there was going to be any withdrawal at all? Did you think that the necessity of a rearguard action was being contemplated by the Dictator of Britain? I did not. Until defeat turned into rout—absolute—the whole world was being told hour after hour by the BBC that the situation was well in hand, and fresh victories were served up with every transmission.... We have long recognized the fact that the British people have been deceived, but isn't it a slightly novel experience to see them treated as congenital imbeciles? ... As the bloody and battered fragments of what was once the British Expeditionary Force drift back in wreckage to the shores of England, it is not impossible that the public will turn savagely upon the men who have so cruelly and unscrupulously deceived it.[122]

Joyce reserved his greatest vitriol for Churchill:

> Is it not a little amusing to think of the trumpetings and flour-

ishings with which Churchill became Prime Minister of
Britain? *He* was the man to frighten Hitler. *He* was the provi-
dential leader who was going to lead Britain to victory. Look
at him today, unclean and miserable figure that he is, and contrast his contemptible appearance with the bright hopes that
his propagandists aroused in the minds of people foolish
enough to believe that this darling of Jewish finance could
really set the might of National Socialist Germany at
naught.[123]

Reichsradio's management hoped to duplicate the success of the
European Service on the North American continent. Unlike today's
radios, it was common for radio sets of the period to include shortwave bands for international listening. Who could speak to these
American and Canadian listeners in terms that they could understand?
American expatriates in Berlin were few at the outset of the war as
most were trying to flee Germany in the face of hostilities, but the
Radio Department of the Foreign Office did find some willing candi-
dates. One of the first was Frederick William Kaltenbach, an Iowa-
born German-American teacher fired from his job at a Dubuque high
school in 1935 for leading a brown-shirted student organization based
on the Hitler Youth. Angered by his termination, Kaltenbach left the
US for Germany as an avowed convert to National Socialism and
began his service for the Reich reading press releases in English.
Dubbed "Lord Hee Haw" for his folksy style, he was cast as the
American equivalent of William Joyce.

Another recruit was Edward Leo Delaney, an Illinois-born actor
and author of dime-store novels, who began broadcasting for the
Germans under the alias "E.D. Ward" in late 1939. Kaltenbach,
Delaney and a Foreign Office official who would have a defining role
in the creation of "Axis Sally," Dr. Max Otto Koischwitz, dominated
the USA Zone's commentaries early in the war.[124]

On September 8, 1939, Hitler issued a decree stating that von
Ribbentrop's Foreign Office would be responsible for the general
guidelines and instructions of all foreign propaganda (radio, film,
newspapers and pamphlets) for the duration of the war. Ribbentrop's
political victory over Goebbels exacerbated an already vicious rivalry

between the two ministers. Moreover, Hitler decreed that those instructions would be "adopted unchanged and implemented."[125] In order to ensure that the guidelines were carried out, the Führer specified that von Ribbentrop assign "competent officials as liaisons" to the Propaganda Ministry.[126] This development signaled a considerable loss of influence and control for Goebbels, who regarded these liaisons as spies for his arch-enemy.

Although the Propaganda Minister still retained control over domestic propaganda and efforts in Bohemia, Moravia, the Government General in Poland and the occupied countries of Western Europe, he experienced a bureaucratic defeat he found hard to take. Intensely critical of the Foreign Office overseers, the minister found their input "stupid," "intellectual" and far too gentle on the Jewish Question. To circumvent their influence, the *Reichsminister* held daily conferences where he directly communicated his personal orders to department heads without interference. The two staffs at times engaged in violent disagreements. In one instance, Goebbels ordered that one Foreign Office representative be physically removed from a studio for meddling in his broadcasts.[127]

Despite the efforts of Kaltenbach and Delaney, the Foreign Office was dissatisfied with the quality of the USA Zone's speakers as early as March 1940. Several of the announcers had distinct and, in certain cases, thick German accents. Dr. Markus Timmler, head of the Radio and Culture section, expressed as much in a memorandum to the USA Zone management:

> There are not enough speakers who have a command of English with an American accent. The current speakers are also used for the announcement of the German news. Hence, those announcers are limited from the start because they do not have a command of American English, but speak enough German. It results in speakers with a German accent to which the American listeners are especially sensitive, which ruins the effect of even the best news material.
>
> The same applies in certain cases to speakers with Oxford accents who are not appropriate for American broadcasts. Hence, it is urgently recommended to not use announcers for

two languages, but to search for high-class speakers who have a very good command of American English ...

It is advised of the importance of our American newscasts to use as far as possible American-born speakers.[128]

Enter "Midge"

Within a month of Dr. Timmler's critique, a down-on-her-luck Mildred Gillars entered the cavernous headquarters of the Reichsradio Corporation. The broadcasting complex consisted of three major buildings: *Das Grosse Haus* (the "Big House"), the "Deutschland House" and a large barracks that housed several radio studios. The Big House had hundreds of rooms that accommodated the organizational maze that was the corporation. It was only one of the buildings devoted to Germany's massive overseas broadcasting service, which broadcast daily around the clock.

Johannes Schmidt-Hansen, the manager of the European Section, asked the nervous actress to audition at the microphone. Her mellifluous voice and command of English impressed Schmidt-Hansen and he told her that she would be getting a phone call with a formal offer. Mildred was skeptical: "I had been promised things like that for years and years along Broadway; since practically nothing ever materializes, I just thought it was another one of those things."[129] When the call finally came, she was told to report to the station the next day (May 6) at the rate of 18 Reichmarks per performance. Her duties were originally limited to station identification and the introduction of records and musical performances.

She began as a shift announcer for two nights a week and for the next seven months eked out a living on a per show basis. Her ease at the microphone was such that she was promoted within three months to be the first female host of a musical variety program on the European Service. Her income rose as she took on more work, and she was offered substantially more for political broadcasts. Over the next four and a half years, she would clock over 10,000 hours of broadcasting to become the highest paid radio personality on the Overseas Service. Paid from a cashier's window in the broadcasting complex, she was eligible for the ration coupons that would become more and more critical to daily life as the war progressed.

In those early days, Mildred was a "cut and dried" announcer, longing for the day when she could work with what she called "live bands instead of dead records." At the beginning of her employment, she was a popular figure by all accounts, and her radio colleagues remembered her as light-hearted and friendly. Easily given to teasing and joking in the studio, her attitude was in direct contrast to the tense atmosphere created by Goebbels and his underlings: "She did not take her job very seriously and made fun of a great many things in Nazi Germany," a musician recalled after the war.

At times her comments could be reckless, and she gained a reputation as a "loose cannon." "I often had to warn her that her speeches about Goebbels would be very dangerous for her," a colleague recalled.[130] Another orchestra member remembered that she would sign off the broadcast with the words *Heil Hitlerchen* in what he described as an "absolutely joking manner."[131] Werner Berger, the chief director of radio plays, described her political and social views at the time:

> Miss Gillars was not a narrow-minded National Socialist, for within artists' circles it was not customary to hold one's tongue, and one did not need to be careful in front of her. As far as I remember, she was probably convinced of the theories of National Socialist ideology, which, in her opinion, were ideal.[132]

However, there was an unstable and volatile side to her nature. Berger continued:

> At times she had sentimental attacks, which could develop into hysterical outbursts. Perhaps it was the pressure of the doubt about her conviction that led her to this.[133]

Berger's intimation that German officials suspected that her political conversion might not be genuine may have stemmed from what they knew about her personal life. It was not politics that would wed Mildred Gillars to the German cause, but a man.

The Professor

Shortly after she joined Reichsradio in 1940, Mildred appeared as an actress in a series of ten radio dramas entitled *Dr. Anders and Little Margaret*, written by the commentator and Foreign Office official Max Otto Koischwitz. From a dramatic standpoint, the plays were poorly written. "Most of those things were so boring," she remembered in 1949.[134] Unimpressed by the plays, she was drawn to the dark-haired, moody intellectual. An erudite Silesian-born scholar, Koischwitz emigrated from Germany to the United States in 1924. Unable to earn a living in the Weimar Republic, he taught German Literature and Drama courses at New York University, Columbia University and Hunter College.

Shortly after arriving in New York, he gained a reputation as a prolific writer and entertaining lecturer. In 1926, he married a Swiss-born governess named Erna (Bea) Keller who would bear him three daughters. By the time he was appointed to a full-time position as an assistant professor in 1928, he was already one of Hunter's most popular instructors. The couple resided in Sunnyside, Queens where Erna kept house and raised the children while Koischwitz wrote and taught. The young professor also had a reputation for pursuing the female students who frequently idolized him.

John Carver Edwards, in his book *Berlin Calling*, described the demise of Koischwitz's academic career in the United States. Before 1933, he was known to be an enthusiastic mentor to Jewish students. He even unsuccessfully recommended one Jewish student for foreign study in Germany. When word of the persecution of Jews started to leak out of Germany shortly after Hitler became Chancellor, Koischwitz angrily denounced such repression to his class. Over the course of the next few years, however, he grew to support the new order ever more vocally.

According to Edwards, the theme of the preservation of German "blood and soil" was prevalent in Koischwitz's writings long before the Nazi accession to power. Recurring trips back to his native land reinforced his deepening conversion to National Socialism. However, his changing political views did not interfere with his efforts to become a naturalized American citizen. In 1935, he took the oath to become a US citizen, effectively removing any danger of deportation for his increasingly unpopular political views.

The timing of his naturalization was fortuitous because it was in 1935 that he came to the attention of the popular newspaper columnist and radio personality Walter Winchell. Winchell, one of the most powerful journalists in the United States, and Jewish, did not hesitate to point to Koischwitz as an example of Nazi infiltration into higher learning. The professor strenuously denied Winchell's accusations. Now a newly minted US citizen, Koischwitz returned to Germany in 1935 and again in 1937 for "study"—each time without Erna and the children, without fear of being denied re-entry.[135]

Mildred would later attribute his repeated trips to Germany to his "love for the land."

> He loved his country very, very much, with a depth that I have seldom seen in another human being, and the soil of Germany was precious to him. He loved the mountains with the intensity that a man may love a woman.... The German landscape pulled him back every year.[136]

Essentially an economic migrant to America, Koischwitz's loyalty to the United States was virtually non-existent. It was at the time of his frequent trips to Germany that Koischwitz aroused the interest of anti-Fascist groups who took note of his use of the classroom as a platform for his political views. Koischwitz peppered his lectures with pro-Nazi rhetoric, much to the dismay of the Hunter student body, faculty and administration. By 1939, it had become increasingly difficult for the college administration to defend him and his views. Only the Chairman of the German Department, Adolphe Büsse, championed his cause in the name of "academic freedom."

In the classroom, students who challenged his ideas were either harangued or ignored.[137] Despite his naturalization and the administration's repeated attempts to defend Koischwitz in the name of "academic liberty," Hunter College did not grant him a full professorship. Instead, he was tenured as an Assistant Professor in 1938, the same year he was feted by the student body as the "Outstanding Professor of 1938." Koischwitz saw the slight as an effort to stall his career prospects and to punish him for his unpopular political views. The tension between Hunter and Koischwitz came to a head a year later when the undergraduate newspaper condemned Fascism in its pages and challenged all members of the German Department to publicly do the same. Chairman Büsse and Koischwitz both refused. The anti-Fascist American Council against Nazi Propaganda wrote to Hunter College President George N. Shuster, warning that Koischwitz was a subversive and/or foreign agent, and that it had photo static copies of his activities. Shuster responded that Koischwitz was solely guilty of "Hitlerite sympathies" rather than outright subversion.[138]

The Anti-Nazi League also petitioned New York State's Department of Education regarding the Professor, stating that "whether, under the circumstances, he is a fit person to remain a teacher of youth in the City of New York, is we believe, of major importance, particularly at this time when Nazi-inspired incitements of racial hatred and fratricidal strife are so much to the fore."[139]

Hunter finally granted Koischwitz an unpaid six-month leave of absence to return again to Germany, effective as of September 1, 1939, the day that Hitler's armies invaded Poland. Although he was scheduled to return on January 31, 1940, it was apparent from the farewell party given by friends and colleagues that the leave might well be permanent. Unlike his other journeys, his wife and three daughters joined him. His staunchest supporter at Hunter, Chairman Büsse, also fled the US for Germany to live with his daughter and her husband—a Nazi official.

Within months, Koischwitz was reported to be living in Denmark on the German border awaiting the opportunity to re-enter the United States (Erna and the children remained in Germany). When the Professor returned to Berlin, he was hired almost immediately by the Foreign Office to work for the English service of the German Overseas Radio. *The Hour*, a newsletter devoted to identifying Fascist and Nazi fifth-columnists in the United States, speculated that the Professor feared American justice:

> The proper authorities in the United States were preparing to take action with regard to his Nazi propagandistic activities if

and when he returned. Photo static evidence of his activities, collected by *The Hour*, was kept ready for such action. Perhaps learning of the impending action, and needed by Hitler in the Scandinavian countries and the Nazi Reich, Assistant Professor Otto Koischwitz chose not to return.[140]

Three days before his official resignation from Hunter took effect, Koischwitz made his debut broadcast as Reichsradio's newest acquisition, "Mr. O.K." (*A.k.a.* Dr. Anders).[141] By June 1940 he was the host of *The College Hour, O.K. Speaks* and other "educational" programs.[142] The educational series was aimed at young people of college age and mixed the Professor's extensive knowledge of German literature and history with a healthy dose of National Socialist opinion.

As Koischwitz's career blossomed as a radio personality, and eventually into a position as the Foreign Office's chief liaison to Reichsradio, Mildred's responsibilities increased. In 1941 she became the host of *Club of Notions*, a music and variety program produced by the Overseas Service that was heard frequently in the US.

Supported by the Lutz Templin Orchestra and other combos, she introduced big band hits and standards played live in the studio. After years of working to survive and pursue her career as an actress, she was employed in a position where she was well liked and respected for her work. As her duties increased, she emerged from the poverty that characterized most of her adult life into a comfortable financial existence.

While walking through the halls of the Big House on her way to the *Sender Bremen* studios in late 1940, she encountered Professor Koischwitz for the first time since their radio plays. Stopping the shapely American woman he teased, "It's not very nice of you to never have any time for my fireside chats."

Replying that she was unaware of his talks, she responded in kind: "[I] thanked him for his interest, and told him he'd never asked me."

"I'd like to go on record now as having asked," Koischwitz flirtatiously responded.[143] Although she was attracted to the scholar, whom she described as "gallant" and "charming," Mildred did not see him again socially until December 1942.

Without a Country

As the United States became more deeply involved in aiding Britain in its war effort, Mildred's position in Germany became increasingly precarious. She was walking a tightrope between her status as citizen of a "neutral" nation and German government employee. Throughout 1940, she had kept her US papers in order, applying for permission to stay in Germany five days after being hired. Failing to state that she was an employee of the German government, she instead swore that she was still Brigitte Horney's personal assistant.

In the spring of 1941, she brought her passport to be renewed by the United States consulate in Berlin. She approached a consular secretary and mentioned in an offhand manner that she was working for the German Radio. "I didn't see anything wrong with it," she claimed.[144] The secretary asked her to return the following day. It was there that Mildred encountered a vice consul named Vaughn who brusquely "snatched" the passport out of her hand. Angered by her reluctance to be repatriated to America in the face of the coming war, she claimed the official took the passport, threw it into his desk drawer and refused to return it to her.

"He just snatched it from me so violently that I knew there was something wrong," she remembered in 1949. "I even wanted to get it back, and he opened a drawer in a great hurry, and the passport just disappeared in the drawer, and the drawer was shut and that was that."[145] The vice consul had been tipped off by the secretary about the true nature of her work and reclaimed the passport. Mildred was nonplussed. "He offered no explanation. That's why I couldn't understand his very gruff and uncivil manner," she recalled.[146] With only a receipt for the passport, she walked out of the consulate with little proof of her American citizenship.

Embassy personnel in Berlin were inundated by American citizens attempting to leave Germany at the outbreak of war, as well as droves of Jewish refugees seeking asylum from their Nazi tormentors. William Russell, in his 1941 memoir of his experiences at the American Embassy in Berlin, described the animus felt by the consul personnel for the Nazi regime:

I think there is no decent American living who could have worked in our Berlin immigration section without acquiring a deep hatred for the government which drove these people like cattle from unfriendly consulate to unfriendly consulate, from blocked border to blocked border. Nothing was too petty for the mighty German government so long as it could do some harm to a harried Jew.[147]

The Vice Consul was revolted by the sight of an American citizen requesting an *extension* to her passport in order to further aid that detested government. The level of repression against Jews had increased exponentially since the beginning of the war, and was common knowledge among Berliners. Dr. Goebbels, in his role as Gauleiter (regional party leader) of the capital city, demanded draconian measures against the remaining 70,000 Jews still in Berlin as of 1940 (19,000 of which still had some kind of employment).[148] Ostensibly angered by the fact that returning front-line soldiers could witness Jews freely roaming the streets of the Reich, he beseeched Hitler to order their immediate deportation to the East. However, a lack of transport and the need for Jewish labor in war-related industries postponed such an effort.

Goebbels was undaunted in his effort to show the remaining Jews no mercy. On September 1, 1941, the decree was issued that the yellow Star of David be worn in public at all times throughout the Greater Reich. By October, Jews were required to have special permission to ride public transportation. On December 21, 1941, a further decree forbade Jews from using public telephones. Early 1942 brought the expropriation of Jewish private property designated by the state as "luxury goods," and in April they were forbidden to ride subways and buses altogether. The average Berliner could not help but notice the stage being set for the complete removal of Jews from their midst.

Despite her willingness to remain and witness the repression, Mildred was not immune from the suspicion of the German authorities. Shortly after the confiscation of her papers, an acquaintance mentioned that the Gestapo was investigating her presence in Berlin:

I was told by someone that I'd come to the attention of the
secret service … this woman told me I must never breathe it to
anyone … she told me to see a certain Major Denner at a certain address—that he would see me privately. [The woman]
said that he would give any kind of passport if you will do
espionage work.

When I met him he was very charming. He said, "What
kind of papers have you?" I said, "Well, I have none." He
asked, "Don't you think we're rather generous to let you run
around without papers?" I told him "yes." He asked me if I
didn't realize the danger I was in. I said "yes."

Denner made her an offer. She would be given a passport and
funds if she would agree to participate in an effort to land German
agents on American shores for the purpose of sabotage. Denner questioned her knowledge of American defense industries and, noting that
she came from Ohio, wanted to know about the Wright Airplane
Works in Dayton. She refused, telling Denner "I want you know that
though I work for the German radio, I would not—even if it meant my
death—do anything against my country."[149] Still under the delusion
that her function as an announcer was not a compromising or disloy-
al act, she remained adamant that there was a distinct difference
between being a performer and being a traitor.[150]
Although Mildred would later insist that she had no money at the
time to return to the US, and claimed that she would face certain
poverty in America, her friend Erwin Christiani told American interrogators of another reason for her stubborn insistence on remaining in
Germany:

At the time, as the USA were going to come into the war, there
was given occasion to all American citizens living in Berlin to
leave Germany. Miss Gillars was, at that time, in full desperation because she wanted to return to her home country, and on
the other hand, she could not. She had a big confidence in me,
so she told me private things, which she will never tell to the
Court.[151]

By late 1941, Mildred had become involved with Dr. Paul Karlson, an Estonia-born physicist and chemist:

> The main reason was that she was in love [with] a certain German Natural Philosopher, who had declared that he wanted to marry her. This man told her that if she would return to America, he would never marry her.[152]

Karlson, who had become a German citizen, was not about to abandon his adopted home to go to America with the 39-year-old ex-actress. Christiani, a radio technician who befriended Mildred when she began working at *Sender Bremen*, was asked for his advice. He told US military interrogators, "I said to her that if she were really sure her friend would marry her, it would be better for her future if she would remain in Germany, as she had no relations in the USA."[153-4] Christiani pointed out that her advanced age and diminishing marriage prospects played a central role in her decision rather than political conviction.

As the final boats boarded to evacuate Americans from Nazi Germany, Mildred chose to remain in the hope of a marriage proposal that would never come. Karlson had reportedly been conscripted and sent to the Eastern Front, leaving without asking her to marry. She would become increasingly dependent on her employers at the broadcasting house and especially on Otto Koischwitz—a dependence that would become total on December 7, 1941.

Pearl Harbor

Mildred was working in the studio when the news was broadcast that Japan had attacked Pearl Harbor. America's entry into the war was imminent. Stunned, she broke down in front of her colleagues. She loudly denounced the Japanese and became hysterical. "I told them what I thought about Japan and that the Germans would soon find out about them," she recalled. "The shock was terrific. I lost all discretion and I went back to my apartment."[155] Angered by the turn of events and trapped in a situation that she could not escape, she committed an offense that could have resulted in immediate arrest and deportation to a concentration camp. Her situation had changed dramatically. She was no longer the representative of a neutral power whose sympathies were merely questionable, but an enemy national. At her apartment that evening, she received a phone call from a monitor at the station who told her not to report to work the next day and advised, "You had better stay in bed."[156]

Her outburst did not go unnoticed by the management of Reichsradio. Johannes Schmidt-Hansen called her into his office to discipline her for her remarks about Germany's ally in the Far East. What happened next would become an object of controversy. According to Mildred, Schmidt-Hansen demanded that she sign an oath of allegiance to the German Reich. Faced with the prospect of joblessness or possible deportation to a prison camp, she felt that she had no choice but to produce an oath.

"I knew what the results would have to be," she said later, "and I could see by the hardness in his flinty eyes at that moment that it would be best of all to leave and make my decision somewhere else, and I did leave his office."[157] It was clear from their conversation that she could not return to work without her signature on an oath of allegiance. She phoned Karlson and explained her plight:

> I phoned him and went, having said I have something very serious to discuss with him, which I did not care to discuss on the phone, because you could not know if your phone was being watched. I talked to him and his mother and one of his sisters who was there, and then they retired after we had a cup of tea, and we went into the library, and he sat down at the typewriter and wrote in German what I submitted then the next day to Mr. Schmidt-Hansen ... something to the effect that: I swear my allegiance to Germany, and signed Mildred Gillars.[158]

She dropped the document off at Schmidt-Hansen's office on December 9 and returned to work. One day later, Hitler declared war on the United States.

Mildred cited the signing of the oath as a pivotal event in her transition from radio announcer to propagandist. Until then, she maintained that she had "not done anything in the least bit propagandistic."[159] In her portrayal of events, she rose to the defense of her beloved America when it was under attack. Risking her job and freedom, she advised her German bosses not to trust the Japanese. Her account casts her as the valiant defender of the United States who relented only to save her life and job. It was the first of a series of self-serving rationalizations that she would later use throughout her life to justify her actions. Each explanation would emphasize her "love for America," her opposition to the war, her hatred of Roosevelt, and her assertion that it was the United States that abandoned her as war approached—not the other way around.

CHAPTER 5

Smiling Through

"Between the two wars, Fascism and Nazism attracted human derelicts as a flame attracts a moth. Most of the Nazi hierarchy consisted of derelicts from the First War, who could not find a place in the Germany of the Republic. Nazism offered them, as it offered our American traitors, a chance to become somebody. It offered them a career and it offered them something ready-made on which to vent their hates."
—William L. Shirer[160]

DECEMBER 1942–AUGUST 1943

Even before the United States entered the war, Max Otto Koischwitz was a rising star at the German Foreign Office. He left behind a stalled academic career in the United States to become an important player on the periphery of the Third Reich's inner circle. It was not uncommon for the former professor to fly to Hitler's headquarters to discuss radio content with Foreign Minister Joachim von Ribbentrop. Although Koischwitz held several different titles within the organizational maze of the radio corporation, he was the *de facto* liaison between the Foreign Office and Reichsradio. He was, as Mildred proudly boasted, "the man who interviewed Ribbentrop personally on matters concerning the broadcasting company which displeased him or pleased him, as the case may be."[161]

On February 23, 1942 he was promoted to manager for political broadcasting to the USA Zone.[162] His mission was to improve the shortwave broadcasts and increase their appeal to American GIs and their families back home. Although the other American commentators (Kaltenbach, Chandler, et al.) were effective broadcasters, Koischwitz sought to bring a voice to the mix that would attract the lonely soldier far from home. He hoped to make Mildred his spokeswoman for that purpose but he would first have to persuade her to abandon her reluctance to broadcast propaganda to her native land. There were also bureaucratic obstacles to overcome. Johannes Schmidt-Hansen, her manager at *Sender Bremen*, did not want to give up one of the European Service's most talented broadcasters to another department without a fight.

During 1942, Mildred became Mistress of Ceremonies (the title then used for the host of a show) for an increasing number of programs. *Club of Notions* was replaced by the war-focused music/variety show *Smiling Through*. Aimed at the ladies in the audience, it dealt with cultural events in Germany, and entertainment. Political content was minimal until December 1942, when Koischwitz came on board as producer and changed the format. Renamed *Home Sweet Home,* "O.K." took the show in a decidedly propagandistic direction.

As American men faced fierce battles in the deserts of North Africa, *Home Sweet Home* was designed to arouse homesickness in the soldiers. Opening with a quintessentially American sound—the moaning of a lonely train whistle—*Home Sweet Home* was a tug on the heartstrings that played on the desires, fears and jealousies of the fighting men. Jazz and swing, while outlawed by the Nazi regime as a "degenerate" art form, were a staple (albeit in an "Aryanized" incarnation) on *Home Sweet Home*. Speaking in a breathless voice, Midge portrayed herself as a much younger but experienced woman. She played the vixen behind the microphone, taunting the men on the front lines and casting doubt in their minds about their mission, their wives and girlfriends, and their prospects after the war. In one early broadcast, she told the GIs:

Hello, Gang. This is Midge, calling the American Expeditionary Forces in the four corners of the world tonight with their little "Home Sweet Home" program. Well, kids, you know I'd like to say to you "Pack Up Your Troubles In Your Old Kit Bag," but I know that that little old kit bag is much too small to hold all the trouble you kids have got ...

Well I'm afraid that [your girl] will never surrender till you kids surrender. How about it? There's no getting the Germans down. You've been trying for a long time now; and you remember what was told to you before you went to Africa—that it would be a walk away for you boys. Well, was it? ... Well, if we women had our way, there would be no wars anyhow ... I just wonder if [she] isn't sort of running away with one of the 4-Fs back home and you know just as well as I do that if the cases were reversed you wouldn't go on waiting year after year either, would you?[163]

Complete with a live orchestra, *Home Sweet Home* marked the culmination of Mildred Gillars' transformation from down-on-her-luck actress to the woman known to the world as Axis Sally—the insidious, hateful, anti-Semitic golden girl of Nazism. On one show in early 1943, she treated Dick, her bandleader, to her particular brand of pacifism and defeatism:

Gee, Dick, I'm afraid, you'll be giving them ... some very bad ideas. They'll just get all kind of woozy and would like to throw down those little old guns and toddle off home. Well, that would be the right thing for them to do after all, because they're certainly not making any headway here in the sector right now.... Gee, I'd never have a war if I could do anything to prevent it and I think most women are like that.[164]

It was during Christmas 1942 when her conversion to propagandist became complete, that the romantic relationship between the lonely announcer and her married mentor caught fire. She was a solitary figure in the studio. "As I was unmarried and had no home," she remembered, "I was free to work on Christmas Day and give the other girls a chance to be with their families."[165]

The romance blossomed quickly as the two met frequently at the coffee house located near the Deutschland House in the broadcasting complex. Eventually the two became inseparable. They dined together at the Hotel Adlon, a favorite haunt of the Nazi elite and the foreign diplomatic corps on Unter den Linden near the Brandenburg Gate. He personally directed her broadcasts and soon expanded her role to become the host of *Morocco Sendung* (Morocco Calling), another offering for the troops in North Africa. The Professor worked overtime attempting to wrest his prize announcer from the European Service.

"[From March to July 1943] Professor Koischwitz was trying to get me away from *Sender Bremen* and to have all my time concentrated on programs to the USA. So we had many talks about it, around Deutschland House and in this coffee house."[166] The pressure on her to join the USA Zone full-time became so intense that she later described it as a constant source of discord between the couple. Koischwitz used his considerable pull within the Foreign Office eventually to outmaneuver Schmidt-Hansen.

"After long negotiations ... Schmidt-Hansen finally agreed to release me from *Sender Bremen* until 8.30 in the evening. This caused a great deal of trouble in the studio because of the times," she later remembered.[167] Her schedule was frantic, finishing *Morocco Sendung* at the Deutschland House and then running over to the "Big House" to start her nightly duties for the Overseas Service.

Mildred was not the only radio broadcaster who was influenced to change loyalties as the result of a romantic liaison. Before the 1938 *Anschluss*, Robert H. Best was a correspondent in Vienna for the *Chicago Tribune* and a bachelor. His engagement to an attractive Austrian woman and devout Nazi named Erna Maurer (along with disappointing career reversals) likely played a central role in his decision to remain. William L. Shirer, the CBS Radio correspondent, recalled that when American reporters were interned at Bad Nauheim during the first days of America's involvement in the war, Best mentioned to the other internees that his fiancée owned land in Austria that she could not abandon.[168]

Best left Bad Nauheim and reemerged as "Mr. Guess Who," the host of the *Best Berlin Broadcast* for *Sender Bremen*, much to the shock of all who knew him in Vienna. While interned, Best offered his services to the regime. He was interviewed by Werner Plack, a liaison responsible for recruiting English-speaking radio personalities. Several years before, Plack had briefly been an actor and wine merchant in Los Angeles and was reputed to be skilled at vetting prospective announcers. Best had been a radio correspondent for Radio Vienna, and his prior experience made him an ideal candidate for Reichsradio. This man, whose closest friend and protégé before the war was Jewish and who was never regarded as an anti-Semite by his fellow correspondents, became one of the crudest commentators on the German radio. The tone of his diatribes resulted in instances where the Foreign Office took issue with the overt, unsophisticated anti-Semitism displayed in his broadcasts.

Neither were the British immune to the charms of the *frauleins*. Norman Baille-Stewart was a British army officer who fell deeply in love with a German woman. Shortly thereafter, he offered his services to Germany as a spy. He sold military secrets during travels to Holland and Germany and was arrested in 1933. After imprisonment in the Tower of London, he was released in 1937 and fled to Germany in search of the woman he loved. He briefly broadcast for the European Service (until December 1939) and then Nazi "black" propaganda efforts from 1942 on under the sobriquet "Lancer."

In Mildred's case, as in the others, a German began a romantic relationship with a lonely and unattached enemy national to influence the object of their "affection" to, in the words of American journalist Dorothy Thompson, "go Nazi." Whether these relationships were born out of romantic love or service to the Reich may never be conclusively known, but they nevertheless served as effective recruiting tools.

As Koischwitz and Midge drank coffee and made plans, the remnant of Berlin's Jewish population served as slave labor in the city's war production factories. Goebbels, in his role as Gauleiter of Berlin, was infuriated that his city was not yet *Judenfrei* (Jew-free) and actively pressed the Gestapo and SS to remove the remaining Jews from factory work and dispatch them to the East for extermination. The factories were to be kept running by importing Poles to replace the murdered Jews. By the beginning of 1943 there were approximately 10,000 Jews remaining in the capital working at war-related jobs. In a mass roundup, trucks went through the streets of the city and Jewish men, women and children were pulled out of their homes and work-places for deportation. The arrests extended to the *mischling* (those whom the Reich determined were of partial-Jewish ancestry) and those married to non-Jews.

In March the regime was forced to relent on the matter of those Jews married to Gentiles, as hundreds of angry wives congregated on Rosenstrasse demanding the return of their husbands. Fearing the wrath of the female workforce that the Nazis relied on for political support and factory work, it was thought to be politically wise to release the husbands and wives of the protesters. These violent mass arrests, like so many others that preceded them, could not have gone unnoticed by the couple whose political and romantic alliance grew stronger by the day. In fact, while Berlin's Jews were being sent to their fate, Mildred's broadcast of May 18, 1943 stressed Jewish culpability for the war and the misfortune that had befallen America:

This is Berlin Calling. Berlin calling the American mothers, wives and sweethearts. And I'd just like to say, girls, that when Berlin calls it pays to listen. When Berlin calls it pays to listen in because there's an American girl sitting at the microphone every Tuesday evening at the same time with a few words of truth to her countrywomen back home. Girls, you all know, of course, by now that it is a very serious situation and there must be some reason for my being here in Berlin, some reason why I'm not sitting at home with you at the little sewing bees knitting socks for our men over in French North Africa.

Yes, girls, there is a reason, and it's this: it's because I'm not on the side of President Roosevelt. I'm not on the side of Roosevelt and his Jewish friends and his British friends, because I've been brought up to be a 100 percent American girl; conscious of everything American, conscious of her friends, conscious of her enemies. And the enemies are pre-cisely those people who are fighting against Germany today, and in case you don't know it, indirectly against America too, because a ... defeat for Germany would mean a defeat for America. Believe me, it would be the very beginning ... of the ... end of America and all of her civilization and that's why, girls, I'm staying over here and having these little heart to heart talks with you once a week....

Gee, girls, isn't it a darn shame? All the sweet old American summer atmosphere which the boys are missing now? Just imagine sitting out on the old ... ah ... back porch in a sweet old rocking chair listening to the birds and twilight? Instead of that the boys are over there in the hot, sunny desert, longing for home and for what? Fighting for our friends? Well, well, well, since when are the British our friends? Now, girls, come on, be honest. As one American to another, do you love the British? Why, of course the answer is "no." Do the British love us? Well, I should say not! But we are fighting for them. We are shedding our good young blood for this "kike" war, for this British war. Oh, girls, why don't you wake up? I mean, after all, the women can do something, can't they? Have you tried to ... realize where the ... ah ... situation is leading us to? Because it is the downfall of civilization if it goes on like that. After all, let the British get out of their own mess girls, and let "God Save The King"; if he's worthy of it, I'm sure God can. At least, there's no reason for we Americans to get mixed up in British messes. Don't you agree ...?[169]

... I love America but I do not love Roosevelt and all of his "kike" boyfriends who have thrown us into this awful turmoil.[170]

Mildred's resistance to political broadcasting weakened not only because of her infatuation with Koischwitz, but also due to pressures stemming from her status as an enemy national without papers. An incident in a Berlin train station in the fall of 1942 may have played a role in her decision to yield. After a day of shopping for antiques, she walked through the station and realized that she had left her food ration coupons in a nearby coffee shop.

"I went into a phone booth and called the shop. While I was talking, I noticed people gathering around the booth. While the shopkeeper was telling me she'd found the tickets, I noticed the crowd getting larger—more and more faces appeared.[171] A man suddenly yelled out, 'You can tell by her accent, she's an American.'[172] He tore open the door to the telephone booth and grabbed hold of my arm, and said, 'I'm from the Gestapo, come with me.'"[173] Frightened, she argued, "You can't do this to me. I'm with the radio company." Producing her Reichsradio identification card, the agent examined it, brushed it away, and proceeded to arrest her.

Recalling an earlier incident when she was accused of sabotage for neglecting to read a few lines of scripted text in her broadcast, she protested. "I told the agent that I had to call the radio station—that if I didn't show up for the broadcast—that would be sabotage."[174] The agent allowed her to call her manager, Schmidt-Hansen. She turned the telephone over to the agent and, as they spoke, Mildred suddenly saw a man in the crowd motioning to her. Taking advantage of the confusion, the stranger grabbed her wrist and pushed her into the open doors of a departing train. Frightened and shaking, she returned to the broadcasting studio. The agent arrived at the *Rundfunkhaus* a few minutes later. After a few minutes of discussion with Schmidt-Hansen, the agent apologized to Midge and left, saying, "Well, ten times out of eleven you're wrong, but the eleventh time you're right."[175] The incident was a sobering reminder of the precariousness of her position in Germany and her dependence on her superiors at Reichsradio to move about freely without arrest or harassment.

While their relationship deepened, Otto Koischwitz kept a disturbing secret from his mistress. The Professor began the affair with his star announcer with the full knowledge that his wife Erna was pregnant with his fourth child. Despite the impending birth, he professed his love to Mildred in two letters from his boyhood home in Silesia. Troubled by the situation, he went away in April 1943 on a weekend trip to what he termed his "Mount Olympus":

There was a particular mountain in Silesia which had played a fateful role in his life ever since his childhood; and he said that every time he had a spiritual problem, since the early days of his youth, he had gone to this particular mountain, which he called his Mount Olympus, and had conferred with himself and considered the problem and found the answer, and he realized at that time, in the spring of '43, what was happening and reverted back to his boyhood habit of going to his Mount

Olympus. He got the answer, that God favored his love.[176]

Koischwitz's love may have been favored by Providence, but the fortunes of the Wehrmacht were not. The remnants of the Sixth Army surrendered at Stalingrad on February 2, 1943, and Hitler's government declared three days of national mourning for the fallen. German cities were under attack by Allied bombers: Wilhelmshaven on January 27, Berlin on January 30 in daylight raids; Essen and the Ruhr on March 5. Even Joseph Goebbels's propaganda machine could not disguise the desperate turn of events. The message had to be retooled to prepare the *Volk* for the sacrifices that lay ahead. Hitler, enraged by the reversals on the Eastern Front, disappeared from view. It was left to Goebbels to proclaim the new message to a carefully selected group of Nazi party loyalists at the *Berliner Sportpalast* (Sports Palace) on February 18. Known as the "Total War" speech, it set the theme for all radio propaganda for the duration of the war:

> I speak first to the world, and proclaim three theses regarding our fight against the Bolshevist danger in the East. The first thesis: Were the German army not in a position to break the danger from the East, the Reich would fall to Bolshevism, and all Europe shortly afterwards. Second: the German army, the German people and their allies alone have the strength to save Europe from this threat. Third: Danger is a motivating force. We must act quickly and decisively, or it will be too late ... Now people rise up, and let the storm break loose![177]

In Goebbels' estimation, Germany would be the final defense against the Bolshevization of Europe and the destruction of Western civilization. "Total war" would require sacrifice to the last man, woman and child. There would be no turning back. "Total war" meant victory or total destruction for the German nation.

Family Affair

Not content with merely recruiting his mistress, Koischwitz did not hesitate to use his children as soldiers in the propaganda war. His eldest daughter, Stella, had been recruited as an actress in her father's radio plays as early as 1940, playing the part of Mildred's daughter. By early 1943, Koischwitz had cast all three of his daughters in a new show called *Seven at the Mike* with Mildred fittingly cast as Mistress of Ceremonies.

Seven at the Mike was aimed at the wives and mothers of America. The children sang and a panel of women, including Lord Haw Haw's wife, Margaret Cairns Joyce, discussed the social and cultural dimensions of wartime German life. Although it is not known definitively whether Erna Koischwitz knew of the romantic relationship between her husband and Midge, it is unlikely that his history of philandering had gone unnoticed at home. Nevertheless, her children were coaxed by her husband to work side by side with his paramour.

The first day of March 1943 was a holiday in the German Reich dedicated to honoring the Luftwaffe. American and British air forces marked the day with fierce air strikes on the German capital. Although the bombing was only a foretaste of what was to come, over 700 men, women and children perished in the attack.[178] Several residential areas and the Berlin Zoo were damaged. Fearing further attacks, Koischwitz arranged for the evacuation of his wife and children to Silesia. Dispatching his family to the countryside also made it easier to conceal Erna's pregnancy from Midge. Left without her on-air "family," the show was renamed *Midge at the Mike* in April.

Transformed into a program of primarily political commentary, *Midge at the Mike* was a "heart-to-heart" talk with the mothers, wives and sweethearts of America about the war, the current political situation, and the nefarious ways of Franklin Roosevelt and his "Jewish advisors." It would also feature some of the vilest anti-Semitic rhetoric ever broadcast on German Radio. With Erna and the girls out of Berlin, forty-two-year-old Mildred finally had her man and a starring role to herself.

A Woman of Privilege

With a high-ranking Foreign Office official as her patron, Mildred had more control over the content of her broadcasts than the rest of her American colleagues. She could thus be difficult and egotistical—even a prima donna. In the large barracks of the "Big House," one of her tasks was to introduce the commentaries of Robert H. Best. Best, whose diatribes against Roosevelt and his administration were crudely anti-Semitic, had the temerity to criticize her "talks" and made suggestions on how to improve her Jew-baiting skills.

"Mr. Best even came up to me while a piece of music was being played and suggested that I say this or I say that. And I did not like the spirit in which I was working up there, interrupted by other people's suggestions," she remembered.[179] Best coached her to "dress up" her commentaries: "I was told to use the word 'kike' and I said I didn't like it and considered it to be very undignified, and I would not say it in private life, and I didn't see why I should say it in a broadcast."[180]

Best's meddling resulted in Mildred successfully lobbying Koischwitz to gradually eliminate all other speakers from the *Morocco Sendung* and the *Home Sweet Home* broadcasts. When the Foreign Office protested the removal of Best from the broadcast, the Professor took up her cause. "Professor Koischwitz cooperated with me to the greatest extent of his ability to force my ideas through," she recalled. "If Professor Koischwitz had not helped me, I am sure that my days would have been numbered at the broadcasting company."[181] It was probably not Best's racist terminology that annoyed her most, since she used the terms "kike" and "Jew" liberally in later broadcasts, but the insolence of the former newspaper correspondent in questioning the quality of her work.

Her financial fortunes increased as her involvement in propaganda deepened. For broadcasts with "political content," she received as much as 60 to 80 RM, effectively tripling her income.[182] At the height of her influence, she was earning 3,000 RM per month, a sizable sum in wartime Germany.[183] She was making so much that she was subject to a confiscatory tax.

"No single person in Germany wanted to earn two thousand marks anyway. If you couldn't earn 50,000, then you certainly didn't want to earn 3,000, because the taxes jumped relatively to such an extent that an unmarried person had to pay terrific taxes," she remembered in 1949.[184] Even with the privations of the war, however, she was earning a comfortable sum for the first time in her life. In addition to the rations of butter and cheese provided monthly by the government, she had ample means to buy what she needed on the black market.

Mildred did not shy away from using her relationship with Koischwitz to settle scores and gain influence in the studio. She raised hackles with her superiors in the Foreign Office when she convinced the Professor to provide American magazines and newspapers to assist her in the preparation of her commentaries. Listening to foreign broadcasts was punishable by death, and access to foreign media was severely limited to high party officials, salaried commentators and radio department heads. Essentially a *per diem* employee, Mildred was not high enough in the hierarchy to meet the requirements. Although she later claimed that she sought the magazines in order to avoid being influenced by German propaganda, it is clear that she was extraordinarily privileged.

"I would read the American magazines and 'O.K.' would suggest that I give a little talk on this article, that article, something that Mrs. Roosevelt had said...." The magazines were never kept at the radio studio, but kept under wraps so that no one but the higher strata of the party could see them. "They were very careful about their magazines, and they weren't supposed to be anywhere where announcers, secretaries or anyone else could get at them. They were considered pretty secret material," she recalled.[185] Since the radio broadcasting company was overseen by representatives of Goebbels's Propaganda Ministry, Ribbentrop's Foreign Office, and eventually a representative from Himmler's SS, it is unlikely that these transgressions would have been ignored if it were not for the access provided by her important mentor.

Moreover, the Foreign Office was shocked to discover that, thanks to Koischwitz, she was working without a script or the supervision of a censor. When Karl Schotte, the manager of the Overseas Service, discovered the freedom that Koischwitz had bestowed on his paramour, he flew into a rage.

"The top blew off everything," Mildred remembered. "Schotte ... just went raving around the place and said 'How did this happen; are you completely mad?'"[186] Confident of her position, she told Schotte that Koischwitz reached an agreement with her when she started working for him—no censor and no propaganda. Schotte went to

Horst Cleinow, the head of the USA Zone, and ordered that she work from a script and that Schotte himself censor all of her shows. Dreading the repercussions of such liberties, Schotte told Cleinow that "nothing like that had ever been done and that it was mad to think it could be done in wartime."[187]

In August 1943, Schotte's failure to read and censor two sentences in an announcer's script resulted in his being dispatched to a concentration camp for sloppy censorship. There are varying accounts of the incident that led to Schotte's arrest. One account claims that a female announcer ad-libbed to an audience of American women and inadvertently mentioned the privations that German women faced as the war progressed. The last thing the Propaganda Ministry wanted was news of the bleak economic situation on the German home front reaching the enemy via one of its own broadcasts.

Another account came from Eduard Dietze, Dr. Winkelnkemper's deputy at the RRG (*Reichsrundfunkgesellschaft*, or German Broadcasting Company). A few days before the August 1943 Quebec Conference between Churchill and Roosevelt, a scriptwriter named Harl wrote that Germany could consider altering its National Socialist policies in return for a negotiated peace. Schotte had read and approved the script. When the Associated Press picked up the text of the broadcast, they published a story citing the item an "olive branch" signaling Germany's willingness to sue for peace. Goebbels and von Ribbentrop were furious, and the Propaganda Minister ordered the arrest of the manager who allowed the script to be broadcast. Although Winkelnkemper defended Schotte by claiming that the manager never read the script, he was sent to a concentration camp. Karl Schotte was released from the camp on Christmas 1943 and allowed to return to the Overseas Service as a producer of entertainment programs.[188] After the incident, Winkelnkemper ordered a mandatory review of each script and recording by an additional censor prior to each broadcast.

"O.K." Indicted

In a small, undistinguished house in Silver Spring, Maryland, radio technicians monitored the broadcasts of the German Overseas Service. Every audible Axis broadcast was examined for content and recorded on acetate disc for future use. Those recordings would lead to the identification of the American expatriates who assisted the German Reich and the Italian Fascists in their war against the United States. As the tide of battle had finally turned in favor of the Allies, Attorney General Francis Biddle determined that the time was right to put the "radio traitors" on notice that there would be a price to pay for their collaboration.

On July 26, 1943, the Justice Department announced a Federal indictment for treason against eight Americans: Max Otto Koischwitz, Frederick W. Kaltenbach, Robert H. Best, Edward Leo Delaney, Douglas Chandler, Constance Drexel, Jane Anderson and the renowned poet Ezra Pound. Reichsradio employed all except Pound at some time after December 11, 1941, the day Hitler declared war on the US. Ezra Pound, an American who had lived as an expatriate in London, Paris and Rapallo, Italy since 1908, was featured on the Italian Radio in several disjointed, obscure and at times, unintelligible commentaries against Franklin Roosevelt, America's involvement in the war and Jewish finance. The Attorney General's statement accused Koischwitz and his cohorts of betraying "the first and most sacred obligation of citizenship."[189] The indictment did not include Axis Sally, who had yet to be identified by the FCC analysts. The indictments appeared on the front page of *The New York Times* and the now-fugitive commentators learned of their status as accused traitors in short order.

With her lover wanted for treason, and the possibility of a German defeat becoming increasingly real, the pressures on Mildred cannot be underestimated. In addition, the likelihood that Koischwitz would ever leave his wife became even more remote when she discovered in August 1943 that Erna was giving birth to his fourth child. A boy named Max Otto Koischwitz was born in a hospital in Silesia on August 15, only to die a few hours later. Mildred's friend and colleague, Erwin Christiani, later revealed to US investigators that Mildred had attempted suicide. Christiani speculated that "her friend" (no longer Paul Karlson, but Koischwitz) had reneged on his promise to marry:

Later on, in 1943, her friend had obviously broken his promise, I guess, for in that year she had tried to commit suicide. It was prevented by her colleague, Miss Ria Kloss, who entered her residence in the certain night by force, because she had got some notion about the intention of Miss Gillars, and shut off the gas valve.[190]

Ria Kloss, a 25-year-old strawberry blonde, was one of Mildred's closest friends at the studio. Forcing her way into the apartment, she discovered Mildred passed out on the floor and took steps to revive her. Mildred had found out only the day before the birth of Koischwitz's son that Erna was pregnant, and the death of the infant must have been a double shock. Christiani never knew the complete details of what had occurred for he was sent to the Eastern front within days of the incident.* Nine days later on August 24, 1943, Erna Koischwitz herself was killed when a massive Allied air attack hit the hospital where she was recovering.[191]

*Christiani does not specify the exact month of the 1943 suicide attempt but the pressures on Mildred reached critical mass with her discovery of Erna Koischwitz's pregnancy on the day before the child's birth, followed by the horrible death of both mother and infant. On the afternoon of the fatal air raid, Mildred, the Professor and Stella sat in a Berlin movie house watching a film.

CHAPTER 6

Did You Raise Your Sons to Be Murderers?

"Well folks, that's what comes of this war, of course ... they're coming in by the hundreds, these American boys, who day after day are flying over Germany in their terror raids trying to extinguish a whole race, killing ruthlessly helpless women and children.... I ask you American women if you brought up your boys to be murderers? Have you? Because that is what they are becoming."

—Axis Sally (February 26, 1944)[192]

By the summer of 1943 the war had taken an increasingly personal toll on Mildred Gillars and Max Otto Koischwitz. In May, Mildred's apartment had been heavily damaged in an air raid. Arriving home from work at 3 a.m. she found the place in ruins. "Where I originally had two rooms," she remembered, "I had just one room because the walls had collapsed and everything in the place [was] smashed to smithereens. It was just a heap of debris, but at least the outside walls were still standing."[193] The Berlin broadcasting complex was a prime target for British and American raiders. During one broadcast that summer, Mildred was on the air as a bomb destroyed a building across the street from the studios. Forced to continue the program without missing a beat, she watched in horror as the structure burned to the ground.

The air attacks on Berlin gained in intensity throughout the year. The raids began on January 30 when British Mosquitoes harassed the tenth anniversary celebration of Hitler's rule in daylight raids. On August 23 and 24 the RAF sent 719 planes over the capital and dropped over 1,700 tons of explosives. Despite the heavy air defenses surrounding the city, the bombardment left Berliners shaken. 854 people died in the attacks and virtually every government building on the Wilhelmstrasse was damaged. As a result, the Overseas Service staff was evacuated to the Berlin suburb Köenigs Wusterhausen a few miles from the transmitters at Zeesen.

Instead of the spacious, barracks-like quarters of the *Funkhaus*, these suburban studios were located in the cramped basement of a post office. Reichsradio personnel lived and worked out of a small inn in nearby Gussow. The major commentators of the Overseas Service were dispatched to locations across the Reich. Douglas Chandler ("Paul Revere") and Robert H. Best were sent to Vienna. William Joyce ("Lord Haw Haw") worked from the studios of Radio Luxembourg, transmitting his commentaries via landline for transmission to Great Britain. The already damaged Berlin broadcasting complex was hit again in a series of raids in November–December 1943—bombings that killed 2,700 Berliners and left a quarter million homeless.[194]

The war's reverses were particularly devastating to Otto Koischwitz. In July, his wife Erna was killed in her hospital bed as she recovered from the tragic childbirth. The hospital was destroyed and everyone in it perished.[195] His newborn son was dead. Indicted for treason in the United States, he faced the possibility of trial and execution. The widespread fame among the troops of the American woman who spoke to them nightly meant that an indictment of Axis Sally would follow. Defeat followed defeat for the *Wehrmacht* in the summer and fall of 1943. In Western Europe, the resignation of Mussolini in July was followed by the Italian surrender in September. In the East, the Germans' last great attempt to wrest the strategic initiative from the Red Army failed with the loss of hundreds of tanks at the Battle of Kursk.

As prospects for a Nazi victory faded, it was essential that Midge put a different face on her service to Germany. She approached Koischwitz with an idea:

We very often talked about America … and I told him that I

felt that my only reason for being was to go to prisoner of war camps, if he could arrange it. He knew that I wasn't a propagandist, and that I certainly had no ambition in that direction, and I told him that the only thing which would be able to give me a little happiness in all this war was to have the feeling that I was being of some service to the people in my own country, and he said that he would do the very best he could do. Negotiations went on for a long, long time ... it was not until Halloween day of '43 that we made our first visit to a prisoner of war camp.[196]

When Karl Schotte was sent to a concentration camp in August, Koischwitz was named to replace him as the permanent head of the USA Zone. His new status enabled him to gain the necessary approval to go to the POW camps and travel with Midge to Holland, Belgium and France. Using his influence in the Foreign Office, he obtained an alien passport (*Fremdenpass*) for Mildred in October of 1943—a highly unusual privilege for a foreign national with no papers. She had first applied for one after the US consulate retained her American passport in 1941, but she received no response. With the intervention of the newly promoted department head, her passport was granted almost a full two years later.

It was not long before Dr. Goebbels expressed his dissatisfaction with a Foreign Office employee managing the USA Zone. The Propaganda Minister demanded that O.K. cut all his ties to the Foreign Office or resign. The former professor resigned as manager to join Midge on her travels to prison camps and hospitals, recording prisoner interviews on erasable cylinders that functioned as the 1940s equivalent of magnetic recording tape. At the end of the tour, the couple brought the recordings back to *Köenigs Wusterhausen* where the completed programs were assembled with Midge providing introductory and closing comments.

It was Halloween day in a camp near Frankfurt-on-the-Oder when Midge, the Professor and two accompanying technicians had their first meeting with a group of American prisoners of war. The group had lunch with an imprisoned American corporal and some of his comrades. Mildred remembered the meal as "quite gay and friendly" as the men expressed surprise at the sound of a woman speaking English. Despite some early reluctance, a few prisoners eventually agreed to record messages. Unfortunately, the Foreign Office official who approved the trips listened to the recordings and complained about the lack of political and military content. The criticism led to the introduction of commentary at the beginning and end of each broadcast, where Midge would customize the broadcast to suit the current propaganda line.

Mildred's radio series *Christmas Bells of 1943* debuted on the first Sunday of December and continued through the holiday season. German Radio's Yuletide gift to GI wives and mothers was monitored by shortwave listeners in the United States and Canada. The listeners sent letters to the families relaying their words. A number of these messages reached the prisoners' families thanks to the efforts of these dedicated hobbyists. The Foreign Office and the Reichsradio's management viewed the Christmas offering as a propaganda success and immediately granted permission to the couple to gather interviews for a program to be called *Easter Bells of 1944*.

Holland provided a welcome refuge from the dangers of Berlin and became the couple's favorite destination for work and play. Their first visit took place on November 29—just in time to celebrate Midge's 43rd birthday. After a short visit to a camp in Braunschweig in January, they returned to Hilversum on February 19—this time to celebrate O.K.'s birthday. Seven months after the death of her mother, Koischwitz's eldest daughter Stella joined the couple for a ten-day trip. The grueling treks to the prison camps and hospitals left little time to sleep, and there were signs that the strain of the past months had an effect on the Professor's health. Koischwitz had been diagnosed with incipient tuberculosis in 1929 and the privations of war did not help his already fragile constitution. Mildred regularly petitioned Adelbert Houben, the second in command of the Overseas Service, for an advance on travel expenses. She explained later that the money was spent obtaining food for the Professor from the black market:

> Professor Koischwitz was not a very strong person and need-
> ed very nourishing food, of which he didn't have too much in
> Germany, and to buy the type of food which he needed and

which would give him strength was very, very expensive. I didn't want him to feel what a burden it was on me. I have always spent money for other things and not for food, but I cooperated with him, and our eating in Holland was a very expensive affair.[197]

Houben was annoyed by her constant requests for additional funds and even asked Mildred's friend and colleague Hans von Richter for an explanation of where the money was going. At the time, Midge was earning a combined sum that rivaled only the salary of Dr. Anton Winkelnkemper, the head of the entire Overseas Service who reported directly to Goebbels. In the Netherlands, she was able to obtain enough food to sustain her beloved Professor, but by the time she returned to Germany she was "broke as usual."[198]

Three weeks before Easter, the two broadcasters traveled to Pomerania to visit an *Arbeitskommando* (work detail) where twenty Americans were working on a large German estate. The visitors from Reichsradio dined with the wife of the estate owner and then went out to the barracks to visit the prisoners' quarters, which Mildred cagily described as "bohemian." Although this visit to the farm was reportedly a pleasant experience, it was a trip to the main camp in March 1944 that brought Mildred Gillars face to face with the anger and resentment of the men she entertained.

Stalag IIB

On an autobahn one and a half miles west of the city of Hammerstein sat one of the most brutal prisoner of war camps in Germany: Stalag IIB. Renowned for its cruelty, the camp was reeling from the execution of eight American prisoners in late 1943 for an "attempted escape." American witnesses at the scene described the incident as cold-blooded murder rather than an escape attempt. Two of the dead soldiers were thrown into the latrine where they remained decomposing in the sun for days as a warning to the other prisoners.[199]

Food rations were minimal, with each prisoner receiving 300 grams of bread and 500 grams of potatoes per day. Twice a week, they were given 300 grams of meat, 20 grams of margarine and a minimal

amount of cheese once a week. The food was distributed once at mid-
day with only ersatz coffee for breakfast. Only Red Cross food
parcels—one per prisoner per week—kept the men from utter starvation. At war's end, the US War Department cited the camp's treatment
of American prisoners as "worse ... than at any other camp established for American POWs before the Battle of the Bulge. Harshness
at the *Stalag* deteriorated into outright brutality and murder on some
of the *Kommandos*. Beatings of Americans on *Kommandos* by their
German overseers were too numerous to list but records indicate that
10 Americans in work detachments were shot to death."[200]

Master Sergeant Robert Ehalt was Adjutant to the Camp Officer
at *Stalag* IIB in March 1944. Ehalt, taken prisoner at Anzio three
months earlier, walked into the camp office to find Medical Officer
Robert Capparell joined by a "Teutonic-looking" man and a woman.
The man and woman were seeking recorded interviews with the prisoners for a special Easter broadcast. The man was introduced to the
Americans as the editor of "O.K." magazine. ("O.K." or *Overseas Kid*
magazine was a four to six page broadsheet edited by Koischwitz
aimed at Allied prisoners of war and distributed throughout the
German camps beginning in March 1943.)

Mildred did not identify herself, and the American soldiers were
immediately suspicious. She made no secret that she wanted the prisoners to say that the Germans were treating them well and giving them
adequate food. After chatting with the officers for several minutes, she
told them that she was born in Maine and had lived in Greenwich
Village before the war. When Ehalt and Capparell asked her directly if
she was Sally from the *Sally and Phil* show on the German radio, she
quickly changed the subject. (That show, aka *Jerry's Calling*, featured
the woman who would become known as the Rome Axis Sally—Rita
Luisa Zucca.)

Convinced that the woman before them was none other than Axis
Sally, Ehalt refused to permit the men to cooperate without first
obtaining permission from the senior American officer in the region.
They made a call to Colonel Drake, who was interned at *Offlag 64* in
Poland. A medical officer was called in to help verify that the voice on
the line was indeed that of the colonel. While the Professor and the

medical officer were speaking to Colonel Drake, Ehalt and Capparell engaged in small talk with the evasive woman. Annoyed that she kept referring to "we Americans" and "us Americans," Capparell asked Mildred why she was freely walking around if she was such a good American. She only replied that she was an "idealist."[201] She noted that the conditions at the camp were not good and told them that she would do what she could to improve them.

Koischwitz returned after a few minutes and told Ehalt that Colonel Drake said that he would leave it up to the US camp leadership to decide whether or not to participate in the recordings. Ehalt made the final decision and flatly refused. Koischwitz exploded in anger, grabbed his bag of equipment and announced that they were leaving. As they walked through a barracks holding over 250 American prisoners, the men howled, catcalled and shouted obscenities at Mildred and Koischwitz. In the midst of this torrent of abuse, one soldier handed her a gift—a carton of Chesterfield cigarettes. Thanking the soldier, she opened the box only to find it filled with horse manure. Revolted, she threw the "gift" to the ground and turned to the screaming prisoners saying "What a bunch of ungrateful people these American people are!"[202]

Despite the fracas at Stalag IIB, their travels eventually yielded enough interviews to provide several programs for the *Easter Bells* show. On Easter Sunday, Mildred spent the entire day in the small makeshift studio in the post office basement assembling 28 programs of interviews with captured servicemen for future use. She described the day in an idyllic light:

> I started very early in the morning. Professor Koischwitz was in my room in Köenigs Wusterhausen. He had his watercolors with him and a little character doll, which I had brought from Holland; and while I was broadcasting he sat in my room and painted watercolors. And I rushed home at noon and got lunch, looked at the painting he had been doing and went back to the studio and broadcast some more. [I] came back and got dinner for us, and then went back to the studio, so that he was alone the whole of Easter Sunday with his painting.[203]

The widowed Professor painted in the peace of Mildred's room as Germany placed its hopes in an Atlantic Wall of steel and iron to halt an Allied invasion of France. It was April 19, 1944, and D-Day was less than eight weeks away.

Medical Reports

In late 1943, the German High Command requested that the Overseas Service broadcast medical reports of captured and injured Allied fliers shot down over Germany and German-occupied territory. In the hope of Allied reciprocation and propaganda gains, the name, service number and type of injury of the wounded were broadcast, as well as a description of their condition. The shows would highlight the humanitarian efforts of those German doctors and nurses who saved the lives of the captured airmen. Although the announcement of the names of three captured prisoners of war was standard boilerplate at the end of each English newscast since the beginning of hostilities, it was the first time that the wounded were used as a propaganda tool. Like a carrot dangled at the beginning of each broadcast, the news announcer held out the possibility of hearing the name of a loved one in return for not turning the dial each evening.

The *Medical Reports* program was effective propaganda not only due to the details being given about the captured men but also the fact that the deliverer of the news was the woman now known to GIs throughout the European Theater as "Axis Sally." The names were given to her by the military and occasionally the reports included the names of fliers who died in hospital. The horrible human damage of the war was described to the families of the dead and injured in grim, almost sadistic detail:

> And now my second death message concerns Pilot George E. Jones. I fortunately have his service number—that may help somewhat in identifying him—it is 13022168T43. Mr. Jones was brought on the 26th of November 1943. His left upper leg had been completely crushed; he had received severe injuries to the right leg and his left hand was also totally crushed. He died on the 27th of November 1943 and this report was made out

by the doctors and went through on the 28th of November. Of course, you know that ... ah ... among fliers the pilot is the last one to bail out, and so of course naturally the machine can be in ... a terrible state by the time he gets his parachute on and is ready to make what in this case was a fatal jump. I'm sorry, very sorry, that I don't have the address of his parents and I do hope that they will get the news soon, although perhaps it is better for them if the news is somewhat delayed.[204]

Her detailed descriptions of the wounds suffered by the captured men were tinged with cynicism and bitterness toward the men who brought America into the war. Staff Sergeant Manuel Rosen of Santa Monica, California was the subject of a message to his next-of-kin—his sister Sylvia Edinger:

Miss Edinger, your brother got his left leg crushed below the knee and the right leg broken below the knee. Well, that's pretty bad if he got both of his legs so badly wounded. Of course, the left one sounds bad where the doctors say that it was crushed below the knee. Let's hope he won't have to lose it, but I suppose it's quite probable.[205]

Her voice became strident and emphatic as she related the carnage she had witnessed in German hospitals and prison camps:

How many very mutilated boys have I seen and they've said to me ... "I don't care how I get back ... just so I get back." You see that's the way they think now. What do you suppose they'll think in later years when there are no jobs for cripples? That's the question.

The reports also reflected her own bitterness toward America for the destruction that the United States had wrought in Germany:

Here is word, now, for Johnsonburg, Pennsylvania ... Johnsonburg ... the report is about Lieutenant William H. Kupole or Lupole, L-U-P-O-L-E, I believe it is, born on the 14th of

February, 1922 in Johnsburg, Pennsylvania. Well, that was a nice little Valentine for his mother at that time. And how little did she ever dream that she'd be asked to sacrifice him for Roosevelt and his Jewish cohorts. Well, he's going to remember the American government for the rest of his life, for his right leg had to be amputated below the knee, and the anklebone in his left leg was broken. The left leg has been placed in a walking cast, and the patient is doing exercises with an artificial limb fitted to the right leg.... Now his mother lives at 235 West Center Street, in Johnsonburg, Pennsylvania ...

Well, Mrs. Lupole, you've seen nothing of this war. You only read Jewish propaganda in your newspaper. But if you've been listening to this broadcast then you know that for many weeks I went from war hospital to war hospital, from one prisoner-of-war camp to another prisoner-of-war camp in France and I saw your boys; saw the pitiful state of untold thousands of them.... Ah yes ... only that is to say thousands I talk of. There are hundreds and hundreds of thousands of them, scattered all over Europe, scattered all over the world, asked to sacrifice their youth, asked to sacrifice their future, because when they get back they will be in no state to take up a job of any consequence.

The voice of Max Otto Koischwitz, the naturalized American citizen who turned his back on his adopted country dominates her message. His ideas, poured into the ear of his lover, were dutifully repeated in unaccented English for American consumption. Lambasting the country that denied the genius of National Socialism and cast aside one of its leading scholars, she further condemns the American people:

And you people are so short-sighted. You know so little about politics, about history, about what is going on in Europe, about the great role which Germany is playing in the future of the Western Continent. Well, if you folks want to fight, to aid and abet the decline of the West, well you are certainly taking the right action. Germany has vision. Germany has culture. Germany has supplied all of Europe, to say nothing of

America and other Western countries with culture. I ask you Americans. What have you done for posterity? Can you answer me? Here are the three things for which you people are known all over the world—money, jazz and Hollywood. Compare your contributions with the contributions of Germany to the world throughout the ages ... and so you want to sacrifice your sons to try to destroy this great country, Germany? Folks, it is a responsibility that you should have never taken on your shoulders. It's the blackest page in the world's history. America should hang her head in shame.

Think it over America. Will you?[206]

Who was to blame for the carnage? Even the parents of the dead and wounded soldiers bear responsibility:

Well, after all, you American parents wanted it, didn't you? And so day after day your boys have to pile through showers of flak ... thousands and thousands of feet up in the air ... sometimes the ship explodes, they're burned alive in the airplane or they bail out and only break their legs, and arms, and so on. Well, you seem to think you've got a grudge against Germany? You prefer perhaps the Jews? You'd like to crony around with them. You prefer Communism. You prefer Bolshevism. Well ... that's no America for me, I must say, and I'd rather die for Germany than live for one hundred years on milk and honey in the Jewish America of today.[207]

At her very core, Mildred Gillars was a survivor. The notion that she would "die for Germany" rather than live in America rings false, as if it were scripted by Koischwitz—a man who had left the "milk and honey" of America for the vision and culture of the Fatherland.

The Mystery of Axis Sally

Across Sicily, Italy and France, the GIs knew the unmistakable voice of "Axis Sally." The sobriquet came into wide use after the November 8, 1942 landing of Allied troops in North Africa. Aided by intelligence

provided by the German military and its allies, Sally seemed to intu-
itively know the movements of US ships, transports, men and material even before they reached their destination. William Scofield, an
American soldier in Italy at the time, recalled the frustration of the
military men when encountering that "all-knowing" voice:

> When we had been sailing several North Atlantic convoys our
> orders for this convoy were to go into the Mediterranean. And
> I recall that as we went through Gibraltar, through the strait,
> there were three or four Spanish fishing boats, so of course
> they immediately put ashore so they could relay their news to
> Berlin as to what was going on, which the Spaniards did all the
> time. And aboard our ship, we were saying "Well, wonder
> how long before we're going to hear about this from 'Axis
> Sally'." And within an hour and a half or so, we're listening to
> the short wave and on she came describing in detail what our
> convoy was like. We had just passed through Gibraltar, the
> types of ships, the number of ships and so forth and what the
> deck cargos were, so in that sense they [the broadcasts] had a
> very irritating role....[208]

Other ex-GIs recalled similar instances. Sam Resnick, an American
soldier in the 100th Infantry Division, had been dispatched to France
under a shroud of secrecy. The men traveled without their insignias
and identification papers in unmarked transports. No stone was left
unturned to ensure that their arrival in Marseilles went undiscovered
by the enemy. As the men listened to the swing music broadcast by
Berlin Radio in a small French village, a voice suddenly came over the
air. It was the familiar voice of Axis Sally: "The men of the 100th
Infantry Division are welcome to France and I hope you have a good
night's sleep on the outskirts of the village of [*she identifies the village*]
because you will need all of your strength tomorrow."[209]

As the troops advanced across Western Europe, the voice of the
woman on the radio reminded the American officers that the Germans
knew their positions. Whether the information was garnered from
German sympathizers in Marseilles or from espionage within
American ranks may never be known, but the announcements gave

Axis Sally an insidious aspect to her carefully crafted mystique. Resnick remembered, "We fooled everyone, including ourselves, but not the lady on the radio, Axis Sally."[210] As Mildred once told a surprised prisoner of war, "You see ... I know everything."

Axis Sally had become more than a radio personality. She had become a figure of almost mythic proportions and endless fascination to the servicemen. Who was this woman who claimed American origin but mouthed the Nazi line? Every soldier and sailor heard her but never saw her. She provided entertainment and music and mystery. In one broadcast on December 9, 1943, Koischwitz answered a letter from a listener about the woman who called herself Midge but they called "Sally":

> O.K.:   Midge does look as gorgeous as she sounds ... her hair is the blackest black imaginable ... her skin is rather white; it's the Irish type ...[211]

He then asked her to describe herself:

> MIDGE: Well, ah.... I think I'm just an armful.
> O.K.:   Oh, well, ah.... I prefer some figure, you know ... to be a little more precise.
> MIDGE: Would you? Oh, you deal in figures ... well, I hope you like my figure?[212]

This exchange is a glimpse into the intimacy between the two as well as an example of Mildred's dogged insistence on maintaining her mystique. She later acknowledged that she knew that she was referred to by the servicemen as Sally or Axis Sally, and determinedly sought to maintain the opacity of her image. The 43-year-old announcer was no longer the youthful showgirl who once trod the boards of Broadway's vaudeville stages, but wanted to keep the image of a young coquette.

Avoiding direct answers about her age and physical appearance, the true nature of Axis Sally would always be left to the imagination. It also made it more difficult for American authorities to identify the woman at the microphone.

A January 1944 article in the *Saturday Evening Post* brought the name Axis Sally to the attention of millions of American civilians. An article entitled "No Other Gal Like Axis Sal," written by an Air Force weather observer named Corporal Edward Van Dyne, described the effect that her voice had on himself and his fellow servicemen. After describing the fare offered by the BBC and the Voice of America as dry and uninteresting, he relates his happy experience listening to Axis Sally to the folks at home.

> Axis Sally is a different proposition. Sally is a dandy—the sweetheart of the AEF. She plays nothing but swing, and good swing! ... She has a voice that oozes like honey out of a big wooden spoon. She dwells on the home, sweetheart and mother themes: "Homesick soldier? Throw down your gun and go back to the good old U.S.A.," she says by implication.
>
> "Why is America still in the wrong camp?" Sally wistfully and repeatedly inquires. She sounds genuinely concerned, hurt, deeply perplexed. Sally is at a loss to understand our attitude in this war and our failure to appreciate Hitler and his good works.
>
> Sally's goo is spiced neatly with little dabs of menace, though. One of her favorite routines is to paint a warm, glowing picture of a little nest in the United States that might be yours; of the waiting wife, the little ones, the log fire.
>
> "You'll get back to all that when the war's over," she says dreamily, then hisses "if you're still alive."
>
> Doctor Goebbels no doubt believes that Sally is rapidly undermining the morale of the American doughboy. I think the effect is directly opposite. We get an enormous bang out of her. We love her.[213]

Although no one knew the identity of the "voice," Mildred had finally achieved the notoriety that always eluded her in America. The myth of Axis Sally found its way from the battlefields of Sicily and North Africa to one of the most widely read American publications and her persona became bigger than that of a mere announcer. The fantasy translated to a tiny illustrative drawing next to Corporal Van Dyne's words—a young pretty blonde with a girl-next-door demeanor addressing the microphone and reading from a piece of paper—a script adorned with a swastika.

Fame and success always leads to imitators—especially in a medium like radio where faces are unseen and scenarios are created in the mind. Axis Sally had her imitators as well. Mildred became incensed when she discovered in late 1943 that another female broadcaster for the German government had been calling herself Sally and Axis Sally. Broadcasting from Rome, the soft voice of a young woman teamed up with an older man, repeating the successful formula that O.K. and Midge had pioneered in Berlin. Closer to the bloodshed on the Italian and North African front, Sally and George attacked the broken promises of Franklin D. Roosevelt, read the names of captured Allied soldiers and answered the letters of listeners.

Soon thereafter, American fighting troops were greeted ashore with propaganda leaflets beckoning the men to listen in to the show known as *Jerry's Front*. Without question, these leaflets identified the Rome broadcaster as the one and only Axis Sally. In January 1944, "Sally's Complementary Return Ticket" used the mysterious Axis Sally to beckon GIs to surrender as the surest way to return home:

SALLY, the RADIO GIRL from station "Jerry's Front" invites you to a FREE RETURN TRIP TO AMERICA via Germany. Sally says, "YOU CAN LIVE IN PEACE and COMFORT at one of the camps operated under the auspices of the International Red Cross." She thinks you ought to take a long, woolen blanket, some underwear and an extra pair of pants. DON'T HESITATE to make good use of this offer while there is a chance. "SUMMER IN GERMANY IS THE PERFECTION OF THE BEAUTIFUL." (Mark Twain)[214]

Two months later, military propagandists issued another leaflet complete with a broadcasting schedule:

What about Sally? GIs Radio Dial: You won't see her but every evening you can hear her most fascinating voice. If you'd like to get a sweet kiss from Sally – tune into Jerry's Front.[215]

When Koischwitz informed Mildred of the Rome Axis Sally's expropriation of her persona, she was angry and fearful that she would be held accountable for the words of another:

> I felt that I could be responsible for anything that I said and I didn't want any confusion after the end of the war as to what I said.... It caused a great deal of trouble. And I said, either this girl in Rome would stop calling herself Axis Sally or I would leave the microphone, because I was not giving out military information or trying to muddle up the GIs by telling them where their position would be tomorrow.[216]

One could imagine her outrage at the existence of a "lesser" talent reaping the benefits of her hard-won and carefully cultivated fame, but what is most telling about the above statement is her recognition that she would have to answer for her deeds at some time in the future. It had been clear that the *faux* Italian "Sally" had been transmitting detailed military information on Allied military movements that had been gleaned from interrogations or intelligence. Mildred wanted no part of the responsibility for what could be construed as military and logistical aid to the enemy. The war's momentum was changing and she began to fear what the future could hold.

CHAPTER 7

Survivors of the Invasion Front

SUMMER 1944

"Hello, Michael. I am the Berlin Bitch. Why don't you sit down."

Axis Sally gave Corporal Michael Evanick a cigarette and offered him a drink. She summoned Werner Plack and asked for some cognac. Plack brought in a bottle and left them alone. She settled herself on a cot across from the chair where he sat. There were no glasses on hand, so she suggested that they drink out of the bottle, American-style. Sally drank first to assure the young corporal that the liquor was not poisoned.

Two days earlier, a Gestapo officer at the German headquarters in Chartres, France had questioned Michael Evanick. Captured on D-Day, Evanick had been transported to a series of prisons and stockades prior to arriving at Chartres. The agent asked him whether he had ever listened to German propaganda:

> The Gestapo man questioned me regarding the German political system, their military and propaganda set-up and asked if I had ever listened to German propaganda. I answered I had listened to "Sally" as did many other soldiers. He asked me if I wanted to meet her and I said, yes.[217]

Evanick looked at the attractive brunette sitting opposite him. As she spoke, she crossed her legs, exposing her lack of underwear. He thought her immodest. On learning that Evanick lived on East 13th Street in New York City, she mentioned that she had worked in Greenwich Village. She brought up the name of a nightclub and told him to say "hello" to its owner when he returned to the States.

She asked about the living conditions at the camp. The corporal complained about the lack of water and food. Sally assured him that conditions would improve when the prisoners were moved to a permanent camp, where there would be "clean sheets, good food, good treatment, showers and Red Cross packages every week."[218] She then asked if he would like to record a message for his family back in New York. Evanick consented, and the Professor and two technicians walked in to set up the microphone and equipment. The three men then left and Evanick and Sally were again alone.

"Michael, aren't you feeling happy that you are a prisoner of war and don't have to fight any more?" the interview began.

Evanick bristled. "No ma'am, I do not because I feel a hundred percent better when I am in the front lines. At least I am not hungry and starving for being hungry, and I got whatever I needed."[219]

Enraged, Sally knocked the microphone to the ground and the recording stopped. Attempting to regain her composure, she had another glass of cognac and lit a cigarette. Within a matter of minutes, she was speaking to Evanick again as though nothing had happened.

"What do you do in the camp on a day like this?" she asked him.

"We sit in the sun," Evanick replied.

Satisfied that she would finally get some useful material, Sally switched the microphone back on and continued the questioning:

"SALLY":	What do you do in camp on days like this?
EVANICK:	We are just sitting in the sun, burning ourselves to death, because we are hungry, and are watching the American planes come over and bomb every five minutes.[220]

Reddened with anger, she threw the microphone on the floor, cursed the young man, and told him to get out. Evanick's refusal to go along with the line of questioning combined with the knowledge that the Allied forces were advancing daily, had obviously pushed Mildred Gillars to the breaking point. The resistance of a single soldier was now visibly rattling a woman who had been relatively cool during the catcalls and insults lobbed at her in Stalag IIB a few months before.

Her level of involvement in the German war effort was deepening as well. She was no longer just a radio announcer. Her collaboration with the German military was evident to prisoners who might one day testify against her. In this instance, what Evanick called a Gestapo agent supplied her with an interviewee as the result of a post-capture interrogation. To the agent, Evanick should have been an easy interview—a regular listener, perhaps even a "fan." Instead, he turned out to be one of the most damaging witnesses to Mildred Gillars' wartime activities.

Chartres

Many Allied soldiers taken prisoner during the Normandy invasion were transported eastward to a Catholic monastery located high on a hill above the Church of Notre Dame near St Lô. The POWs dubbed the monastery prison "Starvation Hill," due to the lack of water and food provided by their captors. The monastery functioned as a temporary stockade until the captured could be moved to a permanent camp. As the Allied advance progressed during June and July towards St Lô, prisoners were marched or transported the 160 miles from "Starvation Hill" to the prison camp at Chartres, located 55 miles from the centre of Paris. The camp was originally built by the French to hold Moroccan and other African prisoners.

The prison at Chartres consisted of four warehouses with tar-papered roofs and a few smaller buildings. Barbed wire and wheat fields surrounded the entire complex. Each of the buildings held approximately 800–900 prisoners. The conditions were so cramped that each man had only about five square feet of straw on which to sleep. A wooden barricade and an eight-foot stone wall subdivided the warehouses. Water and food were extremely sparse and medical attention was non-existent.

A day's meal consisted of one cup of coffee at 8 a.m., followed by a bowl of soup and possibly a small piece of bread at 3 p.m. Guards beat the prisoners for the slightest infraction. The German military headquarters where Michael Evanick was interrogated and interviewed was located two miles up the road from the camp.

On July 5, 1944, Mildred Gillars arrived at the Chartres prison camp to conduct live interviews for her new radio series, *Survivors of the Invasion Front*. Until the June invasion, recorded interviews with Allied prisoners were reserved for the Christmas and Easter holidays. *Survivors of the Invasion Front* would present a weekly program of interviews with US soldiers relieved to be out of the battle.

Sergeant Clarence Gale and Corporal Donald Rutter were two of the paratroopers selected by the Germans to be interviewed. Gale, Rutter and their comrades were lined up in their warehouse prison and then marched to a smaller building at the rear of the camp. They walked behind the building and saw Axis Sally playing with a pair of dice.

She was wearing a dark floral print dress and no stockings. With a cheery "Hello boys!" she began speaking to each of the men about their hometown. She seemed to have been in every one of their hometowns at one time or another. Gale noticed that one of the men accompanying her (Koischwitz) ordered around the other two radio technicians but that the American woman did not take orders from him. She seemed to be "just as big a 'big shot' as he."[221]

The friendly, solicitous woman held a microphone and the prisoners could see that its cord ran into the small building housing the recording equipment. Two technicians assisted her, as she offered to send recorded messages home to their families. Gale and Rutter did not recognize her as the woman from Berlin Radio, but they did wonder why the Germans would care to let them send messages home when "they got damn little to eat and nearly no water."[222]

Without giving her name, she passed out Chesterfield cigarettes to the men and stated that she was affiliated with a unit of the Red Cross. Promising the prisoners Red Cross packages in return for their participation, she asked questions such as "What are you fighting for?," "How would you like to be home?" and "Do you think America will win the war?" Making no secret of her political inclinations, this "Red

Cross representative" told the Americans that they were "fools" for fighting against the Nazis, instead of joining forces with the Germans against the Bolsheviks. She argued that they were fighting "England's war," that the June invasion was being repelled, and that the Allies were being driven into the sea. Corporal Rutter recalled that she also remarked that the Germans were bombing New York and Washington.[223] The reality on the front was that American forces were encountering fierce resistance from the Wehrmacht during that first week in July, and the attempt to advance towards St Lô was slowing considerably.

When the interviews were finished, Gale, Rutter and the other prisoners smoked the cigarettes she gave them and listened to the playback. Gale noticed that she "made over the boys" until she got what she wanted. When she was finished with the recordings "her attitude changed, just as though one would turn off the radio. She paid no more attention to them and they were returned to their barracks."[224] The promised Red Cross packages never arrived.

Midge and the Professor had found an effective cover for obtaining interviews with prisoners wary of being seen collaborating with enemy propagandists. In hospitals and makeshift stockades across northern and central France she declared herself a representative of the International Red Cross seeking to improve the conditions of American prisoners behind enemy lines. The Chartres camp was fertile ground for the couple, as they would return there at least two more times to collect interviews in July and August 1944.

One particular broadcast from the Chartres camp was illustrative of this ruse. On August 1 1944, she returned to the camp to collect further interviews. One of those she met was Carl Zimmerman, an infantryman wounded and captured at St. Pierre on July 18. After a few days at "Starvation Hill," Zimmerman was moved east until he ended up at Chartres at the end of July. On August 1 he and nine other prisoners were led behind the small building at the rear of the camp where they encountered a woman with jet-black hair that Zimmerman thought looked like it had been colored with axle grease. She was heavily rouged and looked much younger from a distance than up close. Her neckline was low cut and he felt she dressed "for sex appeal."[225] The woman gave commands in French and the men who accompanied her stated that she was from the French Red Cross. In the actual broadcast, she can be heard speaking to the technicians in a loud voice: "l'attention, l'attention, s'il vous plaît!"[226] She identified herself as Midge[227] and offered to record messages to be broadcast home so that the families might know that they were still alive.

Zimmerman was the second to be interviewed and was the most talkative of the prisoners.

GILLARS:	What's the town, please?
ZIMMERMAN:	Providence, Rhode Island.
GILLARS:	Oh, Providence, Rhode Island. Well, I spent some very happy hours there myself. (*laughs*) Probably not so happy as you.
ZIMMERMAN:	What's that?
GILLARS:	Not so happy as you.
ZIMMERMAN:	Oh, no! (laughs)
GILLARS:	(laughs) Well, it's home to you. And who are you calling in Providence?
ZIMMERMAN:	My wife. Mrs. Blanche Zimmerman
GILLARS:	What street does she live on?
ZIMMERMAN:	62 Doyle Avenue
GILLARS:	How do you spell that avenue?
ZIMMERMAN:	D-O-Y-L-E
GILLARS:	Oh Doyle! An Irish name. All right, what would you like to say to your wife now?
ZIMMERMAN:	Uh, nothing much just that I'm well and happy and, about all, just very happy.
GILLARS:	Well, you are happy you've got through a lot of air raids (unintelligible).
ZIMMERMAN:	Well, after what I've been through I think I'm glad to be alive.
GILLARS:	I'll bet that you're glad for a lot of things.

This exchange is fascinating because it is between a virulently anti-Semitic broadcaster and a prisoner described in an FBI report as having "a very Jewish appearance."[228] One must wonder what Midge knew of the fate of Europe's Jews when she commented, "I'll bet you're glad for a lot of things." Sharing a bed with an official of the Foreign Office, she was very likely exposed to the rumors if not the details surrounding the relocation of Jews to the East.

Midge asked Zimmerman if he was getting enough to eat. In a syrupy tone, she replied, "Well, lots of people aren't, so that is something to be happy about too, isn't it?"

Zimmerman's reply, "Yes, if you call grass soup once a day enough to eat," was edited out of the final broadcast. The *Survivor* interviews were, at times, heavily edited to dispose of comments that did not fit the profile of the happy and thankful prisoner. Zimmerman's response about "grass soup" was just one incident. Listening to the recorded conversations today, the exchanges seem oddly disjointed.

The volatility of Mildred Gillars's emotional state is evident from the broadcasts as well. The exchanges between Midge and the prisoners could go from extremely warm and chatty to cold, cutting and distant in a matter of seconds. Even the editing and splicing of the engineering room could not disguise the sudden change in tone. One prisoner from Ohio who preceded Carl Zimmerman on the August 22, 1944 broadcast made the mistake of assuring his wife that he hoped to be home by Christmas:

MIDGE:	And the town, please?
POW:	Cleveland, Ohio.
MIDGE:	Oh, Cleveland, Ohio? My goodness I know that awfully well. What part? What street?
POW:	42 East 96th Street.
MIDGE:	East 96th Street. And have you got any folks over there?
POW:	My mother and dad.
MIDGE:	Hmmm. Well, I'll give you the microphone. Say what you want to now.
POW:	Well, hello, mom and dad. I'm OK.

> Don't worry too much, mom. I'll be
> home by Christmas! I hope.

Midge's voice suddenly became cold and caustic.

Midge:	Good thing to add the "I hope" isn't it?
POW	... Yeah.
Midge:	Cause you don't want to give them any false hope. Anyway, you're going to get there as fast as you can, anyhow.
POW:	Soon as they end the war....[229]

The idea that Germany would be defeated within four months was not the message that Midge wanted conveyed to the listeners in America or to her superiors in Berlin. For Mildred and Koischwitz, the month of July was filled with visits to prisoner-of-war camps, stockades and hospitals. At Chartres in mid-July, she accidentally lifted up her skirt when a soldier became entangled in the microphone wire. The watching prisoners began to whistle and catcall. She smiled and said tauntingly, "You like that, eh?" then raised her dress up around her thighs revealing her most attractive feature, the long legs of a former showgirl.[230] At the Hospital de la Pitiè near Paris, she interviewed severely wounded soldiers sporting a Red Cross armband.[231]

Meantime, the disappearance of Koischwitz's "breezy" commentaries that summer raised suspicions about the fate of "O.K." William L. Shirer of CBS took notice of the Professor's new role on the frontlines:

> Goebbels, for some reason, sent the Professor to the firing line. As a "front-line reporter," his specialty was broadcasting eye-witness accounts from the various battlefronts on which the Americans were facing Germans. Since General Bradley's Americans began their race through France, I have not been able to catch any more broadcasts by him. Presumably, he began moving too fast to allow for a pause at the microphone.[232]

Koischwitz was unexpectedly called back to Berlin at the end of July 1944. As Midge and O.K. waited for the train, she borrowed some money to buy a rare leather-bound set of books by Goethe. She gave it to him as an early Christmas present because she feared that they might not be together during the holidays. Before he left, Koischwitz made arrangements for the safe evacuation of Mildred with his German Foreign Office colleague, Werner Plack.[233] As the Americans approached the French capital in early August, Plack abandoned her. When she reminded him of his promise to Koischwitz to drive her back to Germany in his car, he refused, saying, "I am sorry. I have no room. There is so much baggage."[234] In a panic, she telephoned Koischwitz in Berlin.

"When I telephoned Berlin," she would remember, "I had a feeling that something had happened. I asked for Dr. Koischwitz and at that moment I knew that I'd never hear his voice again...."[235]

A voice came on the line: "Professor Koischwitz is dead."[236] Mildred immediately fled Paris on August 15 for Holland in a military convoy. She then boarded a train bound for Berlin, paying for her ticket by bribing a conductor with coffee.[237] Despite rumors of suicide, Koischwitz died in the Berlin-Spandau Hospital on August 31, 1944 of tuberculosis and heart failure.[238] Crushed by the death, Mildred barely arrived in Berlin in time for his funeral on September 4.

Max Otto Koischwitz died alone. The war had taken his wife and infant son. The Germany he loved was crumbling around him. Although it is plausible that he could have taken his own life, it is more likely that Koischwitz, who had been diagnosed with incipient tuberculosis in 1929, and was looking for interviews with POWs in the sickrooms of the Hospital de la Pitié not more than four to five weeks before his death, had finally succumbed.[239] It is also possible that the deteriorating sanitary conditions in wartime Europe played a role in aggravating his already fragile state. Either way, Midge was now without the man to whom she had cast her fate. Her lover—the man who convinced her to betray her nation, who protected her and provided her access to the highest echelons of German society—was gone.

CHAPTER 8

Alone

"Well Sally, we'll be in Berlin soon—with a great big
kiss for you—if you have any kisser left."
—Corporal Edward Van Dyne in the
Saturday Evening Post, January 1944[240]

"Our fate is rolling in from the East ..."
—Anonymous diarist, Berlin, April 20, 1945[241]

SEPTEMBER 1944–JANUARY 1947

As Mildred said goodbye to Max Otto Koischwitz in September 1944, Allied forces were closing in on the Reich. On the Western Front, the US First Army stood north of Aachen poised to breach 400-plus kilometers of fortifications known as the Westwall. Patton's Third Army had reached Metz farther south, while Montgomery's British-Canadian forces were pushing into Belgium and Holland. The advance would slow in the ensuing months, culminating in the last great German offensive, in the sector of the Ardennes.

In the East, the military situation was dire. Following the destruction of Army Group Center that summer after a huge Soviet offensive, the *Wehrmacht* was in retreat from Finland and the Baltics, Ukraine and the Balkans. By October, Riga and Belgrade were in Soviet hands, while the Red Army had advanced to the outskirts of Warsaw. Despite the self-delusion that characterized Hitler's inner circle in the last months of the war, more practical leadership prepared for the inevitable siege of Berlin. On October 18, the *Volkssturm* (Home Guard) announced the imminent call-up of all males between the age of 16 and 60 for the final defense of German soil.[242]

It was in that desperate autumn that Axis Sally returned to the microphone. Shaken and grieving from the loss of her mentor and protector, she feared an Allied victory. Her attitude began to change toward her superiors at *Reichsradio*. Returning to the studios at *Köenigs Wusterhausen*, she was called into a meeting with Johannes Schmidt-Hansen and Eduard Dietze. In a blatant appeal to her ego, the two radio executives had plans for their "star"—a transfer to a new clandestine station in the Black Forest aimed at the advancing Allied forces:

> They were opening a new station in the Black Forest and they were spending enormous sums of money on it, and said it was going to make me a world radio star and I told Mr. Schmidt-Hansen that I wasn't the least interested in becoming that, and that I wanted nothing to do with the station.[243]

Schmidt-Hansen's description of the new effort amounted to nothing less than psychological warfare on the advancing US soldiers. "The soldiers would have the impression that this female voice was right in the bivouac with them," she recalled.[244] Mildred was unmoved by the flattery and Dietze testily invoked the name of her late lover, insisting that Professor Koischwitz would not approve of such intransigence. She stood her ground:

> I told them that I would have nothing whatever to do with it, and I would appreciate it very much if they wouldn't beg me, and that I was just going to continue until the end of the war with these broadcasts which had been inaugurated with Professor Koischwitz—that and nothing more.[245]

Although some of her colleagues did transfer to the Black Forest operation, it was clear that Mildred was no longer willing to bend to a regime whose time was short. Her resistance would increase in January 1945 when she would be forced to associate for the first time with a man she deemed to be a traitor.

Lieutenant Monti Reports for Duty

On October 2, 1944, an American flier based in Karachi went AWOL (absent without leave). Lt. Martin James Monti, a St. Louis native and ardent isolationist, had enlisted as an air cadet in 1943 at a time he was certain to be drafted. A difficult and undisciplined soldier, Monti was posted to India while many of his friends in training were sent to the Italian front. After being denied a transfer request to Italy, he snuck aboard a military transport bound for Cairo, and made his way by land to Tripoli. He then boarded a ship to Naples where, once again, he requested a transfer and was denied. Unwilling to return to India, Monti commandeered a P-38 reconnaissance aircraft and flew it into enemy airspace. Landing the plane near Milan, Monti surrendered. His German interrogators were eventually convinced that his flight was a voluntary defection and began to look for a use for the young airman. A military propaganda unit steered Monti to the Overseas Service in the hope that he might have some value in its radio efforts. Although one manager of Reichsradio's North American section, Heinrich Schafhausen, found Monti "immature and lacking in general education," he was hired as a commentator for the USA Zone.[246]

By January 1945 Monti had become the latest addition to the staff of American announcers at Reichsradio. Mildred viewed the lieutenant with intense suspicion:

> This man (Monti) came into the room. He said "Hello." I just looked at him, turned around and walked out of the office without speaking. This was my one and only contact with him … directly after that, I conferred with Houben [Adelbert Houben. Program Controller for the Overseas Service] and told him I was aware that a former American flier was now working at our station. I said, "That man is either a spy or a

traitor and I refuse to work with either one. If you've been thinking I was a traitor all these years, I'm sorry it has taken me so long to find it out because I've never considered myself one and I don't think my German co-workers consider me one.[247]

Emboldened by Germany's worsening position, Mildred gave Houben an ultimatum: "Either Monti is removed or I go."[248] Houben could not possibly overturn a decision made by the highest levels of the propaganda apparatus—especially at the behest of a recalcitrant employee. Mildred stormed out of the office and announced, "I have made my last broadcast."[249]

Within days, she was called to Berlin to answer to Kurt-Georg Kiesinger, the Foreign Office's liaison with the Propaganda Ministry for Overseas Broadcasting. Kiesinger (who went on to become the Chancellor of West Germany in 1966) tried to assuage her concerns about Monti, but to no avail. After the meeting at the Foreign Office she visited the Propaganda Ministry to collect her weekly food ration coupons. Horst Cleinow, the manager of the Overseas Service, ordered her food rations withheld until she returned to work.[250] A few days later, a letter arrived summoning her to an interview with the Gestapo. Mildred immediately telephoned Dr. Anton Winkelnkemper, the head of the broadcasting service and Cleinow's superior, to plead her case:

Dr. Winkelnkemper pleaded with me to come up to his office ... and he tried to persuade me to go back to work, and I remained adamant: "If you can keep the Gestapo away from me, I will be grateful to you, and if you cannot, I will take the consequences." And I went home after that, and I was in constant touch with Mr. Kiesinger of the Foreign Office and Dr. Winkelnkemper who took care of the Gestapo, and finally persuaded me to return to work and said that Mr. Monti was not working at the microphone.[251]

Mildred narrowly escaped the consequences of her intransigence when the young American lieutenant turned out to be a total failure on the air. Due to a breathtaking lack of skill as a radio commentator and analyst, Monti was on the radio only a few times in early 1945. He proved to be a dull speaker with a limited intellect and an underwhelming command of the English language. Not long after his failure as a radio propagandist, he moved on to become one of the few Americans to join the *Waffen SS*. After the German surrender, US forces arrested Monti still dressed in his SS uniform. (In 1948 he was convicted of treason and sentenced to 25 years in prison, though was paroled in 1960.)

Meantime, Mildred feared that Monti could be a spy sent by the Allies posing as a defector, and if so he would be a witness to her actions. If he was a genuine defector, she could not afford to be associated with him. Her refusal to work with him could protect her from the testimony of a potential eyewitness, as well as support her contention that her wartime deeds were not motivated by treasonous intent. She could use the incident to point out a distinction that she had made long ago in her own mind: *Monti is a vile traitor but I am different—I am an entertainer.* Later, she would explain her visceral distaste for Monti by claiming "I don't like unclean people."[252]

By February 1945, the German offensive in the Ardennes, known as the Battle of the Bulge, had been rolled back to its starting point, after it had only temporarily succeeded in delaying the Allies' relentless advance toward the Rhine. Hans Fritzsche, the head of the Propaganda Ministry's broadcasting division, authorized a travel pass for Mildred in preparation for the coming evacuation from Berlin. Once more, she visited Hans and Georgia von Richter's home at Castle Schackendorf.

The terrible pounding of day and night air attacks convinced the couple that the time had come to flee to the west. Suffering from nervous exhaustion, the von Richters were leaving for a posh sanatorium in the southwest spa town of Bad Mergentheim. The meeting was bittersweet for Mildred, who had dined with Koischwitz at the von Richters' home in happier days. As Hans von Richter said farewell, he took Midge's hand and tried to relieve her fears:

> Well, Midge, it will soon be over, and you have our address at
> Bad Mergentheim, and the three of us will stick together for-

ever; you have nothing to worry about. Georgia and I are your friends.

Leaving Mildred with the assurance of their undying loyalty and friendship, the couple drove off to escape the coming storm.

* * *

By April 16, the long-awaited Soviet advance into the capital had begun. Hitler issued a final decree to the men on the frontlines:

> SOLDIERS OF THE GERMAN EASTERN FRONT:
> The Jewish Bolshevik archenemy has gone over to the attack with his masses for the last time. He attempts to smash Germany and to eradicate our nation. You soldiers from the east today already know yourselves to a large extent what fate is threatening, above all, German women, girls and children. While old men and children are being murdered, women and girls are humiliated to the status of barracks prostitutes.[253]

That night, Mildred left her apartment at 7 Bonnerstrasse for the last time. Her furniture and remaining possessions were left behind. With the Soviets only kilometers away from the outskirts of the city, the radio studio was her only refuge. As a military target, the radio facilities were protected against Russian shelling and air attack. In late April, musician Walter Leschetitzky was patrolling the *Köenigs Wusterhausen* studios. In the midst of the final battle, the *SS* and *Volkssturm* were conscripting every man and boy regardless of age or condition. Those who refused to join in the defense of the city were hanged for "desertion," "treason" or "defeatism." Leschetitzky was one of those conscripted and assigned to the Combat Transmitter group (SS) to defend the radio station. Despite the massive artillery barrage, Reichsradio was still holding on.

Two years earlier, Leschetitzky had been a musician with the Lutz-Templin Orchestra, a fifteen-piece band that provided much of the accompaniment for Midge's *Home Sweet Home* program. During his days as a musician for the show, he never spoke to the shapely brunette in the announcer's booth. He would see her face one more time as the Reich fell. As Leschetitzky made his way through the upper floor of the building, he discovered an extremely distressed woman hiding in the nearly empty broadcasting house. He related his story to military interrogators after the war:

> There I met a very disturbed looking woman ... She told me during the course of a short conversation that she was so afraid of the Americans because she had said so much against them in the broadcasts. Our conversation was very brief.... She had said that she was afraid of the Americans because she was an American.[254]

Suddenly, a tank alarm sounded and Leschetitzky left the woman to return to his post. A few days after this encounter, a terrified Mildred Gillars ended her broadcasting career—leaving through the studio's back exit as the Red Army stormed through the front door.[255]

In Berlin, Soviet troops had also closed in on the bunker in which the Nazi high command huddled. Hitler, along with Eva Braun, committed suicide on April 30, and the next day Goebbels did likewise, after first killing his six children and his wife.

Radio Fugitives

The unconditional surrender of all German forces on May 8 turned the American and British radio commentators for Reichsradio into fugitives. Robert H. Best, Douglas Chandler, Frederick Kaltenbach, William Joyce ("Lord Haw Haw"), Margaret Joyce ("Lady Haw Haw"), Ezra Pound, John Amery and others went into hiding at various points across the decimated Reich. One by one, they would be tracked down to answer for their crimes. Unlike their American counterparts, the British government was not averse to administering the hangman's noose to their radio propagandists.

William Joyce was arrested on May 28, 1945 when he made the mistake of speaking in English to two British officers looking for firewood in a forest near Flensburg on the Danish border. The two

Tommies were shocked to hear the unmistakable voice of "Lord Haw Haw" from the bedraggled refugee, and immediately asked if he was William Joyce. When he reached into his pocket to retrieve the false identity papers supplied to him by the Nazis, one of the soldiers opened fire and wounded Joyce in the hand. During a three-day trial at the Old Bailey, it was discovered that the accused had actually been born in New York City (making him legally an American citizen). Nevertheless, William Joyce was found guilty of treason and sent to the gallows on January 3, 1946.

Another Briton, John Amery, fared no better. The troubled son of an English statesman who had fought alongside Franco in the Spanish Civil War, Amery turned on King and Country to broadcast for the Nazis. He was notable for his recruitment of British prisoners of war for his brainchild—"The Legion of St George." Later known as the British Free Corps, or *Freikorps*, the "Legion of St George" was a National Socialist paramilitary force assembled to join forces with the Germans against the Bolshevik enemy to save Western civilization. Amery, accompanied by a lovely young Frenchwoman, traveled to prisoner-of-war camps across the Reich to convince the unstable of mind and conviction to join his motley band. After the war, Amery stood in the dock for only eight minutes when he shocked the court and the nation by pleading guilty to treason. British law did not allow an alternative sentence for the crime. A guilty plea was tantamount to suicide. Three weeks later, Amery was executed.

Although the American radio traitors were sought out and arrested as swiftly as their British counterparts, the question of what to do with them was a troublesome one for the Army Counter-Intelligence Corps (CIC) and the US Justice Department. As early as 1943, there had been an active debate in the Attorney General's office over whether a conviction could be won on the merits of "mere words" broadcast over the radio. In past cases, the expression of unpopular political opinion during wartime had been insufficient to reach the level of treason. Justice Department attorney Oscar R. Ewing convinced a doubtful Attorney General Frances Biddle that technological advances such as radio meant that words and ideas damaging to the war effort could be spread far and wide—and thus provide the "aid and comfort" required by the Constitution to prove treason.

Ewing recalled his discussions with the Attorney General:

> I got the idea that we ought to prosecute those American citizens who were broadcasting Nazi propaganda and Fascist propaganda from abroad. So, I went to Attorney General Francis Biddle and suggested that these broadcasters be indicted for treason. He answered my suggestion by saying "I don't think we can make a case stick because there are some Civil War cases which hold that mere words do not constitute the overt act that is an essential element of the crime of treason." ... I explained to Mr. Biddle why I thought we could make the case. I argued that those Civil War cases involved nothing more than a man getting on a stump and talking to a crowd of people that were within the normal range of his voice. I felt this was quite different from words spoken into a microphone that could project the words all over the world; furthermore, that propaganda had become a definite weapon of warfare, and that anyone who used that weapon against his own country should be prosecuted for treason. When I had finished, the Attorney General said, "Well, I think you've got a point...."[256]

The Attorney General asked the FCC to monitor and record all Axis broadcasts from the listening post in Silver Hill, Maryland to collect evidence for future prosecutions. Not long after Ewing's conversation with Biddle, the July 1943 indictments against Max Otto Koischwitz, Fred Kaltenbach, Douglas Chandler, Robert H. Best, Jane Anderson, Constance Drexel, Edward Delaney and Ezra Pound were passed down.

Closed Doors

From the moment she left the studio, Mildred Gillars was a wanted woman and a risk to all who sheltered her. Although Koischwitz was dead, it would not be long before the indicted man's paramour would be identified and sought by military authorities. The Professor's eldest daughter, Stella, was living in her father's Berlin apartment when a desperate and disheveled Midge arrived at the door. After her father's passing in September 1944, Stella had been earning a living by read-ing news items for Reichsradio. When she saw her father's ex-mistress at her door, Stella demanded that the fugitive leave the apartment and not return. As she left, Mildred mused to Stella that she might "lose herself" in the Soviet sector to avoid the Americans.

Confronted with the brutality that greeted German women and the epidemic of mass rape that raged through occupied Berlin, Mildred would soon find that the Soviet soldiers would not offer her safety or respite. Russian propagandists exhorted the victorious soldiers to take their revenge ("Soldiers of the Red Army—German Women Are Yours," one poster exhorted) and the men took full advantage.[257] It is estimated that of the 2.7 million Germans who remained in Berlin that April, two million were women.[258] Estimates of the number of women treated for rape in Berlin range from 95,000 to 130,000.[259] German girls and women hid in the nighttime to avoid the drunken soldiers, venturing out for water and food in the morning while the victorious revelers slept it off.

Antony Beevor recounts the experience of a young newsreader at the "Big House"—the massive broadcasting complex on the Masurenallee—who remained in the studios during the last days of the Reich. Women composed two-thirds of the remaining staff in the *Rundfunkhaus* and the final week of broadcasting was rife with drunken and indiscriminate sexual encounters in the sound archives. Those young women who were still virgins preferred to surrender their chastity to a German man rather than the invaders.[260] Similar disso-lution took place throughout Berlin in the dark cellars and shelters that were located in almost every square. The fear of impending death stripped personal conduct to its most primitive.

The terror faced by German women in the months between the surrender in May and the arrival of US, British and Free French troops in July, may explain the lack of detail in Mildred's account of her own personal experience during this time. Although she would describe this period in general as one of "sheer starvation" and "great tragedy," she was remarkably reticent about describing specific events in detail. Her talent for florid and highly detailed storytelling failed her when dis-cussing this period. It is as if a dark hole had appeared in her history that only she would fully know.

She descended into the filthy cellars and shelters that dotted
Berlin, seeking whatever food and water she could barter or scavenge.
Reeking of urine and excrement, the cellars were a hell with intermit-
tent light and no water. The dead—some from suicide, some from
sickness or war wounds—were crowded together with the living until
shortly after the city's capitulation. Mildred struggled to survive, bar-
tering her jewelry and clothes for food on the black market. Even the
fraternity pin given to her by Calvin Elliott, her college fiancé, was
traded for food.[261] Her travel pass bore the name "Barbara Mome,"
a former stage name that Koischwitz was fond of.

An estimated 20 million homeless German refugees trod the
bomb-cratered roads of Germany in those days. Mildred disappeared
into their number heading west to evade the Soviet conquerors and she
experienced the hunger and fear that rose out of the chaos. Hitch-
hiking southwest over 200 kilometers, she went to visit her friends
Hans and Georgia von Richter in Bad Mergentheim.

Hungry and shabbily dressed, her hair was now gray and matted.
The maid greeted her at the door. Mildred asked to see her old friends.
The maid said that Frau von Richter was working but Herr von
Richter was available. Hans walked into the reception room and did
not recognize the destitute woman who had dined at his home less
than a year before. "Can I help you?" he asked. Realizing that it was
his old friend Midge, Hans apologized for not recognizing her.
However, the man who swore his loyal friendship less than a year
before would not offer her a place to stay. He explained that his wife
Georgia was now working for the Allied Military Government and it
would be simply too risky for the couple to harbor a fugitive sought
by the Americans.

Another Sally

By the fall of 1945, the Justice Department sent investigators to
Occupied Germany to locate those Americans named in the treason
indictment of July 1943, as well as other unnamed individuals suspected of collusion with the enemy. On February 29, 1946, President
Truman's new Attorney General, Tom Clark, announced that 22 additional Americans were sought for pro-Nazi broadcasts made from

Berlin, Munich, Vienna and Paris. Clark expressed his determination to hunt down all of the suspected traitors and vowed to "bring every single American who played the Axis game to trial."[262] He appointed Timothy A. McInerney, the Department of Justice's Director of Public Information, to go to Europe and begin the process of assembling evidence against the collaborators.

One of McInerney's most difficult tasks was to initiate the search for Axis Sally. As early as June 1944, the CIC was receiving tips about possible suspects. One lead came from an infantryman who reported that a middle-aged woman calling herself "Berniece" claimed that she was Axis Sally as she caroused with American enlisted men at the Red Cross Club in Rome.[263] After several false starts, the mystery seemed to be solved when on July 7, 1945, US military police in Turin, Italy arrested a cross-eyed woman of 33. The unmarried woman, carrying a six-month-old baby, admitted freely that she was the infamous radio host.

A New York-born Italian-American, Rita Luisa Zucca was the Rome-based announcer who had enraged Mildred Gillars less than two years before, when she heard that Zucca was calling herself "Sally." Rita was the daughter of Constantine Zucca, a Manhattan restaurateur who owned Zucca's Italian Gardens at 118 West 49th Street. She had attended an Italian convent school in Florence from 1925 to 1930 and then returned to New York to work in her father's restaurant. She briefly worked for the entertainment publication *New York—What to Watch* before leaving again for Italy in 1938.

She worked as a typist in Italy for three years before deciding to renounce her American citizenship. According to Rita, her decision was rooted in a wish to save her family's property from expropriation by the Fascist government:

> In June 1941, I understood that Mussolini had put out an order that property of foreigners, including Americans, would be confiscated by the Italian Government. My family had considerable property at Raveno and Turin. I renounced my American citizenship in order to save our property, since it was my understanding that if one member of the family was an Italian citizen, the property would be saved.[264]

In May, Rita informed the American Vice Counsel in Rome that she planned to remain in Italy, and on June 9, signed a statement renouncing her US citizenship. Six months later, she met an Italian soldier, Siro Mariottini, and fell in love with him. Rita was working at a cultural publication in Rome and planned to marry Mariottini after the war's end, but lost her job in March 1942 for copying an anti-Fascist pamphlet. Unemployed for almost a year, she was hired as a radio announcer for the EIAR (Radio Roma) in February 1943. The station wanted fluent English announcers for a new program aimed at American and British soldiers in Tunisia. *The Sally and Phil Show* (a.k.a. *Jerry's Front Calling*) was immensely popular among Allied troops on the North African front, and Zucca was the recipient of military intelligence for use on her show.

In one instance, it was Rita Zucca on *Jerry's Front* who addressed the Allied troops on the night before the invasion of Sicily (July 8, 1943). Calling "the wonderful boys of the 504th Parachute Regiment," "Sally" told the soldiers that "Colonel Willis Mitchell's playboys [the 61st Troop Carrier Group] are going to carry you to certain death. We know where and when you are jumping and you will be wiped out."[265] The propaganda value of this revelation backfired because she told the men that their regiment had been wiped out—one hour before the first plane took off. During the subsequent Italian campaign, the Rome Axis Sally seemed to know the names and ranks of American soldiers in the 3rd, 4th, 34th and 47th divisions on their way to Naples. General Eisenhower, the Supreme Allied Commander, was concerned that her propaganda would adversely affect the morale of the troops on the bloody Italian front. Every night, Zucca signed off her broadcasts "with a sweet kiss from Sally."[266]

Rita attempted to resign from EIAR in August 1943, a month before the Allied invasion of the Italian mainland. Her superiors demanded that she remain at the microphone until a replacement announcer could be found. Financial pressures, however, forced her to return to radio in January 1944. Rita told US interrogators in 1945: "I was unemployed a long time and had sold my jewels to meet the demands of my lover, Siro Mariottini, who was constantly nagging me for more money."[267] This time, she found herself working directly for the Germans.

Her manager, the new head of Anglo-American broadcasting, was Dr. George Goedel, who had created the program *Jerry's Front Calling*. Sally (Zucca) and George (Goedel) were the hosts, and the format was almost identical to the "Midge" programs emanating from Berlin. Goedel wrote the scripts in longhand for Rita, as well as radio plays critical of Franklin Roosevelt and the US–British alliance. George and Sally also read the names of captured prisoners of war, bantered back and forth about the effects of the war on the American home front, and played "hot" jazz and swing. Like their counterparts to the north, Zucca and Goedel had their own band, Jerry's Swinging Tigers, as well as a vocal group consisting of three Italian sisters called The Three Doves of Peace. Although Goedel never told Rita Zucca where he received direction for the propaganda content of the program, she always assumed he took his orders from the German Embassy in Rome.

With Rome threatened by Allied forces, the cast and crew of *Jerry's Front* left for Florence where they moved into the Hotel Excelsior. Ten days later, they were forced to move on to Milan. Resuming the program from that city on June 17, 1944, they stayed only a few months. On September 15, Rita Zucca fled to the sliver of northern Italy known as Mussolini's "Social Republic." Her show and its personnel became part of a German military propaganda unit dubbed the "Liberty Station." The Italian "Sally" was feted as the guest of honor at a party broadcast from a castle in Fino Mornasco (near Como). The live show sent out the sounds of merriment, laughter and clinking glasses across the ether to the advancing American forces. Other Reichsradio personalities, including the British broadcaster John Amery, took part in the festivities.

These strange broadcasts were indicative of the desperation of the dying regime. During one of these *danses macabres*, the familiar, honeyed voice of an American girl came over the radio to the troops on the frontlines. It was a very pregnant Rita Zucca who took the microphone and told the GIs:

Hello, boys ... how are you tonight? A lousy night it sure is ... Axis Sally is talking to you ... you poor silly dumb lambs, well on your way to be slaughtered![268]

Her baby, fathered by Mariottini, was born on December 15, 1944. Rita returned to the studio 40 days after the birth and continued broadcasting until her final show on April 25, 1945. With Italian partisans a few miles away, she fled Fino. On May 5, she quietly boarded a train to Milan where she was met at the station by one of her cousins. He took her to safety at the family home in Turin where she remained until her capture.

Rita Zucca and her child were ushered into IV Corps Military Police Headquarters. "When I saw her coming through the door I said to myself, 'What the hell is this, another rape case?'" an officer remembered. The MPs found her and her baby, now six months old, staying with her aunt and uncle in Turin. Wearing an American field jacket, blue print dress and sandals, Rita was loaded into a jeep with her child on her lap for the overnight drive to Rome. Although the *Stars and Stripes* military newspaper was forbidden to interview the prisoner, the paper described the feminine charms of this particular Axis Sally. One officer observed that she was "really stacked," while the correspondent noted, "True, her left eye is inclined to wander— but that cooey, sexy voice really has something to back it up." As the jeep pulled out for the long drive, the American soldiers gave her and her baby eight blankets to protect them against the night air.

Immediately, the American press and military announced in no uncertain terms that Rita Zucca was *the* Axis Sally, and emphasized that the sultry voice that greeted the doughboys on the beach at Anzio belonged to the cross-eyed mother of a newborn infant.[269] Zucca was pictured in front of a large radio and a baby's cradle in *Stars and Stripes*. Her picture graced *The New York Times* of June 14, 1945 with the heading "Reminder of Anzio." Newspapers in the United States demolished the Axis Sally mystique by claiming that the actual woman was nothing like the fantasies of a million GIs. "Soft-Voiced 'Sally from Berlin' Found to Be Ugly Ex-N.Y. Girl" was a typical headline, with stories describing the young mother as "ugly and unattractive in person as her voice was appealing."[270] One *Stars and Stripes* writer called Zucca "cross-eyed, bow-legged and sallow-skinned."

Nevertheless, Rita was more fortunate than Mildred Gillars would ever be. The Zucca family hired a New York lawyer, Max Spekle, on her behalf. Spekle traveled to Washington to investigate the evidence against her. The press was allowed to tout the successful arrest of the woman who had tormented and teased soldiers throughout the war, but it soon became clear to the Justice Department that Zucca could not be prosecuted for treason in an American court. When the FBI discovered documentation of her 1941 renunciation of citizenship, J. Edgar Hoover informed the Justice Department that a treason case was impossible. Only a month after Rita Zucca's arrest, Hoover wrote to the Assistant Attorney General:

> In view of the fact that [she] has lost her American citizenship, no efforts are being made at the present time to develop a treason case against her. In the absence of a request from you, no further action will be taken regarding this individual.[271]

The US Government's case against Zucca was closed. On September 30, 1945, Rita was tried and found guilty by an Italian court of collaboration. Based on the testimony of three American soldiers over two days, Rita Luisa Zucca was sentenced to four years and five months in an Italian jail. She would serve only nine months, after the Italian government declared a general amnesty for collaborators in 1946.

Although Mildred Gillars took no part in the Italian broadcasts and divulged no military intelligence over the air, she would shoulder the blame for both women. When an American soldier heard Axis Sally broadcast their supposedly secret location at Anzio, Como and a score of other places on the Italian peninsula, he likely heard Rita Zucca rather than Mildred Gillars. Mildred was remarkably prescient when she threatened resignation in 1944 because of Rita Zucca's use of her moniker. The victorious Americans would not care which Axis Sally or Tokyo Rose actually made the most vicious or treasonous statements. The women who "played the Axis game" would have to pay for their crimes. It would prove to be uneven, inexact justice all around.

With one Axis Sally evading American law, the Justice Department was doubly determined to locate other employees of Reichsradio. The CIC dispatched Special Agent Hans Wintzen to Berlin to search for the woman who would replace Rita Zucca as the embodiment of Axis

Sally in the minds of the American public. Wintzen knew that the shrewd, self-assured mother in the custody of the IV Army Corps was not the only female voice that FCC radio monitors at Silver Hill had intercepted night after night.

In August 1945, the search was on but the CIC had only one lead. Raymond Kurtz, a B-17 pilot who had been shot down and captured by the Germans recalled that he was told that the woman who had visited his prison camp was Midge of *Midge at the Mike*. Kurtz remembered that the woman used an alias: Barbara Mome.[272] A "Wanted" poster went up in all occupied sectors of Berlin.

On March 4, 1946, CIC received a tip that she had been seen in the British Sector. Wintzen had a plan: the fugitive had distributed her property among friends across the city. As a person without identification papers, she would have to purchase food through the black market. Barbara Mome was selling her property at various antique shops on consignment to obtain hard currency. Wintzen decided to keep an eye on those shops. Certain that she would eventually emerge from hiding to collect her money or reclaim the property, he believed it was only a matter of time before she would be caught.

After weeks of waiting and watching, Wintzen received a tip from a former neighbor that "Barbara" had left some belongings in a basement storeroom adjacent to her former apartment at 7 Bonnerstrasse. Agent Wintzen questioned the building superintendent and was told that the American had asked for her possessions to be stored away in a safe place when she left the apartment for the last time. Wintzen and the superintendent walked into the storeroom to find seven acetate records containing full programs featuring the voice of Axis Sally.[273] The discovery, if admissible in court, would prove to be a treasure trove of evidence against her. The storeroom also contained an expired US passport—showing her real name—that had been in the possession of her Nazi Party block leader.

Wintzen interviewed her neighbors, friends and colleagues and asked about her "habits, behavior and other little peculiarities." He reported:

> Gillars had actually visited some of these people subsequent to
> May 1945 and had picked up or deposited some of her prop-

erty with various ones among them.... [She] revealed absolutely nothing to them concerning her present address, her present activities, where she was going to or coming from, or exactly what other people she was in the habit of visiting.[274]

The CIC compiled a list of addresses visited by Mildred since May 1945 and set up twenty-four-hour surveillance on those places. When agents were not available, German police were used to stake out the homes. CIC received tips that she had been seen at "different restaurants, beauty shops and other business establishments" in the Kurfurstendamm section of Berlin. The tips helped to narrow down the search to a small section of the city.

The investigation hit pay dirt when the agents found a small table that had belonged to Mildred in an antique shop hidden away on an isolated side street. The store owner gave the CIC the name of the friend who had sold the table to the shop. "Under intensive interrogation," the final report said, "this person eventually admitted having sold the item for Gillars and after a long 'coaxing' by the investigators, also revealed Gillars' present address."[275]

After eleven desperate months on the run, Mildred had settled into a room rented out by a woman and her sister in the British Sector of Berlin. In the cramped conditions that existed after the capitulation, it was not uncommon for strangers to share rooms in single homes and apartments. On March 15, 1946, Mildred returned late in the evening and rang the doorbell. A German plainclothes detective paced outside. Ushered in by the landlady's sister, she found a pale, shaking American soldier in the living room. He pointed a revolver directly at her.

Special Agent Robert Abeles, accompanied by the German policeman, announced, "Miss Gillars, you are under arrest." Momentarily stunned, she reacted with a murmured "Oh ..." and asked if she could take one possession with her—a photo of Max Otto Koischwitz.[276] The agent granted her request and Mildred Gillars went to prison—clutching a photograph of the man she called her "destiny."

Her first night in jail was spent in British confinement. As she slept, another prisoner stole the picture of the dead Professor. Sleep was almost impossible as the lights were kept on all night in the cells. The following morning she was transported to the Wannsee Internment Camp outside Berlin where Hans Wintzen interrogated her for an hour. Another Justice Department lawyer, Victor C. Woerheide entered the room:

"Well, I have heard that you would have given yourself up if you had known that you would have received something to smoke."

"Yes, Mr. Woerheide," Mildred said, "that is more or less the truth."

"Well, it was quite a long search and now we have you."

"You see, I have no experience in this sort of thing," she replied. "I would just like to know, is there such a thing as eating?"[277]

Woerheide apologized and asked a soldier to bring in a hamburger. She had not eaten since her arrest and was famished. She recalled: "I remember digging my bicuspids into the hamburger and making the remark that it was the first meat I had tasted in three months."[278]

As she left her first interrogation, Mildred admiringly told the agents, "I'll take my hat off to the U.S. investigators. They certainly knew a lot about me."[279]

Reporters were ushered into the Interrogation Center to get their first look at the latest incarnation of Axis Sally.

"When I came to Germany in 1934," she told the press, "I had never heard of Hitler. I still don't know anything about politics—I am an artist."

Asked for her reaction to the possibility of the death penalty, she was fatalistic and, as always, highly quotable. "I have always liked to travel, seeking new adventures, and I think death might be the most exciting adventure of all."[280] Sadly, she added, "It doesn't matter. I have lost everything anyhow."[281]

She told the press that her motive for broadcasting was "peace" and declared, "My conscience is clear, and I don't have anything to hide.... Everything I did, I did of my own free will."[282]

On her third day of captivity, a reporter from *Stars and Stripes* visited her cell to see the mythic figure in the flesh. Relishing the moment, the Army reporter taunted her, "Well, well, well, so you are Axis Sally. Well, I just would like to tell you, Sally, that we are all looking forward to your hanging and it is going to be some field day in Washington."[283]

Although the newspapers printed photos of Mildred playing cards with her guards, she was frequently tormented by those GIs seeking to give the "Berlin Bitch" a piece of their mind. She remembered, "From the very beginning, I had only heard of hanging and death, and that I would never need my things, and that I would never eat again."[284]

"I never thought he would die ..."

Emaciated and still weak from her days in hiding, Axis Sally trudged into a small interrogation room at CIC Headquarters in Berlin. It was April 2, 1946, and although she had given CIC a written statement, Samuel Ely and Helen McRae had more questions. Deprived of even military legal counsel, she answered each question openly—even supplying the names of her managers and supervisors at Radio Berlin. Ely and McRae asked about her background.

She did not know if her mother was alive or dead and told the two interrogators that her father died "a long time ago ... we did not get along very well."[285] The prisoner matter-of-factly explained her choice to remain in Germany:

> MG   It was just that it was time to make a decision. It was very hard but also it was only chance that I had not married a German and then I would have been a German woman. There were millions of such cases in the world. The war for me was one against England and the Jews.
>
> Q.   *And you decided to stay with Germany rather than the United States?*
>
> MG   Well, I didn't have a passport anyway. It had been taken away from me.
>
> Q   *You feel that Germany was the right side rather than the United States?*
>
> MG   Well, I can't get the Jews out of my mind. But women are not versed in politics. It would not be interesting to carry on a political conversation with me. When I don't know a subject thoroughly, I don't care to discuss it.

Q   *Did you ever think about taking out German citizenship?*

MG   I definitely planned to marry a German, you see, but it never occurred to me—the possibility—I never thought he would die.[286]

Ely and McCrae asked about a play she recorded prior to the Allied invasion of France. Mildred was particularly proud of her performance in *Vision of Invasion* and even told her questioners that she hoped that there was a copy of the recording back in the United States. The original recording on a magnetic band was destroyed during the frantic retreat from Paris in August 1944 and she was concerned that her best acting had been lost to posterity. Never thinking that her participation as an actress in a dramatic work penned by another could be construed as an act of treason, she made it clear to the CIC that it was considered some of her best work—by herself and her Nazi masters. She told Ely and McCue that Radio Berlin paid the actors more for that play than for any other show of its kind.

The questioning turned to her motives. Her cooperation waned as the questions became accusatory and damning:

Q   All [programs] to the United States were aimed at making people dissatisfied with the war and an effort to make them think the United States was on the wrong side and to make the boys dissatisfied who were in the army. They all had that purpose in mind?[287]

Fixing a stare on the interrogators, she fell silent. The interview was over.

Exhausted and her health failing, she was treated in the Camp Wannsee hospital for three weeks, including one week in the psychiatric ward. Her confinement was difficult, with inedible food and substandard living conditions. She recalled, "The bathroom door could not even be closed … with an armed guard outside."[288]

In July, she was transferred to the Oberursel Internment Camp near Frankfurt am Main. The conditions at Oberursel were not much

Above left: Mildred and her mother, Mae Gillars, circa 1909.
Right: Mildred as a teenager.
Below: Young Mildred in her first communion dress.
All photos courtesy of the Washingtoniana Division, DC Public Library

Mildred Gillars as an
actress and showgirl.
*Courtesy of the
Washingtoniana Division,
DC Public Library*

A young Mildred
Gillars performs
in Ohio Wesleyan
University's
production of
"Mrs. Dane's
Defense" in
December 1920.
*Ohio Wesleyan
Historical
Collection*

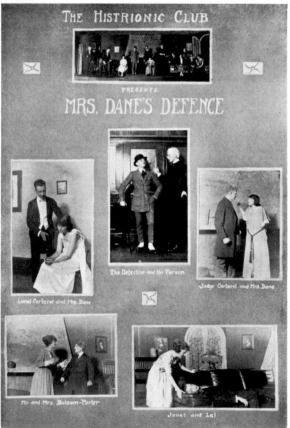

Above left: Charles M. Newcomb was the Professor of Oratory at Ohio Wesleyan who encouraged young Mildred to pursue acting.
Le Bijou 1919, Courtesy: Ohio Wesleyan University Historical Collection, Ohio Wesleyan University Archives, Delaware, Ohio

Right: Mildred at "the height of her theatrical career," in the outfit worn in the Gertrude Vanderbilt show in Washington, a musical comedy which played at the old Belasco Theatre in the early 20's.
Courtesy of the Washingtoniana Division, DC Public Library

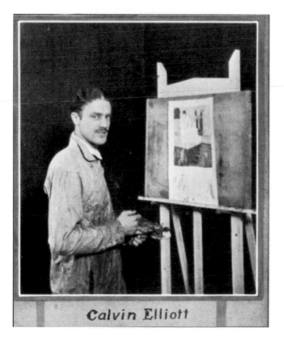

Calvin "Kelly" Elliott was engaged to Mildred Gillars while at Ohio Wesleyan University. He later became an interior decorator but never recovered from the loss of his college sweetheart.
Le Bijou 1919, Courtesy: Ohio Wesleyan University Historical Collection, Ohio Wesleyan University Archives, Delaware, Ohio

Mildred Gillars working as an "artist's model" in New York, circa 1928.
Library of Congress

Mildred Gillars rides a tractor in Algiers, 1933. She first traveled to the country as the companion of an English-Jewish diplomat, though later claimed otherwise. *Courtesy of the Washingtoniana Division, DC Public Library*

"Better grab this dame quick. I understand she built up a terrific following among the boys during the war!"

Cartoon published January 27, 1947 after Axis Sally's Christmas release.
Papers of Bill Mauldin (Library of Congress)
Cartoon Drawings (Library of Congress)

In March 1946, the US Counter-Intelligence Corps (CIC) posted this "Wanted" poster for Mildred Gillars throughout occupied Berlin.
Library of Congress (New York World collection)

Mildred enjoys an American cigarette after her arrest in March 1946.
Library of Congress

Iva Toguri d'Aquino ("Tokyo Rose") poses in dress and apron (1945).
Library of Congress

Surrounded by military police, "Tokyo Rose" (actually only one of several women known as such) speaks to reporters in 1945. *Library of Congress*

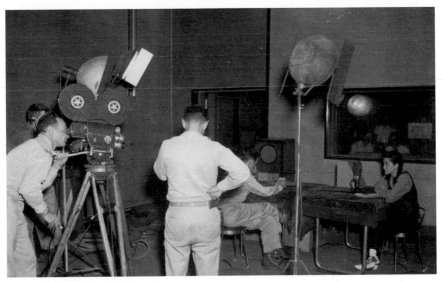

Iva re-enacts a broadcast of the "Zero Hour" by "Orphan Ann" from Radio Tokyo for newsreel cameras in September 1945.
Library of Congress

Matchbook from Zucca's
Restaurant, a popular 1940's
Manhattan eatery owned by
the father of Rita Zucca (the
Rome "Axis Sally").
Courtesy World War II *magazine
and the National Archives*

In Frankfurt-am-Main, "Axis Sally" (Mildred Gillars) bids farewell
to Germany as she is repatriated to the United States. She will
be arrested for treason upon landing in Washington, DC.
To her right is Warrant Officer Catherine Samaha.
The National Archives

Mildred Gillars leaves for Washington to face a grand jury treason inquiry. En route, she told her companion that she "did not expect to be kicked around by anyone, especially her own country."
Photo Credit: Harold Briggs/Stars and Stripes. Photo courtesy: Stars and Stripes.

Above and below: Mildred Gillars ("Axis Sally") responds to reporters'
questions as she leaves the US Commissioner's Office,
following her arrest for treason in August 1948.
Courtesy of Critical Past LLC

A helping hand for "Axis Sally." A Justice Department agent is shown holding the handbag brought from Germany by Mildred Gillars. She is pictured on the sidewalk before her arraignment, August 21, 1948. *Courtesy of the Washingtoniana Division, DC Public Library*

An emotional Edna Mae Herrick after the conviction of her half-sister, Mildred Gillars. *Courtesy of the Washingtoniana Division, DC Public Library*

Axis Sally speaks to reporters at Bolling Field shortly after her arrival and arrest
in Washington DC, August 1948.
National Archives

The jury in the Axis Sally trial leaves the US District Court for lunch. They are (from left): Mrs. Ethel J. Porter, Mrs. Betsy Shenk Rose, Matron Margaret Ferris, Mrs. Carmella George Alley, Stanley R. Kane, Harriet E. Greene, Clifton E. Greaves, Henry G. Davis, Jr., George D. Clark, Mrs. Mildred G. Ashton, Ford H. Flemming, Sr., Marshall Elmer Harris, Norman H. Hedsman, Steward L. Morris and Mrs. Letitia J. Burnani. *Courtesy of the Washingtoniana Division, DC Public Library*

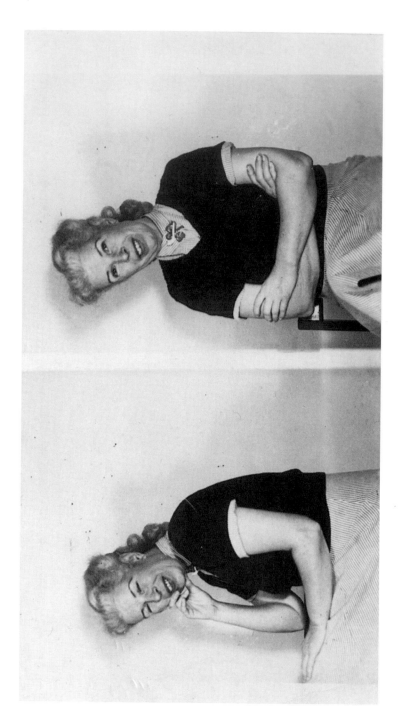

Mildred photographed at Alderson Prison, West Virginia, 1950.
National Archives, College Park, MD

better. During one meal, an inspection officer came to the table and asked the prisoners about the conditions. Mildred and Donald Day complained about the quality of the food in the mess hall. When the inspector left, they were rewarded for their cooperation with two weeks in solitary confinement.

Meanwhile, back in America, news of her arrest brought enquiries into the background of the mysterious Maine-born, Ohio-bred prisoner. The Associated Press contacted Alan Conger, Registrar of Ohio Wesleyan University, for an assessment of her academic record. He told the AP that Mildred had been a problem student who was a "completely undisciplined individual, and noticeably eccentric."[289] This view may have been influenced by patriotism and politics. Mildred's college transcript may be a mixed bag academically, but certainly not one that could be characterized so harshly.

Amnesty

Nearly nine months after her arrest, the CIC announced that Midge and her former colleagues Donald Day and Herbert Burgman would be released for the Christmas holidays. On December 23, 1946, the prisoners were released on the condition that they report back to the Allied Military Government in Frankfurt am Main every two weeks.[290] The Justice Department refused to state publicly whether they still sought to prosecute her. Douglas Chandler (a.k.a. "Paul Revere") and Robert H. Best were slated to be tried first—testing the application of the treason charge to electronic acts such as radio broadcasting. The conviction of two of the most vocal and enthusiastic pro-Nazi broadcasters on the German Radio would establish an important legal precedent that would set the stage for later prosecutions. Without explanation to the press or public, the CIC and the Justice Department approved the release. Alone and with nowhere to go, Mildred was not pleased with the surprising news:

> It wasn't until I got upstairs that I wept and said that I had no place to go, and when I got outside of the barbed wire, I could look to the left or right, it was immaterial, I didn't know which way to go.[291]

She remained in the internment camp for three additional days until December 26. Donald Day made arrangements to go to his home in Bavaria where he shared a small single room with his wife in Bad Tölz. Apologizing to Mildred for not inviting her to Bavaria, he explained that "we just could not have room for you and so God bless you."[292] The old man bid his friend farewell and left the camp.

No one she knew seemed to be left in the area. She remembered:

> I had no one in the American Zone that I knew or where, at least, I was sure that they would have an extra bed ... that was the trouble in Germany. Sometimes four or five people are living in one room, and the friends that I had in the American Zone were all people who had originally lived in Berlin and had lost their homes there, and were to all intents and purposes refugees in the American Zone.[293]

As she greeted reporters at the entrance to the Camp Wannsee compound, Mildred bared her soul and told them of her fear and uncertainty. Wearing a borrowed suit and carrying one mark, 85 pfennig, the highest-paid woman on Nazi radio told the assembled press and photographers of her doubt that she was still an American citizen and questioned whether she was qualified to receive food rations provided to German nationals by the Allied military government. "I have no place to live, but I had some friends in Germany once. Surely some one will extend a helping hand. I planned to go on the German stage when the war was over. Two plays had already been written for me," she told reporters. She explained her unglamorous appearance: "[My hair] turned gray in just a few weeks ... those horrible weeks after the fall of Berlin."[294]

While the description of her plight was meant to evoke sympathy, one of the answers she gave to newsmen would later haunt her. Asked to give her reasons for joining Reichsradio, she spoke neither of the poverty she faced nor the man she loved. Instead, she claimed that her service to the Nazis gave her "the outlet for the dramatic expression I had always sought."[295] Portraying her former employment as a fulfillment of her artistic aspirations could not possibly help any future defense, and the press seized upon her words—putting her statement in the lead paragraph of a *New York Times* article. Mildred walked out into that wet December morning, unknowingly placing her future in even greater jeopardy.

After spending two days at a Frankfurt am Main inn, the destitute woman traveled 48 miles to the small village of Dietz where she found accommodations and was able to get some food rations from past acquaintances. Mildred remained in the picturesque village for 23 days until she was scheduled to report back to the US military authorities. In America, however, the announcement of the Christmas amnesty resulted in an unsubstantiated rumor that she had left Germany and had arrived in Miami, Florida. It made national headlines when the Allied Military Government denied the rumor on January 17 and insisted to the press that "she reported on schedule to our Frankfurt office this afternoon and we can produce her on an hour's notice if necessary."[296]

The false report aroused such outrage that the Attorney General himself acknowledged the rumor and said that if Gillars had indeed fled to Miami she would be arrested immediately for treason. Telegrams poured into the White House for the attention of President Truman, protesting the Christmas release. Charles Robinson, Secretary of the International Hodcarriers, Building and Construction Union, wrote that his members felt that the "traitors, Axis Sally, Mildred Gillars, Herbert Burgman and Donald Day ... should have been executed or given a life sentence at hard labor."[297] A veteran of the 45th Infantry Division wrote to the President that he was "amazed and enraged" that Axis Sally could be released, and other writers were equally opposed to Mildred Gillars re-entering the United States.[298]

The release of Axis Sally had struck a nerve, and the outpouring of emotion was felt all the way from the White House to the Justice and War Departments. In response to the rumor, the Immigration and Naturalization Service was notified to keep an eye out for any attempt by Rita Luisa Zucca or Mildred Gillars to enter the United States. A declassified FBI memorandum dated January 13, 1947 warned that "a boat is due from Italy at 8:00 A.M on 1/14/47 and one from Germany on the morning of 1/15/47, and though they [the INS] had no information indicating the individual in question would be on either of these vessels, they wanted to be prepared."[299]

Immigration officials had already received word from the highest levels of government that the two women were to be barred at entry. Even though the FBI memo states that "Zucca formally renounced her citizenship in June 1941, and apparently the Department was not interested in any treason case against her," the file on Mildred was classified as "pending."[300] Neither woman was welcome in America, but even at that early date only Mildred Gillars rather than the woman who had expropriated her name and style (and who was more likely to have transmitted information of a military nature to Allied troops over the airwaves at Monte Cassino and Anzio) would be prosecuted.

While the Immigration Service was looking for her at American ports, Mildred was on her way back to Frankfurt am Main. Returning to the CIC office on January 23, 1947 to check in and to obtain a pass to go back to Dietz and the French Occupied Zone, she was abruptly held for questioning without explanation. Unaware of the controversy building in the United States surrounding her Christmas amnesty, she was not told that she was under arrest:

> I wasn't arrested. I was locked up ... I was confined again in back of barbed wired all over again.... I kept on going to them and saying, "Why are you doing this? Can I have a lawyer? I am told I am not under arrest, and I have done nothing these 26 days in Dietz but rest and get over the shock of the nine months I have just passed through, and for four and a half months I had nothing but the clothes I had on my back" ... and the Army could not find any pajamas or any stockings, or anything else for me.[301]

Newsmen asked US military authorities to explain their sudden change of course. Ignoring the political pressure emanating from the US Justice Department, the major American press outlets honed in on statements Mildred had made over the past month in what were described as unsolicited interviews. Upon her release, she told the newsmen that the political views she espoused on the air regarding the Communist threat were not only accurate but prophetic:

> I tried to warn America against Communism and Judaism, to

show how they were threatening and undermining America ...
All the things I warned against have become actualities. Oh, if
only those poor GIs who sacrificed their lives and futures had
realized what was going on.[302]

Publicly casting herself as a Cassandra warning against the Soviet
scourge was not the role that the Attorney General and the Justice
Department had in mind when they agreed to release her for
Christmas. The change in public opinion vis-à-vis their former Allies
was fertile ground for the Nazi propaganda line of 1944–45. As early
as September 1945, *The New York Times* published a front-page article entitled:

Pro-German Attitude Grows as US Troops Fraternize—
Survey Show Many GIs Have Less Regard for Allies than for
Former Enemies—One Major Doubts Dachau Crimes

The *Times* reporter blamed the pro-German attitude on fraternization between the US occupation forces and the alluring
"Gretchens":

An alarming and unhealthy symptom of these close relations is
the readiness of the average officer and soldier to spout the
enemy propaganda line. It is amazing how much of it comes
back to one in accents of Brooklyn, Texas or the Middle West.
It is surprising to hear from General George S. Patton that 98
percent of the Nazis—a figure he later corrected to a "majority"—had been forced into the party against their will. It is
equally surprising from a Major in Munich that he does not
believe in those Dachau atrocity tales, although Dachau is only
a few miles away and evidence of the atrocities is still available
for those who care to investigate.... All the old tales the
Germans have been telling about the Russians can be heard
repeated by many of our soldiers and officers, many of whom
have never been in contact with the Red Army and therefore
know nothing but what Germans have been pouring into their
ears.[303]

Some GIs might have been receptive to Mildred's claim of political foresight, but the Justice Department viewed her outspokenness as an affront—a direct and public challenge to the Government. Attorney General Clark could not possibly set her free to spew the Nazi propaganda line on the streets of Germany or possibly dare to re-enter the United States.

Rita Zucca had been more fortunate. She was released early from an Italian jail in August 1946 after serving only nine months of her four and a half year sentence. Claiming that the amnesties just issued by the new Italian government covered her crimes and made her eligible for release, the jurists took mercy on the collaborationist young mother.

The similarities between the two women's stories are striking. Like Gillars, Zucca had "renounced" her citizenship in 1940 to become an Italian subject, just as Mildred signed a loyalty oath to Germany in December 1941 after Pearl Harbor—an oath that she assumed was a sufficient renunciation of her citizenship. Like Gillars, Zucca claimed that her motive in collaborating with the Nazis was not political. She was neither pro-Nazi nor pro-Fascist. Instead, Zucca claimed that a desperate financial situation drove her to the microphone.

What Zucca did not do was doggedly insist that the content of her broadcasts was correct when she denounced the martyred Roosevelt, or implied that the men who fought and died in the armed forces had sacrificed their lives for a Communist victory, or that men of industry and finance had driven America into the war for Jewish monetary gain. Zucca was allowed to fade into obscurity on time-served and avoid prosecution in the United States. The Berlin Axis Sally had to be punished to the fullest extent of the law.

CHAPTER 9

The Stage Is Set

"This is quite a bombardment.... but I'm used to
them, you know. I mean bombs during the war!"
—Mildred Gillars, August 20, 1948[304]

AUGUST–SEPTEMBER 1948

A swarm of news correspondents and photographers surrounded Axis
Sally as she approached the C-54 transport that would take her to
Washington, DC. Drinking in the attention that had eluded her for so
long, she was finally, unquestionably, a celebrity. After almost seven
teen months of uninterrupted imprisonment without trial or counsel,
Mildred lingered in front of the news media—posing for photos and
supplying reporters with snappy quotes. When one reporter inquired
about her wartime activities, she gave the cryptic answer, "When in
Germany, do as the Germans do!"

She wore a "flowing black fur cloak and black slacks," supplied
secondhand by the Army. Like an actress taking her final curtain call,
Sally carried a bouquet of red roses—flowers reportedly sent from a
mysterious friend residing in the French sector of Berlin. Enjoying her
fame, the silver-haired, 47-year-old lady of the stage ignored her
guard's pleas to board the plane.

"Goodbye, Frankfurt!" Axis Sally shouted with a flourish of her
arm. She bade farewell to the press and climbed the stairs into the
waiting plane.[305] Having survived rejection, failure, poverty and the

hell of Germany's collapse, Mildred had achieved the notoriety she had always sought. With the prisoner finally secured on the airplane, Warrant Officer Catherine Samaha and Lt. Franklin Davies signaled to the pilot, and the C-54 took off in a gray drizzle. Although she did not know it, Mildred was saying goodbye to her beloved Germany forever. She came to Berlin fourteen years before as a failed actress with almost nothing to her name. She left Germany with nothing but a name synonymous with treachery.

The repatriation of Axis Sally had been meticulously planned for weeks. The Justice Department wanted to avoid the confusion of December 1946, when the first accused "radio traitors" Douglas Chandler (a.k.a. "Paul Revere") and Robert H. Best, had been flown back to America to stand trial. Federal law demands that an American citizen accused of committing a crime overseas must be tried in the Federal District where he first entered American territory.[306]

Oscar R. Ewing, Special Assistant to Attorney General Tom Clark, specifically requested that the plane fly directly up the Potomac River to land in Washington, DC. The Chandler and Best investigations were based in the District of Columbia and the Grand Jury had already heard witnesses. Ewing wanted to try the men there. Despite repeated requests to stick to the flight plan, the pilot put the plane down at Westover Field near Boston, Massachusetts. The flier claimed that he had to travel farther north because he could not get the aircraft's wheels retracted. Ewing later discovered that the pilot had a girlfriend in Boston and decided to pay her a visit. While the plane was being examined for "mechanical trouble," Chandler and Best spent almost three hours in the airport lounge. The pilot and his girl had a costly reunion at government expense.[307]

The mistake resulted in a legal and logistical nightmare for the Justice Department. Ewing recalled the snafu: "We had to re-indict him up there in Boston because of what this darn pilot had done ... it cost the United States Government at least a hundred thousand dollars because of the expense of bringing the witnesses back again from Germany."[308] German witnesses, who had already testified in Washington, had to be recalled before a newly empanelled Grand Jury in Boston federal court. The pilot's rendezvous also forced J. Edgar Hoover to move the entire FBI investigation to its Boston field office.

The FBI was determined that Axis Sally's transfer would present no such problems. The moment the plane carrying Mildred Gillars was airborne, a telephone call was placed to Washington, where prosecutors immediately sought a warrant for her arrest. The course of the plane was predetermined with refueling stops in the Azores and Bermuda. The flight then traveled northwest over international waters until it traversed the Potomac River. Then, Mildred was to be taken into custody by military police, turned over to the FBI and arraigned by a United States Commissioner at Bolling Field in Washington.

The Justice Department prosecutor assigned to Mildred's case, John M. Kelley, Jr. warned the FBI to "avoid any possible criticism growing out of alleged mistreatment of Miss Gillars, and to ensure that she was given breakfast and, if needed, supplied medical treatment prior to her arraignment.[309] American public opinion had to be taken into consideration. Axis Sally would now be in the public eye, not hidden away in a military internment camp abroad. The government could not risk being accused of mistreating a defenseless woman, no matter how notorious her reputation.

Hitler's Girlfriend

On perhaps the most unusual assignment of her military career, Warrant Officer Catherine Samaha settled into her seat next to Axis Sally. The Woman's Army Corps (WAC) guard, wearing the drab brownish-green of Army issue, jumped when her prisoner pulled a jagged glass mirror and a comb from her handbag. Stunned that a potentially desperate traitor was allowed to board a military plane without a search for contraband, Samaha decided to let her prisoner go ahead and check her makeup.

Visibly exhilarated from the press attention, Mildred engaged the WAC in a long conversation. Catherine Samaha was, like Mildred Gillars, an Ohio native—a fact not lost on the Army commanders who assigned her to the task. In Washington, FBI agents were waiting to debrief the guard upon landing. The details of their conversation were well documented in a memorandum to FBI Director Hoover that was then forwarded on to prosecutors working the case. In her "just between us girls" style, Mildred opened up to the younger woman and provided damaging details about her life in Germany. Her words and actions on the flight to the United States shed light not only on her fragile state of mind that August day but also how American officials deceived a disoriented and isolated prisoner.

As the journey began, Mildred told Samaha that the American authorities in Germany assured her that she was only being taken to the United States for interrogation and that she was not under arrest.[310] With typical bravado, the prisoner defiantly told her young companion that she "did not expect to be kicked around by anyone, especially her own country."[311] Mildred regaled her new friend with quotations from Shakespeare and her knowledge of astrology, noting "The study of the stars is one of my favorite hobbies."[312] Despite the risk of opening up to a representative of the US government, Mildred told the WAC that she had become quite fond of her and proposed that they meet socially in United States. Samaha cagily drew the lonely actress out. The WAC told her FBI debriefers, "I played on her ego and complimented her on her alertness, hair-do, etc."[313] Samaha was greatly amused that Mildred "accepted such flattery with a great deal of enthusiasm."[314]

When the conversation turned to her work for the Germans, Mildred was equally forthcoming. "English was always my first love," she told the guard, "I always made it a point to not acquire a foreign accent." She prided herself on retaining her American manner of speaking. Mildred revealed intimate details of her day-to-day work as a radio broadcaster. She even described the technical processes of her work, describing how she recorded the majority of her broadcasts on what she termed "film rolls" (magnetic recording cylinders or bands). These cylinders were generally erased after transmission and then reused. Mildred doubted that many of them survived.

Samaha told the FBI that Axis Sally "could do anything she wanted in connection with her work; she had a free rein to travel and actually did travel to Holland, Paris, Belgium, Italy and other places and frequently used her recordings as an excuse for such travel.... She realized that she worked for the German government against the United States during the war, but made no direct statement acknowledging her guilt.... [Gillars] stated that she spent six months in Algiers during the war, and although she had never made a live broadcast from

Algiers, the Germans probably used her recordings there."[315]

These were dangerous half-truths that falsely gave the Americans the impression that she was an employee of unquestioned loyalty to the Nazi cause. Mildred was candid as she explained her escape in the face of the Soviet advance:

"I had slipped out the back door of the radio station in Berlin as the Russians were entering the front entrance.... The Russians were very, very anxious to get a hold of me."[316] Although the remark reveals Mildred's egotism, her fears were reasonable considering the fate of her colleague Fred Kaltenbach ("Lord Hee Haw") who fell into Soviet hands after the fall of Berlin. When an attempt to trade two captured SS officers for the radio announcer failed, the Soviets informed the American government in June 1946 that Kaltenbach died in custody, of "natural causes."[317]

Mildred told the officer that she did not keep company with the highest of Nazi officials, but was disarmingly honest about her opinion of Hitler's late wife, Eva Braun. "She severely criticized Eva Braun for her appearance, personality, etc...." Samaha said. "Her attitude showed marked jealousy."[318]

This bit of gossip would prove to be of great interest to J. Edgar Hoover and his friend Walter Winchell.* The newspaper columnist and radio broadcaster for the *New York Daily Mirror* was instrumental in inflaming public opinion against the defendants in the "radio traitor" trials, reserving special venom for the female propagandists. As early as 1947, Winchell repeatedly referred to Axis Sally in his radio show as "Hitler's girlfriend."

Mildred was becoming detached from reality, casting herself as the star with the guard playing the role of personal assistant. "From the beginning of the trip," Samaha claimed, "she more or less took the attitude that I was sort of a personal companion rather than a bodyguard."[319] The prisoner even attempted to order her around on several occasions. She was living in a fantasy world, acting as though she

---

*The symbiotic relationship between Hoover and Winchell is well documented in hundreds of declassified FBI files containing correspondence between the two men. The FBI Director regularly leaked information to Winchell, who in turn lionized Hoover in his columns and radio broadcasts and even floated the Director's name for the Presidency.

were onstage. In her mind, Mildred was no longer the gofer who served the film star Brigitte Horney hand and foot.[320] In her delusion, Axis Sally was the celebrity.

Although it may never be known if Mildred's bizarre behavior ever led the Justice Department to question her fitness to stand trial, the week of psychological tests ordered by the Army Counter-Intelligence Corps were probably enough for both the G-men and the prosecutors. Nevertheless, Samaha's encounter with Axis Sally reveals a woman with a tenuous grip on reality.

Mildred falsely boasted that she was the only broadcaster at the USA Zone who neither used a prepared manuscript nor was censored. Claiming that all of her broadcasts were "ad-libbed" was an extremely damaging admission. She could no longer hope to convince a jury that she was a mere pawn parroting the Propaganda Ministry's line. Douglas Chandler's conviction in June 1947 provided only a limited precedent for the coming trial of Axis Sally. Chandler was in every way an architect and refiner of the propaganda message that went out daily over the airwaves.

Every morning at 11 a.m. Joseph Goebbels met with his department heads to convey that day's message, called the *Tagesparole* or "watchword." The meetings consisted of one long monologue by the *Reichsminister*. The department heads (in the case of radio, Hans Fritzsche) then communicated the "watchword" to their staffs to discuss how to tailor the day's message to their specific audience. Chandler (along with Best and several other Americans including Constance Drexel, Jane Anderson and Edward Delaney) actively participated in the planning meetings. The expatriates helped craft the uniquely American spin that would adorn Goebbels' core message. An admission of responsibility for the authorship of her pro-Nazi screeds could send her to prison for life (as were Chandler and Best), or death in the electric chair.

"I have no one ..."

It was 1:30 in the afternoon when the airplane touched down in Washington. A barrage of questions greeted Axis Sally as she descended the steps onto the tarmac. Posing for photographs, she waved off questions about her future, stating, "Those are very big questions and they require very big answers and I can't say now."

A "lonely and dispirited" figure, she told her story to reporters. "I went to work for Radio Berlin because I am an actress," she explained. "It is very difficult to return under such circumstances, of course. I have been living in a country subject to a great deal of tragedy for the last nine years."[321] To the mothers and fathers of America who had buried their sons as a result of Hitler's aggression, Axis Sally's tears over Germany's nine years of tragedy must have rung hollow. Her first meeting with the press that Saturday afternoon in August 1948 set the tone for how the public and the press would look at the friendless woman over the ensuing months.

She reminisced about her last visit to Washington, DC. Sixteen years earlier she had performed at the National Theater in a play whose name she could not recall. Now she would play the most serious role of her life: defendant. Flanked by Federal agents and military police, US Commissioner Cyril S. Lawrence approached and read out the warrant for her arrest, stating that between December 11, 1941 and May 6, 1945 she "unlawfully, willfully, and treasonably adhered to the government of the German Reich, an enemy of the United States, and did give the said enemy ... aid and comfort."[322]

Her face froze as the Commissioner read out the charges. Lawrence coolly informed her that the charges carried a maximum sentence of death. She fell quiet as she finally comprehended the seriousness of her situation. "If Miss Sisk-Gillars yet realized she faced a possible death penalty," one witness to the proceedings reported, "she did not show it. She listened attentively to the charges for which she had been brought home from Berlin—but she had nothing to say."[323] The Commissioner asked how she chose to respond to the charges against her.

"I wouldn't agree with them," she abruptly replied.[324]

Lawrence then asked if she had any relatives or friends in the United States who could help her prepare her defense.

"As far as I know," she replied, "I have no one here in the United States."

He informed her that the FBI had located her half-sister, Edna Mae

Herrick. Reporters on hand noted that Mildred seemed "surprised and
not very interested" in this revelation, but she was likely wondering
about her absent mother.[325] Unknown to her, Mae Gillars had died in
March 1947. She spent her final years in the Toronto rooming house
she owned and managed, ill and grieving over her imprisoned daughter whose innocence she protested until the day she died.

"When did she get here?" she asked, referring to her half-sister as
she was led away to the District of Columbia Jail.[326]

"A pretty dismal place, that jail—dark, noisy and smelly," was
how one newspaper columnist's description of the District jail that
once held mental patients and violent criminals.[327] Led into a bare cell
to await a hearing, bail was impossible as Federal law proscribed bond
in treason cases. As officers booked her, the Commissioner advised her
to find an attorney as soon as possible. When asked her age, the haggard and gray woman who had survived like an animal in demolished
buildings and internment camps remained an actress to the core.

"Thirty-nine," she told the booking officer, subtracting nine from
her actual age.[328]

* * *

In the small town of Ashtabula, Ohio, a 39-year-old dance instructor
was gazing at a newspaper picture of a woman with a prominent jaw
and smiling eyes that resembled her own.

Edna Mae Herrick was positive that the woman who had arrived
over the weekend from Germany was none other than the delicate
"china doll" she had idolized as a child. The press soon called on the
half-sister of Axis Sally for her reaction to her sibling's return. Ever
loyal, Edna Mae Herrick swore to stand by Mildred:

"I believe if my sister did anything which was treasonable to her
country," she said, "she did it unwillingly. If she is in trouble, I want
to be by her side."[329]

For over a year and a half, Edna Mae and her family had suffered
for the actions of her distant sister. When Mildred was arrested in
March 1946, she was fired from her job for the sole cause of being kin
to Axis Sally. Nine months later, as false rumors of Mildred's arrival
in Miami swirled in the press, she again felt the heat of public outrage.

With her mother's health growing worse day by day, Edna Mae wrote to J. Edgar Hoover in January 1947. Alternately beseeching and defiant in tone, the handwritten letter cited the bitter loss of her own job, the meanness of the American media, and the disastrous effect of the controversy on her mother, Mae:

> *Personally, I feel sorry for the "dog eat dog" attitude of the world today. We seem to have too many churches for the few Christians. Walter Winchell and others apparently feel justified in standing in the judgment seat and making what they think is a patriotic stab. Well, I suppose they have to make their living. It would suit them better to first check by real people. Friends right in New York who knew and loved Mildred. I think the real Democratic news would have been to ask America "why I, an innocent party, was fired from my job when Mildred was arrested in March?" Jews did this to me!— And I, with a young son to support.*
>
> *Whoever this woman is, she must be desperately tired. If it is my sister, I do wish we could have her home soon for a much needed rest. We have very little money and it's frightening to think of what a drag through court will cost. I can't see why, if the American court there could release her, why this additional time and cost must be spent.*
>
> *I hope this letter hasn't annoyed you, but rather will lend light on the subject. I hope with all my heart, Mr. Hoover that you can help before the whole thing kills my mother.*[330]

Less than two months later, Mae Gillars passed away.

Edna Mae and her husband, E. Reid Herrick, were busy building a new house. The unfinished home had no furnace yet, so the family kept warm by lighting three fireplaces. With Mae gone, there was no question that she would support her sister to the bitter end. "It was a mess," Edna Mae recalled in an interview shortly before her death, "but it never entered my mind not to be there for moral support. I don't think Mildred cared one way or another if I was there. I did it for my mother."[331]

Edna Mae packed her bags for the long trip to Washington and the longer wait for Mildred's day in court. She barely knew what to expect after more than a decade of silence. So much had changed. Their mother was dead. The family home in Conneaut had been sold. Her sister, now gray and battered by the cruelty of war, was sitting in a narrow, damp cell built to house prostitutes, thieves and murderers. The effects of her newfound fame on her family always weighed heavily on Mildred's mind. Two years earlier she had spoken of her fear that her actions might harm her family, especially her mother.

"I am hoping my mother will not hear about this at all," she told CIC interrogators in April 1946. "I don't like to run the risk of my relatives and school friends finding out about it. Such notoriety has never been in my family before."[332]

If there was any doubt about the extent to which Mildred Gillars had cut off her relations with family and friends in the United States, it was apparent on the day of her arrival in Washington. As she was booked into jail, she listed a friend, Mrs. E. Arnold of Dietz, Germany (where she found shelter during the 1946 Christmas amnesty), as her next of kin.[333]

The taint of her infamy was impossible to escape. Her mother Mae, heartbroken by her failure to convince her headstrong daughter to return to America in 1939, was only one casualty. The rest of the Hewitson and Gillars families were similarly affected by the shame of being related to Axis Sally, as FBI agents discovered when they visited Mae's brothers in New Brunswick, Canada. Accompanied by an officer of the Royal Canadian Mounted Police, the agents traveled to the province in an attempt to verify Mildred's American nationality. Mae's elder brother, William Hewitson, was an elderly farmer who had not been off his Fredericton property in almost a decade. His 62-year-old younger brother, Joseph, was willing to go to Washington to testify at his niece's trial, but was short of cash and required a fifty dollar cash advance to pay for the train ticket.

Mildred's Uncle Joseph acknowledged that the controversy had hit his family hard. Still, he did not believe that his niece had worked for the Nazis voluntarily and could not fathom "how she could do the things which she is reported to have done."[334] Joseph pleaded with the agents to refrain from contacting his sister, Cora Ross, who was ill in a Nova Scotia hospital. The sickly woman was especially disturbed by news reports concerning her infamous niece. The investigators decided not to pursue the Hewitsons further after the FBI collected enough documentation to confirm her American birth.

Voices from the Past

As Axis Sally settled into her cell, she could not know how close she had come to avoiding prosecution altogether. In January 1947, a troubled Assistant Attorney General Lamar Caudle told Washington columnist Drew Pearson that the Justice Department was having trouble meeting the Constitution's "two witness" requirement for a treason conviction. At the same time, the Army was pressuring his department to drop the charges rather than hold her indefinitely. In 1961, Pearson explained his role in keeping Axis Sally in jail:

> Caudle said they could find no witnesses. No Americans had actually seen Axis Sally broadcast to American troops on behalf of Hitler. Caudle told me of his predicament, and I broadcast an appeal to ex-GIs who had been prisoners of war in German camps and who might have seen Axis Sally in action. Two GIs answered the appeal.[335]

Caudle also sought the help of Walter Winchell. When the Justice Department lawyer mentioned that the Army had requested a reconsideration of Mildred's case, Winchell made sure his audience was duly outraged. Assuming the mantle of spokesman for "Mr. and Mrs. America," the columnist demanded an explanation from the War Department:

> The Department of Justice has denied the application of the Army to drop proceedings against Axis Sally. Secretary Patterson ought to explain the position of his department to the American people. The Gold Star mothers would be particularly interested in whether the War Department should intervene to save the voice which taunted our wounded and dying [that] they were suckers—not heroes.
> Assistant Attorney General Caudle, who turned down the

request, did it with a grin. "We're not taking Sally off your hands," he said, "because among other things I'd have Pearson and Winchell around my neck."[336]

After months of arrest, release and then re-arrest, the Army could not hold Axis Sally indefinitely. The rank and file soldier who enjoyed her music from afar could not give eyewitness testimony to her treachery. Men who saw Axis Sally at work in the flesh were required—the GIs that Mildred sought to help by broadcasting messages to their loved ones as they lingered in a prison camp. Caudle needed the few who were disgusted to see an American woman in league with the enemy that killed and maimed their comrades.

Pearson and Winchell's campaign to see Axis Sally behind bars paid off. Within days of Drew Pearson's January 26 appeal, the columnist received handwritten letters from two former American prisoners of war. Albert J. Lawlor of Stony Brook, NY, had been held in *Stalag VII A* near Furstenberg on the Oder between February 1943 and April 1945. Lawlor described his encounter with Axis Sally:

> A woman came to this camp one day sometime between September 9, 1943 and May 12, 1944 to make a propaganda broadcast. She said her given name was either Midge or Madge and [she was] a typical girl. During her stay at the camp, in company with technicians and other men, one of whom was called "Professor," all of who spoke English very well and who, by their own admission to me, had lived and worked in the United States, they made records to be broadcast to the United States.
>
> I witnessed the entire affair and am willing to try to identify this woman if she is the so-called Axis Sally and keep her and the likes of her out of this country, which we love and they betrayed ... I consider it my duty to do whatever possible.[337]

A few days later, Pearson received another handwritten note from a former Army Ranger named Robert Ehalt, the prisoner of war who refused to let the men of *Stalag IIB* record messages for Midge and the Professor in 1944. He vividly recalled her angry reaction to the horse manure-filled cigarette carton that his fellow prisoners gave her, and her threat that they would soon regret it. Ehalt vowed not to let the haughty collaborator get away:

> I refused to allow her to take these recordings. As she left her parting words were "What a bunch of ungrateful people we Americans were." This woman was Berlin Sally. At the time she visited us she asked the boys to make records saying that we were being treated good and had plenty to eat. Outside of the barracks she had a sound truck already [*sic*] to the USA by short wave.
>
> This woman spoke perfect English and said she had come from America; also that she had lived in NY a long time in Greenwich Village. Her hair was black. The man with her was a German professor. This woman, I believe, came to see what was left of the 1st Ranger Battalion because all through the N. African, Tunisian, Sicily and Italy campaigns [*sic*], she ridiculed the Rangers. I can give you the names of two other GIs who were with me at the time of my conversation with her.

Pearson turned Ehalt and Lawlor's letters over to Victor Woerheide at the Justice Department. Within weeks, FBI agents interviewed the former POWs. Each man recalled more names, and each successive witness recalled the names of other men who participated in the recordings for the *Survivors of the Invasion Front* program. The FCC-recorded tapes from the monitoring station in Silver Spring, Maryland yielded additional names. By June 6, 1947, Pearson could report to his readers that the eyewitness testimony of the former POWs gave the Justice Department "a reasonable chance of conviction."[338]

The publicity resulted in a nationwide campaign of war veterans in American Legion and VFW posts determined to "bar Axis Sally, Nazi-loving war broadcaster, from returning to the United States unless she is brought back to face trial for treason."[339] One resolution from a Legion post in Detroit, Michigan "was offered by Wilson

Elliott, an Air Corps gunner who was forced to listen to her propaganda broadcasts every day for two and a half years in a German prison camp after Elliott's bomber was shot down over Germany."[340] With veterans groups aroused, the political pressure to keep Mildred in jail was mounting in the upcoming presidential election year of 1948.

President Harry Truman was facing an uphill battle for re-election. It had been almost 16 years since a Republican sat in the Oval Office and the emerging threat of international Communism was fertile ground for the GOP. Truman was determined to appear tough on enemies foreign and domestic, and the prosecution of former Nazi collaborators was an effective means of doing just that. September 1948 saw another infamous propagandist, Iva Toguri d'Aquino, brought back to America. Preparations were being made on the West Coast for "Little Orphan Anne"—better known as Tokyo Rose—to be tried in San Francisco for treason. Mrs. D'Aquino landed on American soil only four weeks after Mildred's arrival at Bolling Field. The dramatic and public repatriation of the two women was certain to show the voters that the Truman Administration knew how to deal decisively with traitors and bring them to justice.

A Priceless Service

Not all Americans viewed Axis Sally as a traitor. Throughout the war, a dedicated group of hundreds of amateur ("ham") and short-wave radio hobbyists sat in darkened rooms warmed by the glow of the tubes and dials of their Hallicrafters and Zenith radio sets. With pencils in hand, these average American citizens dutifully monitored the broadcasts of Berlin Radio. Each night, these listeners waded through the German war communiqués, musical interludes and ludicrous commentaries to hear the names of captured and wounded American, Canadian and British troops.

They recorded the names, serial numbers and hometowns of the men. At their own expense, they wrote cards and letters to the families of the imprisoned soldiers informing them that their loved one was captured but alive. In many cases, this correspondence was the first and only news of their lost soldier. Rita Zucca, the Rome "Axis Sally," also regularly read the names of the captured on her show *Jerry's Front*.

In several FBI statements of former prisoners interviewed by Axis Sally, the number of Americans who regularly listened to the wartime broadcasts surprised Hoover's men. One of the prisoners interviewed by Midge, Homer McNamara, told the FBI how his mother had received a telegram from "some radio ham" up in Maine, advising that he had heard McNamara's voice over the radio from Germany and that he was a prisoner of war—and alive."[341] Another ex-soldier, John Patrick Butler, gave the G-men:

> several postcards and letters received by the members of [his] family after the broadcast was made by [Gillars] to the United States, disclosing her interview with Butler. These communications generally reflect that the writers of the communications had heard the ... broadcast and wished to inform the members of the Butler family of Johnny's message to them. These communications would tend to indicate that Mildred Gillars' broadcasts were widely heard by numerous people in the United States.[342]

Of the hundreds of American civilians who listened to the broadcasts of Axis Sally or received information about their loved ones, only two came to her aid. Irwin and Violet Bender of Harrisburg, Pennsylvania regularly listened to Midge during the war. The Benders took up their pens again in defense of the American girl who spoke to them over the airwaves. The couple challenged the validity of the government's claims against Mildred. Like other acts of postwar dissent, the Benders' actions came to the attention of the FBI and J. Edgar Hoover. The mother of a former prisoner of war, Gertrude Laughlin, received one such letter in October 1948:

> Dear Mrs. Laughlin:
> On May 16, 1944, Mildred Gillars read your son's message via the Berlin Short-wave radio in Germany and your letter of appreciation testifies to the benefits derived from that message. This brave woman, known to American "relay-lis-

teners" as "Midge," by which name she identified herself over the German radio, has been "kidnapped" by the Department of Justice and they have "framed" a treason charge against her.

There are certain revengeful persons on the loose here in America who wish to see everyone who brushed elbows with anything German during the war wiped off the face of the earth. This brave woman unfortunately found herself in Europe at the outbreak of the War in Europe (which began long before we entered the war) and when we entered it, this woman found the plight of our boys who were prisoners of war in that country, she cast her lot with our boys and began the humanitarian work of helping the boys write their messages, collecting them from the various camps, and then reading them over the Berlin short-wave radio.

She carried out this priceless service for nearly two years and you as well as thousands of others here in America received the great "aid and comfort" that was to be had in her brave efforts in transmitting these messages of life and hope.

The false charge of "treason" (for the definition of treason carries the charge of giving "aid and comfort to the enemy") is based on her North African broadcasts which were harmless, and there certainly was no "aid and comfort" given to the Germans in all her radio activities ....

I have been working very hard in the defense [sic] of Miss Gillars (whom the Department of Justice has "unfairly" dubbed Axis Sally), and have many influential people helping in the cause. My wife and I listened-in and relayed nearly all the messages "Midge" read via the Berlin short-wave radio during the war, and the thousands of letters of appreciation we have received testify to the fact that Miss Gillars has rendered to the American people a priceless service that can never be repaid. The FBI and their "Alma Mater," the Department of Justice, are trying hard to carry out the wishes of certain vindictive persons to "railroad" this girl to life imprisonment, and even—DEATH.[343]

Laughlin's son, James (no relation to Mildred's future attorney), sent the letter to the FBI and told the Bureau that he was "in no way sympathetic with the contents of the letter."[344] Hoover received similar letters from other families concerned that Bender's message might reflect on their loyalty. One Indianapolis woman passed on the Benders' letter and told agents that she was "not in sympathy with the request." Mrs. William F. Boylan of New York City had more reason to be outraged at the Benders' request for support. Although her son was a prisoner of the Nazis for 22 months and survived the war, he died at home a year later as a direct result of his imprisonment.[345]

Mildred's recordings of POW messages for broadcast from Berlin were not treasonous in and of themselves. The prosecution would have to show that she intentionally used those broadcasts to provide aid and comfort to the German war effort, rather than comfort to heartsick families back home.

Justice Department prosecutors also had serious concerns about the testimony of the former prisoners. An examination of the August 1948 correspondence between the prosecutors and the FBI shows that the memories of those GIs who witnessed her actions in the camps were less vivid than their later trial testimony would indicate. Prosecutor John M. Kelley and his team needed two witnesses to the *same* overt act of treason to get a conviction. Acting Assistant Attorney General Alexander Campbell pointed out the difficulty that the prosecution was experiencing in nailing down the somewhat hazy memories of the former prisoners:

Their encounter with the subject was brief and occurred more than four years ago. Moreover, at the time they were approached by the subject they were underfed and physically exhausted by the ordeal of their capture and the enforced marches which ensued. In view of these factors it is not surprising that reports of investigation submitted by the Bureau following interrogation of these witnesses reflect many omissions and discrepancies. A number of these witnesses were unable to recall either the names or faces of their fellow prisoners who recorded messages at the same time, but express the belief that recognition would probably occur if they could meet face to face. Once these witnesses are brought together for common discussion and reminiscence it is accordingly anticipated that many of said omissions and discrepancies will disappear.[346]

Even before Mildred returned to the United States, Kelley recognized the possible weaknesses of his case and, more so, his witnesses. To attempt to eliminate the discrepancies, the FBI brought together the former prisoners of war into small groups to listen to Axis Sally recordings and meet for "common discussion and reminiscence." These eyewitnesses to a capital case required the reinforcement of the memories of their fellow prisoners. Although the majority of the witnesses were able to identify Mildred Gillars from old photographs, the Justice Department was concerned by the fact that the prisoner's "physical appearance has altered considerably during the period of her incarceration," and the witnesses would no longer be able to recognize her.[347]

Campbell asked that the witnesses view the accused immediately after their arrival in Washington, so that "should some of them wholly fail to identify her, they can be dismissed forthwith."[348] Kelley had reason for concern. The FBI reports of their interviews with some of the ex-prisoners cast a shadow on the witnesses' ability to immediately identify Mildred. When shown recent photographs of her, ex-POW Homer McNamara "failed to pick out the photo of subject Gillars but did select her photo along with one of another woman." In addition, the investigators noted that a photo with her name written on it "struck no familiar note" with McNamara.[349]

Campbell went as far as requesting that the witnesses *hear her voice*, because "in some instances they may have to hear the subject speak before they can be certain one way or another."[350] Axis Sally's voice was heard by literally hundreds of thousands of GIs in Europe and Africa. The ex-POWs were being called to testify about their *personal* contact with her in a prisoner-of-war camp. A familiar voice that spoke to them over the radio for more than three years could not determine whether they could visually recognize her. Despite it all, "common discussion and reminiscence" would be used to turn foggy memories into vivid evidence at trial.

Moreover, prosecutor John Kelley was concerned that these discrepancies might affect his ability to get an indictment from the Grand Jury. In an undated FBI internal memorandum, FBI Special Agent F.J. Baumgardner wrote:

> Mr. Kelley further related that ... there are certain discrepancies in the statements of some of the witnesses, which must, of course, be clarified prior to the appearance of these witnesses before the Grand Jury. He requested that Agents be assigned to interview certain witnesses when they arrive in Washington and endeavor to clear up these discrepancies.[351]

Baumgardner was annoyed at Kelley's use of Bureau agents to get his witnesses stories to mesh. He limited their use, stating, "We do not intend to have these Agents running errands, and they will be instructed to perform only the investigation which appears logical, and if a request is made for any illogical investigation, that the Bureau be advised."[352]

In January 1948, a renewed search began for German witnesses. The CIC's European Command alerted all regions of Occupied Germany to seek out musicians who had participated in Mildred's broadcasts. Despite working daily in the same studio with her, most of the band members did not hear or understand the English content of the messages. The search was largely unfruitful except for information provided by Hermann Rohrbeck, Berlin Radio's orchestral supervisor during the war. Rohrbeck told the CIC that the only people in the studio who understood what she was saying were a Dutch vocalist and a sound engineer.[353] The crooner, Willy DeVries, was to provide damaging testimony at her trial. Several other musicians were located, but they too could not understand the words of the woman in the booth. After months of seeking out her colleagues, the CIC came up with little and called off the search a few months later.

"A stranger in my own country"

The Axis Sally case was sure to dominate the newspapers and radio for months. It was the kind of case that could propel an aggressive, attention-seeking attorney to national prominence. On her second day in the United States, Washington lawyer John M. Holzworth visited Mildred to offer his services. Holzworth presented the jail's superintendent with his card, along with a letter of recommendation on American Civil Liberties Union stationery. The superintendent, Colonel Curtis Reid, kept the FBI informed of all visitors and correspondence to Axis Sally's cell. As a result, a declassified documentary record of the preparations for her defense exists.[354] Holzworth told the quiet, somber prisoner that he represented a "New York organization" willing to pay for her defense. Never disclosing to her the name of the organization, he left the jail and announced to the waiting press that he had been selected to represent Axis Sally at her upcoming trial.

Holzworth was a flamboyant character with a hunger for publicity. A trial lawyer with a reputation as a big-game hunter, he wrote a seminal book on wildlife in 1930 called *The Wild Grizzlies of Alaska*, chronicling his observations of the bears over three summers at Alaska's Glacier Bay. As the Chairman of the National Committee on Protection and Preservation of Wild Life, Holzworth was mentioned in *Time* magazine in 1932 when he chided President Herbert Hoover for taking his grandchildren to visit the bears at the Washington Zoo.[355] A lifelong naturalist in the mold of Teddy Roosevelt, the attorney was the driving force in the bid to make Alaska's Admiralty Island a nature preserve and part of the National Park system.[356] Embarrassingly, he was arrested in 1947 for passing phony checks after he bid $12,500 for the collected oil paintings of the nineteenth-century illustrator Gustave Doré. Holzworth made the newspapers and *Time* magazine again when his dramatic but ill-starred bid beat a genuine bid of over $10,000, but the check bounced.[357]

Back in the spotlight, Holzworth told the press that Axis Sally was "without a cent," and disclosed that he would immediately file for a writ of *habeas corpus*.[358] Holzworth maintained before the Federal District Court that his client became a German citizen by marriage in 1940 and that she no longer owed allegiance to the United States. As a German citizen, Mildred was being illegally held. Holzworth demanded a written justification for her continued imprisonment by September 9, 1948. The attorney also wrote a telegram to Attorney

General Clark claiming that a "very long and costly trial" could be avoided by allowing his client to testify before the grand jury deliberating her fate.

Holzworth also made the curious claim that Army Intelligence had promised Mildred a "clean bill of health" in return for information on Communist espionage activity in the United States. High-ranking German officials had allegedly supplied valuable intelligence to Axis Sally, which she then passed on to CIC. Therefore, her arrest for treason came as a "complete and utter surprise" to his client.[359] These statements would explain Mildred's jaunty claims to her guard that she was not under arrest because the Army had informed her that she was being transported to the US for further interrogation.

Prosecutor Kelley responded that Holzworth was ineligible to request relief because he had not been admitted to practice before the court. Kelley also noted that earlier that same day a "Negro attorney" named Richard W. Tompkins had filed the same request for a writ of *habeas corpus*.[360] When word of the confusion reached the jail, Mildred was incensed. Whether her anger came from the rumors of Holzworth's connections to the ACLU (an organization known for its defense of Communists and African-Americans) or his assertion that she had been married in Germany, she was determined to renounce the lawyer to all and anyone who would hear. Moreover, she was extremely angry about Holzworth's claim that she married a German citizen in 1940. "Why should I lie?" Edna Mae quoted her sister when she appeared before reporters in front of the courthouse, stating that the idea was "cooked up" by the lawyer.[361]

"If Mr. Holzworth should call again, please notify him that I do not care to have any further interviews with him," the angry prisoner told the jail superintendent.[362] Despite the rebuke, Holzworth continued to pursue her. Finally, on August 26, Mildred typed out a letter to the Chief Justice of the District Court requesting assistance in finding competent legal counsel:

> I have been out of the country for more than fifteen (15) years and during this time have virtually lost all contact with family and friends in the United States. This condition, more or less, makes me a stranger in my own country. As you know [*sic*]

doubt have become aware of the conditions surrounding my case through its coverage in the newspapers, this condition is most confusing.

Quite a number of attorneys have contacted me and the officials of the District Jail offering their services in my behalf. I do not know to whom I should turn to for this advice in selecting counsel. It has been recommended that I contact your Honor, the Chief Justice of the District Court for advice in securing counsel.

I would appreciate and be indebted to you if you would kindly furnish me with the names of a few attorneys whom you feel are competent to handle my case involving the various conditions that will arise at my trial.[363]

Her refusal of Holzworth's services damaged any remaining chance that the charges against her might be dropped. As the obstinate prisoner sat in jail without counsel, the prosecutor John Kelley was presenting his case for Mildred Gillars' indictment to the Grand Jury. Time was of the essence. If her defense strategy included the claim that she did not owe allegiance to the United States at the time of her alleged crimes, her written statement to an officer of the court that she was "a stranger in [her] own country" could sabotage that effort and affirm that she was conscious of her obligations to the United States.

As the days passed, her mood worsened. Edna Mae came to visit every day, but they did not discuss her activities in Germany. "I didn't ask any questions. I was not interested. I just wanted to get it over with and get home," she recalled.[364] On August 30, Edna Mae arrived at the District Jail accompanied by attorney Daniel Boone, an associate of Washington attorney James J. Laughlin. Laughlin was one of several court-appointed lawyers in the Sedition Trial of 1944. In that mass trial, vocal opponents of American involvement in World War II on both the Left and the Right had been charged with conspiracy against the United States. Laughlin was assigned to represent one of the thirty men and women named in a mass indictment for conspiracy to demoralize the armed forces and overthrow the United States government.

After a chaotic 102-day trial that ended only after the judge died of a heart attack, the Sedition Trial was the American equivalent of a show trial.[365] Laughlin brought the trial to a standstill when, claiming collusion between the Anti-Defamation League of the B'nai B'rith and the Justice Department, he entered a motion to subpoena all of the ADL's files regarding the sedition cases. Although the judge attempted to ignore Laughlin's request, the attorney commanded headlines when he issued a copy of the motion to the press—placing the focus squarely on the issue of the ADL's role in providing information to the government on which to base the prosecutions.

On paper, Laughlin seemed like the ideal attorney to represent Mildred Gillars: energetic, fearless and brazen in manipulating the media to his client's advantage. While the Sedition Trial proceeded in disarray, only to end with a whimper, the Axis Sally trial was a capital case with an unpopular defendant and a determined prosecutor. The core issues of the case were not the ability of American citizens to voice unpopular viewpoints during wartime, but the responsibilities of a citizen while abroad in the midst of hostilities and the possibility of imprisonment in a concentration camp (and the threat of death that such imprisonment implied). Her case required a sharp legal mind with thorough knowledge of the precedents surrounding the crime of "aid and comfort."

A public defender with a mediocre reputation and a penchant for conspiracy theories was not the best choice for a defendant whose life hung in the balance. Moreover, it would be impossible for any attorney to focus blame on the Anti-Defamation League or any Jewish organization three years after the liberation of Auschwitz, Belsen and Treblinka.

The reunion of the Gillars sisters was marred by the news of their mother's death. It was especially bitter for Mildred to realize that her mother died with the knowledge of her imprisonment as a traitor. Grieving and emotionally drained, she was also troubled by Holzworth's continuing attempts to garner publicity from her case. Holzworth had gone to incredible lengths to get in contact with Edna Mae after Mildred repeatedly refused his visits. When she changed hotels to avoid his pursuit, he reported her missing to the police and sent an alarming telegram to her husband in Ohio stating that she could not be located.

From jail, Mildred angrily dashed off two typewritten letters—one to Holzworth and another to Associate Justice Richmond B. Keech, whom Holzworth had petitioned for the writ of *habeas corpus* only days earlier. She told Keech: "Holzworth has undertaken to appear in your court as my attorney. He is not my lawyer; I have not retained him, and he has so been notified." She further told the judge:

> I am at this time ill and I am desirous of obtaining medical attention. I have been continuously in custody in excess of nineteen months without a hearing, or without any word from my family, or knowledge of my mother's death. To say the least, at present, I am utterly exhausted and in the direst need of a respite.
>
> As I don't know what procedure is necessary, I appeal to your Court to provide, or cause to be provided, proper medical examination and attention, so that I may be able to conduct my defense in a composed state of mind.[366]

Her letter to Holzworth was caustic and accusing; charging that his "unwarranted and unsolicited efforts have inflicted an immeasurable damage to me in prejudicing my rights prior to my defense."[367] Keech requested that the District Jail provide her with a complete medical examination.

On August 31, Justice Keech informed Holzworth that the court no longer recognized him as Mildred's attorney. Within minutes of Keech's order, she was brought before Commissioner Cyril Lawrence who informed her that her hearing would be postponed for two weeks so she could enter the hospital for medical treatment. Lawrence reassured her, "You will not be railroaded. I can assure you, we have in America a system of justice that does not permit anyone to be 'railroaded'."[368] When the Commissioner reread the charges against her, Mildred testily replied, "I told you that I didn't agree with you."[369]

The Grand Jury returned an indictment on ten counts of treason against Axis Sally on Friday, September 10, 1948. After a week of daily visits to her sister's cell and testimony before the Grand Jury, Edna Mae Herrick was ready to go home. As she left for Ohio, she spoke to the press. With tears in her eyes, she spoke on behalf of the imprisoned Axis Sally.

"Mildred firmly denies ever having been anything but an American. I know she is innocent." Quoting her stepsister, she relayed Mildred's position to the assembled reporters, saying: "I never talked politics. I never told those boys to throw down their arms or that their wives or sweethearts were unfaithful.... I never once let them think I was from the Red Cross. I always said I was with Berlin Broadcasting Company'."[370]

Edna Mae took Mildred's denials at face value and explained her motivations for remaining in Germany: "Now I think I understand how she felt. She loved the German people. When hoodlums come in and take over—that's no time to run away."[371] Mildred looked upon the Nazis as "we do Al Capone and his gangsters."[372] Departing Washington, Edna Mae announced to the world: "I am going to stand by her side. I want the world to know that's my stand."[373]

It would be an increasingly difficult stand to take as the trial of Axis Sally drew near.

CHAPTER 10

Destiny

"The Nazi-hired recordings of Axis Sally's broadcasts ... have a not-so-amazing similarity to the opinions spouted by isolationists during the war and before it. If she had made those statements in the U.S. instead of Germany, Sally might have been elected to Congress."
—Walter Winchell, February 7, 1949[374]

JANUARY–MARCH 1949

As Mildred Gillars languished in the District Jail, it must have seemed that the predictions she made five years earlier over a German microphone were coming to pass. The Nazis' post-Normandy propaganda line warned daily of the "Red World" that would inevitably result from an Allied victory. By 1948, half of Germany and practically all Eastern Europe were firmly in the Soviet grip. President Harry S. Truman countered a Communist threat to Greece and Turkey with massive economic aid. Two brutal winters exacerbated the hunger and poverty of Occupied Germany under the Morgenthau Plan. Economic and political turmoil was spreading to the rest of war-ravaged Europe. Not until the proposal of the Marshall Plan in March 1947 did the United States abandon its putative policy against its former enemy and move to rebuild its economy. The geopolitical reality that only Germany could act as a counterweight to Soviet influence in Europe was finally dawning on American policymakers. Those men in the Nazi leadership who believed that Germany's strategic position would

164

ultimately save their skins miscalculated, for it took a crushing Allied victory to launch the chain of events leading to the Cold War.

Galvanized by the new Soviet threat, the US government's efforts to tie up loose ends from the last war were haphazard at best. From September 1945, the Allies actively pursued war criminals and former high-ranking officials responsible for implementing Hitler's policies. The Nuremberg War Crimes Tribunal held surviving members of the party leadership accountable for their crimes against humanity and military aggression. At the same time, the Occupying Powers hoped to address the guilt of mid-level Party functionaries, civil servants, *SS, SA* and *Gestapo*. In the immediate aftermath of the war, almost two million men were forbidden to hold any job above the level of manual laborer—a policy that left West German society without essential technocrats and skilled workers. The creation of *Spruchkammern*, or civilian de-nazification courts, established a mechanism to determine a defendant's political culpability, wartime conduct and fitness to function in the new democracy.

The de-nazification courts were administered by German citizens, many of whom were politically reliable members of Weimar-era parties such as the Social Democratic (SPD) and Catholic Centre (Zentrum) parties. The former Director of the RRG, Hans Fritzsche, was sentenced to nine years at hard labor by one of these courts—despite his acquittal at Nuremberg for war crimes. By 1948, the necessity of rebuilding the defeated nation with knowledgeable and competent officials, industrialists and financiers had taken precedence over the effort to wipe away the stain of Hitlerism.

In time, "de-nazification" became a mere formality. The very week that Axis Sally went on trial in Washington, DC, a German court ordered Hitler's diplomat Franz von Papen to pay a substantial fine. In return, von Papen was granted a clean bill of political health. Even Otto Skorzeny, the legendary commando who, on the Führer's orders, engineered the daring rescue of Mussolini and facilitated the escape of war criminals to Spain and Latin America, was de-nazified *in absentia* in 1952.

In reality, the whitewashing of Nazi pasts began much earlier. As early as September 1945, the American OSS (Office of Strategic Services) was secreting German rocket scientists, weapons experts and intelligence agents out of the former Reich. Given employment and new lives in the United States, the beneficiaries of *Project Paperclip* lived in relative obscurity, safe from Soviet hands. One of *Paperclip's* most illustrious alumni was Dr. Werner von Braun, the rocket scientist who would become the architect of the American space and missile program. Another, Arthur Rudolph, played a central role in the development of the Saturn V rocket that took man to the moon. During the war, Rudolph was responsible for the deaths of thousands of slave laborers at the *Mittelbau-Dora* V-2 rocket plant. Hubertus Strughold was dubbed the "father of US Space Medicine," though he performed medical experiments on prisoners at Dachau.

As American intelligence quietly rehabilitated the political pedigrees of former Nazis and war criminals, a penniless American arrived at the Federal District courthouse in Washington, DC. It was January 24, 1949, and a rush of curious onlookers followed the woman with shoulder-length silver hair as she emerged from a caged prison van. Inside, 105 prospective jurors filled the courtroom. Technicians worked feverishly, stringing the wires of 40 headsets along the expanse of the jury box, judge's bench and attorney's tables. The electronic equipment was to be used to listen to the defendant's wartime handiwork.

Mildred strode into the courtroom and took up her position at the defense table. Her attorney, James Laughlin, greeted her with a long, deep bow. Eight US Marshalls guarded the courtroom's door and windows while a ninth sat only inches behind the accused. Mildred slipped off her black fur-trimmed coat, and quickly turned and smiled at her stepsister, who was sitting in the front row. Her skin, caked with heavy makeup, had an orange tone. *The New Yorker* columnist Richard H. Rovere gave his impression of Axis Sally:

> She has the hair of Mother Machree, and she wears it in the style of Rita Hayworth. At forty-eight, she has the figure of a woman of forty-eight who has worked hard and sacrificed much to keep the figure she had at twenty-four. You wouldn't take her for forty-eight and you wouldn't mistake her for twenty-four. Although she has been in jail for many months,

she has a Miami Beach tan, the cosmetic nature of which is given away by the prison pallor of her hands. Her entire getup—the black dress, the black spiked-heeled shoes, the indigo scarf that she uses for gesturing, the generous applications of lipstick and nail polish—suggests that she is torn by an inner conflict: Although desperately trying to avoid conviction, she is at the same time determined not to destroy the illusion of herself as a woman of mystery, glamour and intrigue.

By all the rules of the game, a woman in Miss Gillars' fix, on trial for her life before a jury that includes five proper-looking members of her own sex, should not be getting herself up like this, but Miss Gillars is following her own course. It is doubtful, however, whether she stands to lose much by this, for the notion of Miss Gillars as a woman of glamour, either sinister or otherwise, is one that—at this stage of the game anyway—only Miss Gillars herself can harbor. The total impression that she makes is not that she is a woman who has spent years in the service of the mighty war machine of the state that was going to endure for a millennium, but that she is a woman who has been fighting an uphill battle to make a living from a dress shop in Queens or a millinery shop in Staten Island.[375]

The strain of the past five years was visible to all. Her fall had been fast and brutal and it showed. Observers marveled at the stark contrast between the aging defendant and the fantasies her voice conjured up among the GIs. One reporter, Andrew Tully, compared her to:

The kind of girl you'd run into in a second-rate tavern on pay night in most any factory town. She is 48 years old, and she looked like any woman of 48 who wants to put it off. Axis Sally's face probably was pretty once, but it obviously had many good times. Somewhere she'd picked up a tan and that helped, but it couldn't hide some sad little wrinkles and that swollen hardness at the cheekbones. And when she tried to put life into her smile, her eyes seemed to protest.[376]

The Curtain Rises

"Now, ladies and gentlemen," Judge Edward M. Curran announced to the court, "this is an important case. This woman is entitled to a fair and impartial jury. Are any of the prospective jurors members of the Jewish race?"[377]

Seven were dismissed.

"Do any of you entertain any prejudice either for or against the policies adopted by Franklin D. Roosevelt or Winston Churchill or any prejudice against Englishmen themselves?"[378]

No one rose. Seven more had already formulated an opinion about the defendant's guilt. Three others were dismissed because they could write, read or speak the German language.[379] Judge Curran then asked if they had ever been a member of any organization that could be described as "German-American." As the judge asked the jury pool to acknowledge any possible bias for or against the woman on trial, he did not reveal his own.

In 1943, Assistant Attorney General Edward Curran had signed the Justice Department's indictment of Max Otto Koischwitz for treason—a name certain to come up in Mildred's case and sufficient reason for his recusal from the case. The jurors did not know that the FBI had thoroughly checked their backgrounds to ensure that they held no politically undesirable views that might favorably affect their opinion of Axis Sally. In his own attempt to weed out biased jurors, James Laughlin asked the judge to include questions that would divine their political and religious attitudes:

> *Did you contribute to bundles of aid to Britain?*
> *Have you ever belonged to B'nai B'rith or any other Jewish organization?*
> *Have you ever written anything about the war crimes trial at Nuremberg?*
> *Do you have any opinion on the Morgenthau Plan for Germany?*
> *Do you have any connection to the new Israeli government?*[380]

Five hours later, a jury of seven men and five women with two alternates of each sex was seated. Although nearly equally divided by gender, no one could say that there was a diversity of political opinion on the panel. A jury pool pre-evaluated by the FBI for unorthodox opinions was one subjected to a political litmus test—not an evaluation of its impartiality.

It was almost four in the afternoon when Mildred stepped back into the prison van to return to her eight-by-ten-foot cell. That evening, her stepsister Edna Mae Herrick dined with the journalist John Bartlow Martin. Martin, on assignment for *McCall's*, was covering the trial for the popular women's magazine. The Justice Department refused his request to interview Axis Sally so he sat down with Edna Mae, who had become a *de facto* spokesman for her sister since her arrival in the United States.

In the restaurant, Martin took copious handwritten notes as she described her sister's formative years—her popularity in school, her close relationship with their mother, and her miserable relationship with her alcoholic stepfather. As she told Martin of her family's troubled history, the restaurant's cashier read aloud from an inaccurate gossip column in a Hearst newspaper.

"It says she did it because she was afraid. She is out on bond. She's walking the streets right now!" the cashier yelled across the room.

"Is that the great American public?" Edna Mae wondered aloud and then fell into a deep silence.

After a few moments, she said, "People used to turn and stare at my sister on the street. I was always so thrilled that she was my sister. She was so wonderful."[381]

Moved by her story, Martin wrote in his notes of Axis Sally's dysfunctional relationship with her stepfather—and Edna Mae's claim that Mildred was "hurt" by him. After hours of conversation with Mrs. Herrick, Martin had no clear answer to the question of how Mildred Gillars became a woman capable of treason, but his conversation with Edna Mae seemed to provide some clues:

> Why did she need success so desperately? We do not know. We return to her childhood, when a loathing for her stepfather may have driven her from home as forcefully as did ambition. But the truth seems to be buried too deep to resurrect: one doubts she herself knows it.[382]

The details of Mildred's youth were there for a reporter to hear, but they would see neither the printed page nor the open air of court. Words that may have painted a fuller, more sympathetic picture of Axis Sally would sit in a journalist's files—unread and unexamined—for almost sixty years.

Sugarcoated Pills

With cool, methodical certainty, Assistant Attorney General John M. Kelley, Jr. laid out the Government's case against Axis Sally. In 1947, Kelley had won the conviction of Boston Mayor James Curley on mail fraud charges, and quickly established a reputation as one of the Justice Department's top young prosecutors. With a flair for mixed metaphor, Kelley compared the defendant's radio work to "sugar-coated pills of propaganda" scattered far and wide to sow "seeds of suspicion and discontent" on the American home front and on the battlefield.[383] Axis Sally denounced "members of the Jewish race, the then-President Roosevelt, Prime Minister Churchill and the British people" for fame and profit.[384]

A failure in show business, Kelley claimed that she coldly sold her birthright to become a well-paid and well-known celebrity. The prosecutor described her meteoric rise in sordid terms. Driven by ambition and greed, she indulged in an affair with a fanatical Nazi—a man with three children and one on the way—to pave her road to the top. She was so successful that, by 1944, Mildred Gillars was the highest paid radio announcer at the broadcasting service.

When Kelley completed his brief opening statement, James Laughlin stood up to address the jury. Laughlin was no stranger to the crumbling green walls of the District Court. In the sweltering spring and summer of 1944, he had been center-stage as a public defender in the great Sedition Trial of that year. In a prosecution personally demanded by President Franklin D. Roosevelt, a motley assemblage of anti-Semites and Nazi sympathizers was put on trial for violation of the Smith Act (which made it a crime to conspire to overthrow the government). A canny lawyer with a talent for publicity, Laughlin revealed to the press that the Anti-Defamation League of the B'nai B'rith provided the FBI with "evidence" against the defendants—supporting his assertion that Jewish interests had instigated the sedition prosecutions in retaliation for the defendants' unpopular views. His public grandstanding resulted in a contempt of court citation. Laughlin made headlines when he defended himself on the contempt charge. Nevertheless, the jury found him guilty.

The chaotic Sedition case ended in mistrial in November of 1944 when Judge Edward Eichler died of a sudden heart attack. The Justice Department refused to pursue the prosecutions further (Roosevelt died in April 1945 and the original impetus for the trial disappeared with the President's death), but the public defender had established a less than sterling reputation among Washington lawyers. Now, Laughlin faced another politically driven case of even greater importance.

In a thunderous voice, Laughlin portrayed Axis Sally as a loyal but misunderstood American trapped in an impossible situation. Like many Americans before the war, he said that Mildred Gillars believed Franklin Roosevelt's promises to keep the nation out of Europe's conflicts. She felt a deep sense of betrayal when the President pursued policies that undercut US neutrality and blatantly tied America's fate to that of Britain. The defense attorney reminded the jury that only a decade earlier her opinion was not at all uncommon: "She said no more and did no more than thousands and perhaps millions in this country said or did," he claimed.[385] Moreover, she was trapped in Hitler's Germany without a valid passport and relied on the good graces of her German hosts. "She had no passport, no money. She had to remain where she was," he emphasized.[386]

At first, Mildred was coaxed by what the attorney called the "magnetic—nay, hypnotic" personality of Dr. Otto Koischwitz. When all of the Professor's charm proved insufficient to convince her to make propaganda broadcasts, she was finally coerced. Laughlin cast O.K. as a calculating Svengali—a Nazi cad who preyed on the hopes and affections of a lonely matron longing for marriage. With his finger pointing at the steel cases containing her broadcasts, Laughlin warned the jury that although the voice might belong to Mildred Gillars, the words and the message were that of Otto Koischwitz.

"The voice is Jacob's voice but the hand is the hand of Esau!" he shouted across the courtroom.[387] "Professor Koischwitz was a dynamic, hypnotic personality. He was a vigorous, determined man with fixed ideas and this defendant was under his influence," the defense lawyer said, pointing at his client.[388] O.K. was a philanderer and ladies' man who promised marriage to his mistress, but suddenly died and left her alone to face Germany's defeat and America's vengeance. At the mention of the Professor's name, Mildred dabbed at her eyes with the flowing indigo scarf she kept wrapped around her neck.

Laughlin insisted that she was only a small cog in the wheel of the Nazi propaganda machine, one that never had "any connection with Hitler, Goebbels, Goering or any others of that unholy lot. She made it plain to the Germans that she would do nothing that was hurtful to the United States government. She was proud to be a citizen of the United States and rejected material for her scripts that she believed harmful." Laughlin asked the jury to reject the government's assertion that Mildred held a highly paid position of great importance, for she lived in "constant fear of her life, under the threat of the Gestapo."

Chief Prosecutor John Kelley's first witness was Adelbert Houben. The 41-year-old former Program Controller at the Overseas Service testified to the financial success of Axis Sally's radio career, claiming that, at her peak, she earned 3,000 Reich marks a month ($1,200 in 1949 dollars)—almost twice the amount of Houben's own salary. Only one man at Reichsradio earned more money than Axis Sally— the Director General of the Overseas Service, Dr. Anton ("Toni") Winkelnkemper.

Houben admitted that he was an enthusiastic National Socialist who joined the party in 1932. He readily told the court that he believed in the party and "everything it stood for," even displaying a reverent tone in his voice when referring to "the Führer." Houben acknowledged that the radio drama *Vision of Invasion* was an attempt "to prevent the invasion by telling the American people and American soldiers that [it] would be a risky task with respect to the lives of the soldiers."[389] Furthermore, Houben made the damaging, yet debatable assertion that no foreigner was ever forced to appear on German radio.

On cross-examination, Laughlin asked the stocky ex-Nazi about his prior experience as a material witness. Noting that he had testified for the prosecution at both the Douglas Chandler and Robert H. Best treason trials in Boston, the confrontational lawyer asked, "You make your living by testifying against people, don't you Mr. Houben?" Offended, Houben sputtered, "What do you mean by that?" Laughlin pointed out that he had collected between $800 and $900 from the US government for his prior appearances. Taking the bait, Houben volunteered that he had earned $2,400 more on his own as a laborer in Philadelphia—an admission sure to fuel further resentment against unapologetic Nazis profiting from the treason prosecutions.[390]

Houben's testimony was momentarily halted while John Kelley read aloud from a list of stipulations agreed to by the defense. The first and most crucial was to inalterably affect the outcome of the trial: both sides agreed that Mildred Gillars was a native-born American citizen and remained so throughout the war. This blanket pronouncement about a woman who privately questioned whether she still held American citizenship effectively removed any possibility of an acquittal under the provisions of the 1940 Nationality Act—a law that allowed the renunciation of American citizenship in favor of the assumption of another nationality. This is what allowed Rita Zucca (the "Rome Axis Sally") to avoid prosecution by the US government.

When Houben's testimony resumed, he told the court of his internment with Mildred in Germany after the war and acknowledged that he felt quite differently about her guilt in those days. Privately, Houben made several statements critical of the government's treatment of her, even calling it "a shame."[391] Houben also admitted that he told Justice Department prosecutors that it was a "mistake" to bring Miss Gillars to trial because she "had done nothing wrong."[392]

Damning Messages

In his opening statement, John Kelley told the jury that it would be Mildred's own words that would convict her. In the corner of the room, a stack of 29 acetates sat near a waiting phonograph. Kelley stated his intention to play only the propaganda portions of the broadcasts, but Laughlin objected. The judge agreed that the entire recording should be played to ensure that the defendant's words remain in context. Only the judge, jury, attorneys and press had access to the forty headphones strung throughout the courtroom. With the mannerisms of a young starlet, Mildred slipped on her pair, resting her chin on folded hands in the style of her idol Theda Bara.[393] Spectators leaned forward to try to hear snippets from reporters' headphones.

Laughlin objected to the introduction of seven recordings as evidence because they were seized by the Counter-Intelligence Corps (CIC) from the basement of Mildred's Berlin apartment house without a search warrant. Judge Curran asked the jury to leave while the court heard testimony from the agent who retrieved the recordings. Special Agent Hans Wintzen came to the stand to describe how he stumbled upon the recordings in a nearby storage room after interviewing the building's superintendent.

Mildred then briefly took the stand and complained to the judge that her apartment and its contents were seized by the Allies and given to a Communist after the German surrender. Curran quickly ruled that although Axis Sally would be tried as an American citizen, the Constitution's protections against warrantless search and seizure did not apply to her. She was a citizen pursued by the American military in a foreign land, and had no such legal protection. After Curran decided that the seven recordings would remain as evidence, the jury returned to the courtroom. Soon, toes were tapping in the jury box as Midge's house band, Dick and His Footwarmers, played Nazified versions of swing and jazz. Between the musical selections, the jury heard the legendary voice for the first time:

> This is Berlin calling, Berlin calling the American wives, mothers and sweethearts. And I'd just like to say, girls, that when Berlin calls, it pays to listen. When Berlin calls, it pays to listen in because there is an American girl sitting at the microphone every Tuesday evening at the same time with a few words of truth to her countrywomen back home.
>
> Girls, you all know, of course, by now that it's a very serious situation and there must be some reason for my being here in Berlin—some reason why I'm not sitting at home with you at the little sewing bees knitting socks for our men over in French North Africa. Yes, girls, there is a reason. I'm not on the side of President Roosevelt, I'm not on the side of Roosevelt and his Jewish friends and his British friends because I've been brought up to be a 100 percent American

girl; conscious of everything American, conscious of her friends, conscious of her enemies.

And the enemies are precisely those people who are fighting against Germany today and in case you don't know it, indirectly against America too, because a defeat for Germany would mean a defeat for America.

Believe me, it would be the very beginning of the end of America and all of her civilization, and that's why, girls, I'm staying over here and having these little heart to heart talks with you once a week.... And that's why I'm just going to put all the energy I can into these few moments I have with you each week and try to get you to see the light of day and to let you realize that you're on the wrong side of the fence....We are shedding our good young blood for this "kike" war, for this British war....

And I say damn Roosevelt, and damn Churchill, and all of their Jews who have made this war possible. And I, as an American girl, will stay over here on this side of the fence, on Germany's side because it's the right side, as I've told you many, many times before ...[394]

Girls, watch out! Become America conscious! Don't forget the beautiful things we have at home which are now in danger of being jeopardized by the Jewish and the British.[395]

With the inference that America's late, beloved president was the leader of a cabal of Jewish homosexuals fresh in the jury's collective mind, prosecutors turned to the July 27, 1944 edition of the *Home Sweet Home* program to illustrate the hidden purpose of the broadcasts:

Well, I'm afraid she'll never surrender 'til you Kids surrender.

Well, how about it?

It is not a bad idea really. After all, you are fighting—it is a tough fight, but there is no getting the Germans down. You have been trying for a long, long time now and you remember what was told to you before you went to Africa; that it would be a walk away for you boys. Well, was it?

They'll just get all kind of woozy and throw down those little old guns and toddle off home. Well, it would be the right thing for them to do after all, because they're certainly not making any headway in the sector right now![396]

By the end of the trial's first week, the court had heard a series of recordings that spanned the length and breadth of Midge's radio career. Friday's proceedings began with the lilting strains of *Lilli Marlene* and ended with the despondent voice of Axis Sally on September 19, 1944 as American forces crossed the Rhine.

So you want to sacrifice your sons to try to destroy that great country, Germany? It is the blackest page in the world's history. America should hang her head in shame. Think it over, America, will you? Well, girls, I'm sorry, but the time has really almost run out.[397]

The Actor as Traitor

"Stop chewing gum!" Judge Curran lashed out at the heavyset Prussian aristocrat in the witness chair. Hans von Richter was nervously chewing a stick of gum as he took the oath. Of all the prosecution witnesses, von Richter and his American-born wife, Georgia, were personally closest to the defendant. The couple knew Midge intimately, had dined with her and Otto Koischwitz at their home, and sadly bade her farewell as Allied troops closed in on the capital. When she was on the run as a haggard and hungry fugitive, Hans von Richter turned her away. Hans and Georgia met in Cleveland, Ohio where he was a dashing German consular officer and she was the daughter of a successful local businessman. When the German Foreign Office transferred him to Brazil, Georgia followed him. The couple lived in Belo Horizonte for two and a half years, and then the Reich called him home to Berlin.

Like all foreign nationals in wartime, Georgia needed ration coupons to survive, and took employment as an announcer for the radio service. On several broadcasts, Mrs. Von Richter joined Midge,

Margaret Joyce ("Lady Haw Haw"), Constance Drexel and others to chat on air about women's concerns and cultural events. Georgia claimed that the content of her radio appearances was never political in nature. Unlike Koischwitz, Hans never demanded that his wife espouse political positions on the air or make propaganda broadcasts to America.

Von Richter spat out the gum and apologized. He testified that he saw Mildred Gillars speak into a Berlin radio microphone "many times." Hans matter-of-factly acknowledged that *Vision of Invasion,* the recording most explicitly aimed at derailing the American war effort, featured her voice. Mildred whispered excitedly into her attorney's ear as von Richter spoke. When Kelley finished his questioning, Laughlin rose to ask the witness if his wife had made broadcasts for the Germans. Von Richter answered in the affirmative and Laughlin delved into their content. Kelley strenuously objected, perhaps fearing the court hearing of other Americans who made similar broadcasts but were not facing the prospect of prison or death. The defense attorney saw his chance to wave the flag of injustice:

"We want to show that his wife's broadcasts were far in excess of anything with which this defendant is charged. There should be equal justice. There should not be persecution of some and exoneration of others."[398]

A torrent of objections rose from the prosecution table. Kelley accused the defense of trying to prejudice the jury. The judge agreed and once again Laughlin was forced to abandon a line of questioning that would have undoubtedly shed light on the motives of the government and the selectivity of its prosecutions. In the midst of the controversy, Hans von Richter defended his wife, stating that she "was a German citizen and under the laws, she was assigned to this task [broadcasting]."[399] Little separated the actions of Mildred Gillars and Georgia von Richter but a marriage certificate, just as a single piece of paper separated the Berlin Axis Sally from Rita Zucca, the Rome Axis Sally. A marriage certificate or a testament of allegiance meant freedom, exoneration and a life uninterrupted. Unfortunately for Midge, Otto Koischwitz was dead. For her, there would be no such escape.

Georgia von Richter spoke to the press and took angry exception to the introduction of her wartime broadcasts into the public record.

Ironically, she also expanded on her role, claiming that her broadcasts were merely "non-political Red Cross" messages from wounded and imprisoned American soldiers. "To compare my broadcasts with those made by Mildred Gillars would be ridiculous. My broadcasts contained no political references or tinges. I interspersed no commentary. I was only concerned with sending the messages of the boys who were prisoners to their parents in the United States," she told the Associated Press in an eerily familiar defense.

Described in the press as a Vassar College graduate from a respectable background, Georgia told reporters that she resisted an offer of extra rations in return for broadcasting propaganda. Notwithstanding her honorable refusal to participate in those programs, the fact remained that her husband was a salaried Foreign Office employee of aristocratic lineage. Unlike the single Mildred Gillars, Georgia did not need the extra rations "to live."[400] Mrs. Von Richter described her radio job as a "nightmare I have been trying to forget for two years," and described Laughlin's effort to drag her into the case as "an effort to discredit the testimony of my husband in Washington." For some, the nightmare was not over.

Hans von Richter left the witness stand, and the judge and jury put on their headphones to listen to *Vision of Invasion*. Penned by Koischwitz, Mildred played an Ohio mother (Evelyn) whose son (Alan) is an American GI destined for the invasion of France. Her husband (Elmer) is blithely accepting of the war but Evelyn, who is something of a psychic, has a disturbing premonition that both her son and the invasion are doomed. Scratchy and at times unintelligible, the recording of *Vision of Invasion* did have moments of clarity that spoke to the core of the government's case.

The radio play began with a portentous voice:

> Why D-Day?
> D stands for Doom and Disaster!
> For Defeat and Death!
> For Dunkirk and Dieppe![401]

The 1942 Dieppe raid claimed the lives of over 6,000 Allied servicemen, and Koischwitz's narrative graphically compared that battle's dead to "roasted geese" and "heads of cabbage on their way to market." The drama opens in Evelyn and Elmer's living room. The radio is playing jaunty swing music when a news announcer breaks in to announce the beginning of the invasion of France. Evelyn is terrified that D-Day will end in disaster for her only son.

> EVELYN: Everyone knows that the invasion is suicide. Even the simplest person knows that. Between 70 and 90 percent of the boys will be killed or crippled for the rest of their lives.
>
> ELMER: What can we do about it?
>
> EVELYN: Bah. We could have done a lot about it. Have we got a government by the people or not? Roosevelt had no right to go to war.[402]

The scene shifts to an American troop ship where her son, Alan, awaits his orders. The young man is despondent and tells a shipmate, "I have a feeling that I shall never see the States again. I was just thinking what mother is doing now."[403] Back in Ohio, the radio continues to play dance music. At her wits' end, Evelyn is unnerved by the blaring orchestra and demands that Elmer shut off the radio. When he refuses, she retires to her bed and dreams of her son:

> EVELYN: I was dreaming, but you are so real, Alan, I'm so happy.
>
> ALAN: It's no dream, mother, our ship is sinking. I only came to say farewell. (*Wailing*) Mother!
>
> EVELYN: Alan! (*Screaming*). The dead bells of Europe's bombed cathedrals are tolling the death knell of America's youth.[404]

Mildred's overwrought hysterics and hackneyed acting won no admirers among the listeners. "Amateur night stuff" and "a monumental bore" were just a sample of the press notices.[405] Her wild sobbing "almost fractured our eardrums," one reporter claimed.[406]

Another wag hoped for Axis Sally's conviction just "to prevent her from going back to radio."[407]

The prosecution then called Ulrich Haupt, the thirty-year-old actor who played the role of Alan in *Vision of Invasion*. Although Haupt confirmed that Mildred had acted in the play, he was not the damning witness the government expected. Haupt's mother was Jewish and the actor had faced the constant threat of deportation to the East. In 1936, he was inducted into the *Wehrmacht* and assigned to the theater. Laughlin asked Haupt what the ramifications would have been had he refused to participate. The witness offered a vivid reminder of the power of the Nazi state:

HAUPT: My mother would have been sent to a concentration camp. My wife and three children would have been sent to concentration camps. I, too, would have been sent to a concentration camp.

LAUGHLIN: And you might have been shot?

HAUPT: That would have been very mild.

LAUGHLIN: But you knew you were participating in Nazi propaganda, didn't you?

HAUPT: Oh, yes sir. Everything you did in Germany whether you were playing in classics or playing a flute, everything was coordinated to fit their purpose.[408]

LAUGHLIN: Do you regard yourself as a Jew?

HAUPT: No, sir.

LAUGHLIN: How were you regarded in Germany?

HAUPT: As not a Jew.

LAUGHLIN: Did you oppose the Nazis?

HAUPT: I certainly did as far as possible.

Haupt's matter-of-fact testimony made it clear that the threat of imprisonment or death was an ever-present reality for an employee of the *Reichsradio*. If Haupt, a German citizen, had reason to fear for the lives of his wife, mother and children, what fate would befall a solitary American woman if she refused to perform *her* duties as instructed?

To limit the damage of Haupt's testimony to his case, John Kelley recalled Adelbert Houben to the stand. Houben was asked to recount the "Schotte incident" of 1943, when Karl Schotte, manager of the USA Zone, was sent to a concentration camp for sloppy censorship. In Houben's version of the incident, Schotte was arrested after failing to edit out a few sentences from a prisoner of war's message to his folks at home. In an atmosphere of increasing paranoia and overlapping oversight by the Foreign Office, the Propaganda Ministry and eventually the SS, the Gestapo feared that the errant script might be a secret code to American forces.

"Isn't it a fact," Laughlin asked Houben, "that Miss Gillars broadcast those messages in the exact form in which they were written and thereby jeopardized her safety?"

When Houben replied in the affirmative, Judge Curran stepped in and asked the witness if it was the manager's job to edit the prisoner messages and pronounce them safe for broadcast—as if the editor or supervisor alone faced the risk of arrest. Once again, Curran assisted the prosecution by blunting the impact of testimony favorable to the defense.[409]

Prisoner Parade

For the next several days, the prosecution focused on Midge's interviews with Allied prisoners of war. Kelley played selections from *Christmas Bells of 1943*, *Easter Bells of 1944* and *Survivors of the Invasion Front*, and then followed the audio with the testimony of the actual former prisoners featured in each broadcast. The first witness was a Canadian officer, Captain Harvey Crossthwaite. In the summer of 1944, he was a wounded prisoner at the Hospital de la Pitié in Paris. Crosthwaite recalled that the defendant arrived at his bedside in a red dress, spoke in the style of a showgirl, and claimed to be recording messages for the International Red Cross.

Prosecutor Kelley then called an American who lost a leg in the Normandy invasion. Gilbert Lee Hansford had been heavily sedated when Midge came to the hospital, but he clearly remembered that she claimed to work for the Red Cross. Another American, John Lynsky, hobbled up to the witness stand on two crutches. Crippled by injuries sustained at the hands of the Germans, Lynsky remembered that she wore "a little Red Cross pin."[410] With the Allies only a few miles from Paris, the witnesses made it clear to the court that it was easier for Midge to find willing interviewees as a Red Cross representative than a Berlin radio personality.

The parade of prisoners continued on for days. Each man told the same basic story, differing only in the small details. Then, a thirty-year-old ex-private with a slight Ukrainian accent took the stand. Michael Evanick, a former infantryman from New York City, stepped up and took the oath. With his wartime diary written in the Ukrainian language admitted into evidence, Evanick told his story about an unusual private meeting with Axis Sally. It was July 15, 1944 in the Chartres prisoner of war camp where Evanick first saw the woman he called the Berlin Babe:

> I saw her in the barracks. There was a German officers' head-quarters there, and that morning a German came there and called my name—called me from the group of prisoners sitting on the outside and took me for interrogation. I was told I was going to be interrogated by somebody else, so when I came in, there were 8 to 10 German officers and soldiers in the room, and they just told me to go into the next room.
>
> When I opened the door, I hear that sweet voice—"Hello Michael." So right away, I would know her, because I have been listening to her, through Africa, Sicily and it was very familiar to me. So she introduced herself to me. "I think you know who I am, I am Sally or whatever otherwise you fellows are calling me"—because we never call her Axis Sally but we have a name "Berlin Babe." So she introduced herself by the name Sally and said, "You are going to know me better by that name."
>
> She told me to sit down, and pulls a chair over at the wall

and I sit down, and there was a German army cot, and she sits there, lifted her leg, and really exposed herself and really, she did not have any undergarments on. She started to talk to me about New York, and places she used to work, and she sung in the Village there. And she said, "By the way, do you care for a drink?" and I say, "Well, I never refuse." So she called in a fellow—she calls him "Professor" and he came in and she sent him for the cognac. He brought the cognac and he opened the bottle and handed it to her, and she made a move for him to walk out.

The bottle was opened and she said, "Sorry we haven't any glasses, but we are going to drink in the American style." And she said, "Well, you're probably going to be afraid to take the first drink from the bottle," and handed the bottle to me. And eventually she said, "It is good stuff. It is 60-year-old cognac."

We talked and she gives me a cigarette, and she started talking to me again about New York and about the places there and said, "How would you like to say hello to your family back home?" And so on, [to] which I said, "I would like it." She opens the door again, called and told the Professor to bring the microphone in…. I said, "I would like to say hello to the people back home," and then she said after I'd finished with that, she said, "Michael, aren't you feeling happy that you are a prisoner of war and don't have to fight anymore?" And I said, "No, ma'am. I do not because I feel one hundred percent better when I am in the front lines, at least I am not hungry and starving for being hungry and I got whatever I needed." So she got mad and just knocked the microphone down which fell toward the cot there.

She started all over talking and asked what did we [the prisoners] do [in the camp]? I said, "I sunbathe." She asked if I would say the same thing and I said yes. She brought the mike and I said, "We are just sitting in the sun, burning ourselves to death, because we are hungry and are watching American planes come over and bomb every five minutes."

So at that time, she threw the microphone down again, which was the last time I spoke into the mike.[411]

On cross-examination, Laughlin asked the witness how he knew
that the woman was wearing no underclothes. Evanick responded,
"Because she was sitting across the room from me, and she just
opened her legs right in front of me and I have to see it. I am not talking about a slip. I am talking about bloomers or whatever you call
it."[412] Laughlin asked if Mildred made any sexual advances toward
him and Evanick said no. The attorney focused on the lurid details of
the soldier's story rather than challenge discrepancies between the
recorded evidence and his testimony.

Evanick claimed that Midge was so angry after he mentioned the
hunger of the American prisoners that she knocked down the microphone stand for a second time and ended the recording session. He
also claimed that he left the angry woman and walked out of the
room. However, the FCC-monitored recording of the program explicitly shows the young GI cheerfully saying, "Goodbye New York!"
in unison with Midge as they ended the interview—a crucial discrep-
ancy that the defense did not exploit. Instead, Laughlin took aim at
the motivation of the witness and Evanick admitted under cross-examination that it was *he* who expressed a keen interest in meeting Axis
Sally. The prisoner told his German interrogators that it was "every
paratrooper's wish was to see her." Two days later, Evanick got his
wish.

The drama continued as a combative, ex-GI named Eugene
McCarthy took the stand. Interned at *Stalag IIB*, McCarthy witnessed
Mildred Gillars and Otto Koischwitz in action as they sought interviews for *Easter Bells of 1944*. McCarthy and his fellow soldiers were
alone with the defendant for more than an hour while O.K. sought
approval for the interviews. The young man testified how a nervous,
chain-smoking Midge attempted small talk with her fellow Americans.
Soon, the small talk disintegrated into a maelstrom of anger and
threats:

> McCARTHY: She [Gillars] asked for an American cigarette,
>   then another.... As we were sitting in the
>   room, a carton of American cigarettes was
>   passed into the room. It was ... passed to her
>   and she was as surprised as we were, won-

dering where the cigarettes came from. She took it and thanked the boys generously until she opened the carton.

KELLEY: What was in it?

McCARTHY: Horse manure.

KELLEY: How did she react?

MCCARTHY: Very surprised and angry.... She said we were the worst bunch of American prisoners she ever ran into ... [that] we treated her terribly for being a woman.... There were quite a few men in the barracks at that time, about 300 men standing on the tables and the bunks outside the "man of confidence's" room. The room was full, and men were going in and out. At the time, the men were very, very angry—as a bunch of GIs will get—and they were saying very vile words.... [She said] "I am leaving!" She turned to the GIs in the barracks; she said, "You will regret this!"[413]

Laughlin tried to mitigate the impact of McCarthy's testimony by accusing the former POW of "bias" against his client. The witness met the accusation with a withering reply:

McCARTHY: If you put 15 months in a prison camp, and you seen your buddies once a month in that camp—one fellow a month shot—and that camp was there 18 months. In 18 months there were 18 men shot, and I saw the way we were treated in there and made to live, and all is just not right, and you see an American person come in and say she is an American working for them; do you think I love that person to sell out her country, no sir?

LAUGHLIN: Now, Mr. Witness, you do not know the cir-
                cumstances under which she was doing that.

MCCARTHY: Well, sir—now, why in that two and a half
                hours, or hour and a half, when the German
                officers and Otto Koischwitz went out, and
                she was in the room by herself, why didn't
                she make a statement to us at that time as to
                what she was being held to?

Laughlin changed the subject and took aim at one of the core
tenets of the prosecution's case. Did Axis Sally's activities adversely
affect the fighting man's morale?

LAUGHLIN: Did she undermine your morale?

McCARTHY: Undermine it. Absolutely.

LAUGHLIN: She did.

McCARTHY: Absolutely.

LAUGHLIN: She caused you to desert.

McCARTHY: To desert? I don't know what you mean.

LAUGHLIN: How did she undermine—

McCARTHY: (Interposing) She lowered herself—

LAUGHLIN   How did she undermine your morale?

McCARTHY: By just seeing her working for them, my
                morale was upset, by this woman working
                for the Germans.

LAUGHLIN: Wasn't your morale at a very low ebb when
                you were in a prison camp anyway?

McCARTHY: No sir. When you see when they take one boy
                and shoot a man, we got clannish and the
                Americans stuck together. We didn't care what
                would happen. Every time another boy was
                shot—we would fight them all the harder.[414]

LAUGHLIN:	Mr. Witness, when did you first know the name of the defendant?
McCARTHY:	When the first FBI agent told me what her actual name was.
LAUGHLIN:	That was 1946?
McCARTHY:	That is right.
LAUGHLIN:	You didn't know it before that?
McCARTHY:	No, I knew her by the [name] Berlin Bitch or Axis Sally.
LAUGHLIN:	Berlin what?
McCARTHY:	Berlin Bitch.

The Court of Public Opinion

Three weeks of testimony had passed and public interest in the trial began to wane. Some commentators expressed doubts about the wisdom of bringing the aging, down-on-her-luck actress to trial at all. *New York Daily News* columnist Ruth Montgomery expressed a common opinion: "A good number are beginning to wonder whether dramatizing the stage-struck propagandist by assigning her the leading role in real life is the best way to render justice." Montgomery suggested stripping Mildred of her citizenship and leaving it at that:

Would it not have been greater punishment, then, to have revoked the American citizenship of Axis Sally and consigned her forever to live—scorned and friendless—in the country to which she sold out? Like Philip Nolan in Edward Everett Hale's "The Man without a Country," Axis Sally might have been eternally forbidden to return to her native land; never again could she have visited her relatives, friends and former neighbors in Maine or Conneaut, Ohio.[415]

Estimating that the Justice Department had already spent one million dollars to bring Axis Sally to trial, Montgomery pointed to the many government witnesses flown in from Germany, some of them formerly enthusiastic Nazis. The US government provided them regular stipends and allowed them to stay and work in the United States as the trials progressed. "None [of the German witnesses] have shown any interest in leaving the land of plenty when the treason trials adjourn. Our government is permitting them to live wherever they choose and take well-paid American jobs. It's a lucky break for the Nazis," she concluded.[416]

Desperate to avoid returning to the privations of occupied Germany, the former colleagues of Chandler, Best and Gillars were more than willing to buttress the government's case. The hypocrisy was not lost on some observers. "Nuremberg had a low opinion of Nazi officials, but it turns out they are expert, reliable and lovable while working for the prosecution."[417]

Even Walter Winchell, whose consistent call for Axis Sally's head made him a virtual press agent for the trial, seemed to sense the changing tenor of public opinion. In one column, Winchell wrote that a member of Mildred's legal team had phoned reporters during the first week of February. The unnamed lawyer told the press that the syndicated columnist had offered to pay Axis Sally's legal expenses out of guilt and remorse. Realizing that the public's thirst for vengeance was not nearly as keen as his own, Winchell was loathe to call off the dogs, instead just chalking it up to basic American decency:

> This repulsive woman is more than a show-off and she should be punished, although we doubt that any U.S. soldier (who was agonized by her voice) wants to see her hanged. It is part of the dignity of this nation that Americans do not want to see a woman hanged. Perhaps it would be punishment enough if she were the first woman without a country. Let her live up to her Nazi broadcasts. Let her live in America but never again be privileged to salute it or call it her own.

Still, there were those who wanted blood. Syndicated columnist Robert Ruark had no reservations about meting out the ultimate punishment to Axis Sally:

The British strung up Haw Haw for a sin no greater than the one that Miss Gillars is charged. If it can be shown that the well-constructed Miss Gillars is guilty, in the Haw Haw manner, she rates a noose or a hot seat or a gas pill or whatever the maximum penalty for broad treason the court is empowered to decree.

Hometown newspapers throughout the country interviewed local veterans to ask what should be done with Miss Gillars. Although embittered by Axis Sally's wartime activities, some vets were reluctant to support a death sentence. "I'd hate to see her get death but if that is what our constitution calls for in case of such a crime—then we will have to abide by the constitution," remarked Louis Doerr, a onetime commander of Am Vets in Mansfield, Ohio. Doerr, formerly assigned to the Army's Psychological Warfare Division, put the charges against Mildred Gillars into perspective, recalling, "At that time, there were a number of women broadcasting over German radio, but Axis Sally was considered by our outfit as being the best propagandist."

Only one announcer used the name Sally regularly—the star of *Jerry's Front*—the former New Yorker Rita Zucca. Other veterans had more detailed memories of Sally's broadcasts. A former seaman who listened at his base in Scotland remarked, "We picked up Axis Sally practically every night. On several occasions she specifically mentioned us in her broadcasts when she urged the Americans at our base to desert and come over to the Nazis."

None of the recordings played at the trial featured her identifying or addressing specific military units. A former Ohio infantryman, Dale Beer, stated that he first heard Axis Sally in France in July 1944 (when Mildred and Koischwitz were in France interviewing hospitalized soldiers and producing their programs in Hilversum, Holland). Beer stated: "During the broadcast she [Sally] mentioned the names of several divisions in our territory, and we were surprised when she didn't name the Ninth Infantry, our outfit."[*]

[*]In fact, a search of the content of recordings and transcripts of Mildred Gillars' broadcasts at the National Archives and the Library of Congress reveals no specific references to military units, naval bases, etc.

* * *

"Mere words do not constitute the crime of treason," James Laughlin posited in his request for a summary acquittal. "Things have come to a pretty pass if a person cannot make an anti-Semitic speech without being charged with treason. Being against President Roosevelt could not be treason. There are the two schools of thought about President Roosevelt—one holds that he was a patriot and a martyr. The other holds that he was the greatest rogue in all history, the greatest fraud and the greatest imposter that ever lived."[418]

Judge Curran denied the request and ruled that the trial proceed. Laughlin asked the government to fly in a number of defense witnesses from Germany, but the judge agreed to only four. Emil Beckman, Franz Schaefer, Maria (Ria) Kloss (who discovered Mildred after her suicide attempt in Berlin) and Erwin Christiani, the radio technician who helped her decide in 1940 whether to return to the United States or remain in Germany. Kloss and Christiani had not yet arrived in the US, so Laughlin impetuously moved the trial forward by calling unused former prisoners on the prosecution's list.

The first of these men was a Northwestern University student named Gunnar Dragsholt. Laughlin asked Dragsholt if at any time Mildred identified herself as a representative of the International Red Cross. He responded that she had not. Satisfied, Laughlin dismissed him, but the 30-year-old veteran did not leave the stand. He had been one of the scores of outraged men who met Axis Sally at *Stalag IIB* during the "horse manure" incident.

Instead of stepping down, the young man pointed at the defendant, shouting over Laughlin's objections, "She threatened us as she left—that American citizen. That woman right there! She threatened us!"[419]

Laughlin angrily tried to stop the out-of-control witness but Kelley rose and asked him to tell his story:

> She told us that she was an American citizen. She said she was doing the thing she was doing out of loyalty and patriotism. She also said she was being paid by the German government. I asked her if it was not strange that if she was an American she could go floating around Germany, while the rest of us

Americans were locked up behind barbed wire. She said she
had high ideals. We called her a traitor and shouted names at
her when she left the camp. She shouted vile names right back
at us.[420]

On Monday, February 21, the defense called the radio scriptwriter
Emil Beckman. Beckman testified that the Gestapo and the SS constantly watched the entire staff of *Reichsradio* and that his superior,
Horst Cleinow, personally threatened him with deportation to a concentration camp. Warned that a mistranslation or any "attempt at
appeasement" was a crime, Cleinow told him, "One false utterance
and you will be put away."[421]

Judge Curran erased the impact of Beckman's testimony by
instructing the jury to disregard it, as Beckman was the person threatened, not Mildred. Although Ulrich Haupt, Adelbert Houben and
other witnesses also testified to the dangers of such "sabotage," Judge
Curran insisted that the jury consider Mildred immune from this men-
acing atmosphere.

The Final Witness

Almost four weeks had passed before the jury heard from the accused.
With few witnesses available to the defense, and the undeniable weight
of the evidence stacked against her, Mildred's only hope was to take
the stand in her own defense. Determined to tell her side of the story,
Axis Sally strode up to the witness box and sat down, forgetting to
take the oath. Laughlin gently asked her to stand and swear to tell the
truth. On that cold February 16, 1949 she abandoned her silence and
her customary black dress. She arrived wearing a smart green sweater,
tan jacket and a black skirt.[422] Her attorney asked her to describe her
rootless childhood. She explained that she never knew her father,
whom she referred to as "Mr. Sisk." Glossing over her bitter, unhappy life with her alcoholic stepfather, Mildred focused instead on her
days of fulfillment on the college stage and years of discouragement
and want in Cleveland and New York.

With only the slightest of detail, Mildred told how she followed
young Bernard Metz to Algiers. When that fleeting romance failed, she

left North Africa with no prospects. When her mother left Europe to return to America, she found herself alone and broke in the newly born Third Reich. America could offer no respite, as the nation remained in the deepest phase of the Great Depression. A constant theme in her testimony was her relentless search for stable employment and financial security—a search that finally culminated in a career on the radio waves.

After several hours of testimony, her story turned to the summer of 1940. Germany was the master of Europe. Dunkirk cast British and Free French forces back to England. All of France was either under Occupation or under Petain's rule. After a long drought, Mildred finally found gainful employment at *Reichsradio* and needed her passport renewed by the American State Department. Jews, intellectuals, leftists and other enemies of the Nazi regime sought refuge in North America. When a vice consul named Vaughn found out about Mildred's collaboration with the hated Nazis, he grabbed her passport and threw it into a drawer. She told the jury that her only option was to return to work. When asked why she thought the consul was so angry, she pled ignorance, stating that she was "confused" by the diplomat's actions.

Mildred explained that she was fortunate to find work in Berlin as a war economy and rationing took hold. She had built a life in Berlin full of friends, especially a physicist named Paul Karlson. After six years of struggle in Germany, there was nothing left for her in the United States but poverty. Although ships left regularly to ferry US citizens home as America moved closer to war, she did not board one. Pearl Harbor would prove to be the point of no return.

With great emotion, Mildred described the shock of December 7, 1941, and how she vehemently expressed her contempt for the Japanese surprise attack to her German colleagues. The Axis alliance virtually guaranteed that Germany would honor its commitments and go to war with America. With the realization that the attack made her an enemy of the German state, she lashed out, "I went to pieces in the studio. I told them what I thought of Japan and what the Germans would find out about them. I expressed myself in a very violent way. The shock was so terrific and I lost all discretion, and then I went home."[423]

What happened after that became one of the main areas of contention between the prosecution and the defense. Mildred got a call that evening from her friend Erwin Christiani, a radio engineer, who advised her not to come in the following day. Only an oath of allegiance to Germany, she claimed, would enable her to continue working and avoid arrest. She then went to her friend Paul and asked him to type up an oath in German. She neither kept a copy of the note nor recalled the exact wording, but she insisted that it happened and that Christiani could back up her story. After a few days off, Mildred testified that she returned to her duties with her written oath in hand. Laughlin asked her to tell the jury why she signed the note.

GILLARS: It is obvious that one has to live somehow, and
             after all …

LAUGHLIN: Did you sign it to save your life?

GILLARS: Well, I signed it in order to live and up to that
             time, I had never done anything in the least bit
             propagandistic.[424]

Her equivocation that she signed the oath in order "to live" rather than to save her life undercut the direction of Laughlin's argument. It was only the first of several missteps by the defendant in which she stubbornly stuck to her own version of events—whether or not they condemned her in the eyes of the law. Laughlin tried to portray the headstrong woman on the stand as a victim at the mercy of a totalitarian regime. At critical junctures, her words and manner belied that image. Her defense repeatedly seemed to be that it was not treason in her own mind or her German compatriots'—thus it was not treason. In Mildred's own mind, she swore allegiance to the Reich to eat another day, to keep a roof above her head—and above all, to evade a concentration camp.

In the first few days of her testimony, Mildred's dramatic tales of life in wartime Berlin garnered more headlines than her line of defense. In a tone reminiscent of a spy film, she told the court of her arrest by the Gestapo in the autumn of 1942. She had lost her food ration coupons while shopping at a Berlin department store. A Gestapo agent overheard her American accent as she spoke on a public telephone. He cried, "You can tell by her accent that she is American" as he forced the door of the phone booth open. With no *Fremdenpass* (identification papers for foreigners) and no US passport, she carried only her Reichsradio identification card.

Panicked, she told the agent that she was late for work, exclaiming, "If I don't get to the station, that'll be sabotage"— an offence that would inevitably land her in a concentration camp. After her manager Johannes Schmidt-Hansen intervened, the Gestapo agent apologized for the misunderstanding and she returned to the studio. The story provided a terrifying illustration of her fragile existence in Germany and her dependence on the good graces of her Nazi masters.

Her assertion that German officials tried to recruit her to provide information on the Wright Airplane Works in Dayton, Ohio and promised her "any kind of passport" in return for espionage and sabotage work stunned the assembled press. Despite Mildred's self-serving monologues, her tale of a second run-in with the Gestapo was gripping.

She described a "charming" agent named Denner who pointed out to the expatriate that she did not have a US passport, and remarked that the German government was "rather generous" by letting an enemy national "run around" Berlin without papers. He offered her a passport in return for espionage work. The revelation made headlines, even in *The New York Times*, as did her flag-waving response: "I want you to know that even though I am working for the German Broadcasting Company I would never, under any circumstances whatsoever, not even if it were to mean my death, do anything against my country."[425]

Assuming the mantle of a female Nathan Hale, she turned down the offer. The story emphasized the compartmentalization in her own mind between entertaining and "idealistic" radio work and overt acts destructive to the United States and its armed forces. In her mind, she performed radio work "to live" and "to survive"—to remain employed and avoid deportation.

The following day (February 24), Laughlin turned his attention to the man most responsible for the creation of Axis Sally—the charismatic Otto Koischwitz. The silver-haired Laughlin asked his visibly distressed client to describe the beginning of her affair with the married father of three. Again, he faced resistance in his attempt to portray her as the lovesick victim of a scheming Lothario.

"When did you first keep company with Professor Koischwitz?" he asked.

"Well, to keep company seems like a strange expression," she said, followed by a long silence. Finally she took a deep breath. "He just grew into my life. It's not always so easy to draw a line of demarcation between admiration, compatibility and love, especially under the circumstances as they were at that time."

Laughlin pressed for a more revealing answer. "When did you first speak words of love?"

Mildred stiffened and protested, "Mr. Laughlin, I wonder if it is necessary to go into all of this. You see, there is such a thing as a person waiting all his life to find another."

When Kelley objected to her non-responsiveness, she snapped back at the prosecutor, "Words of love were not spoken, Mr. Kelley. They were written from Silesia in the spring of '43."

Clearly in love with the dead professor's memory, she waxed poetically about Koischwitz's innate love for the idyllic Silesian countryside and his yearly visits to a mountain he called his "Mount Olympus." Like his Führer's habit of retreating to the "Eagle's Nest," the professor went to his mountain hideaway to commune with nature and contemplate life's mysteries.

Prosecutor Kelley strenuously objected to this hagiography of a dead traitor, and Judge Curran asked Mildred to keep it short. She explained that Koischwitz wrote two letters to her from Silesia that confessed his confusion about their emotional attachment. "He realized in the spring of '43 what was happening and he reverted back to his boyhood habit of going to his Mount Olympus—he got the answer that God favored his love."[426]

Laughlin valiantly fought on against Mildred's frustrating evasiveness. Her refusals clearly annoyed the lawyer when he had to demand an answer from his own client:

LAUGHLIN: Now Miss Gillars, were you in love with Professor Koischwitz?

GILLARS: Mr. Laughlin, it is very difficult to discuss personal things on the witness stand, just as it is difficult to discuss religion or anything else that is sacred to you.

LAUGHLIN: Well, would you care to answer the question?

GILLARS: Of course, I loved him.

LAUGHLIN: And did Professor Koischwitz exert an influence on your life?

GILLARS: I consider Professor Koischwitz to have been my destiny.

LAUGHLIN: Would you care to tell us, Miss Gillars, just what you mean by that?

GILLARS: Well, I believe that people are the result of other human beings who have been in their lives, and I believe that without the presence of Professor Koischwitz in my life I would not be fighting for my life today, and I also believe if you have been happy, then you must be prepared at any time to accept a lifetime of misery. It has to be worth that much to you.[427]

Even after Germany declared war on the United States, Mildred insisted that she remained a simple announcer. Not until Koischwitz witnessed the extent of her talents and realized that he could put her popularity to use did she encounter pressure to perform propaganda. She broadcast chiefly for *Sender Bremen* to Europe and the United Kingdom until the professor took over the USA Zone from the imprisoned Schotte. She "pleaded and begged of Koischwitz to do nothing about [a transfer]." "Please let me stay at the Sender Bremen station," she asked, but Koischwitz would hear none of it.[428]

Finally she relented: "I suppose it is very difficult for a person who has never been in that position [in a dictatorial state] to be able to appreciate my position. You could not just go around saying, 'I don't want to do this' and 'I don't want to do that.'"[429]

When she protested to Koischwitz, he slyly appealed to her artistic sensibilities. "Even Shakespeare and Sophocles could be taken as propaganda," he told his wary accomplice.[430]

A difficult day on the stand ended with a crippling admission. As Mildred effusively extolled the professor's life and work, she drew a direct connection between Koischwitz and Hitler's Foreign Minister. Exaggerating her lover's role, she told the jury that her beloved served as a liaison for Joachim von Ribbentrop.

"He was the go-between for von Ribbentrop and the broadcasting to the American zone. I knew he was in contact with Ribbentrop because he once left me in France to drive to Adolf Hitler's headquarters and meet Ribbentrop."[431]

No one could have been more surprised by her statement than her own attorney who, less than a month before, told the jury that his client never had any association with the "unholy lot" that led the world to slaughter. Instead, she revealed that she intimately loved a man who was welcomed to the Führer's lair.

On the final day of her testimony, John Kelley grabbed his stack of transcripts and read excerpts from Axis Sally's broadcasts. With his voice full of contempt, he read the words "She'll never surrender until you boys surrender.... How 'bout it?" The prosecutor asked, "Did you think that was going to entertain your countrymen in the foxholes?"

Mildred grew combative. "I knew that they were not taking that seriously. I had many written reports on it, and Professor Koischwitz knew it too."

Undeterred, Kelley read from the transcript where Midge wondered if the GIs wives and girlfriends were not "sort of running around with one of the 4-Fs back home." Kelley spat out, "Did you think *that* was going to entertain them?"

GILLARS: I had proof that it did.... I was just clowning.

KELLEY: Were you clowning in your Medical Reports when you gave on the radio a mother's name and told her that her son had died? Then continued to tell her about his sufferings just prior to his death? Were you clowning then?

GILLARS: You know I wasn't.

KELLEY: I don't know. You tell me. Were you clowning
          then?

GILLARS: I was not.

KELLEY: Did you ever want the United States to lose the
          war?

GILLARS: No.

She denied ever posing as a Red Cross worker to deceive wound-ed men to obtain interviews. She insisted that if any of her group had said he or she represented the Red Cross, there would have been no recording, "concentration camp or no concentration camp."[432] Too many men had testified to the contrary. In the days following the June 1944 invasion of France, Allied forces moved so rapidly that many hoped and some believed that the war would be over by Christmas. German armies were in rapid retreat and it only made sense that Axis Sally would have trouble finding willing participants. In the face of so much prisoner testimony, Mildred's heated denials devastated the credibility of her entire testimony.

She denied that she exposed herself to Michael Evanick and she denied that she ever threatened the men of *Stalag IIB* with retaliation for the horse manure incident. In order to believe the defendant, the jury would have to believe that every former prisoner who took the stand against her had lied. John Bartlow Martin wrote in his private notes as he observed her days on the stand that "her aplomb is keen-er at the start of the day.... It wears down to where she almost stops lying at the end of hard days on the stand."[433]

Her power of self-delusion was evident, no more so than when she described her visits to the prisoner-of-war camps. None of the cruelty and hardship experienced by the prisoners appeared in her recollec-tions. She called one "very picturesque, their washing on the line, so very Bohemian"—a world where the inmates peacefully strummed on guitars and mandolins, asked for her autograph and excitedly lined up to be interviewed.[434]

The more she spoke the more divorced from reality she seemed. In one instance, she thanked the Irish "who have suffered for over 900 years" for giving her the strength to face her persecutors. In another, she told the court that *Sender Bremen* owed her hundreds of Reich Marks, and the USA Zone owed her thousands, though the broadcasting company and the regime that created it was ground to dust. Her capacity for self-deception had its limits. When the jury listened to a particularly damaging broadcast where she referred to American pilots as "murderers," Axis Sally fell to the floor unconscious. The judge quickly called a recess and an ambulance rushed her to the jail infirmary. Edna Mae attributed it to a pork chop her sister had eaten for lunch but the attending press drew a direct connection between her illness and the words on the recording.

When Mildred returned to the stand the following day, the shaky witness testified that she became increasingly uncomfortable with her role at the radio station. As the Allies pushed through North Africa and Italy in 1943, she decided to do something for the American boys in captivity. "I begged to be allowed to enter the prisoner of war camps because I wanted to see how the American boys were getting along," she insisted. "The only thing that could bring me a little happiness in the chaos of war was the feeling that I could be of some service to the people of my own country. I told Professor Koischwitz that my only reason for being was to go the prisoner-of-war camps. He knew I was not a propagandist."[135]

The Other Sally

Laughlin introduced the existence of the Rome Axis Sally to the court, and Mildred explained the reasons for her fury at discovering the existence of the other broadcaster. The woman used the name Sally repeatedly in propaganda broadcasts directly aimed at advancing American troops in the field, and designed to confuse and break their will. She told the court that she was enraged that another woman would usurp her notoriety, but the nameless woman's ability to violate the fine line she had established in her own mind between entertainment and treachery was intolerable.

She expressed her belief that there were lines that she simply would not cross, and it was particularly frightening to be in a position where she could not control the statements or actions of the woman in Rome. Mildred told of how she burst into the office of Adelbert Houben to demand that the woman stop using the name Sally.

> I told them: either that girl in Rome would stop calling herself Axis Sally or I would leave the microphone because I was not giving out military information or trying to muddle up GIs by telling them where their position would be tomorrow. My only interest at all times was to try to stay in touch with America, and to do something for them the only way I could in my difficult position.[436]

Laughlin sought to expose the name and story of the "Rome Axis Sally," even bringing up the name Rita Zucca in open court, but Judge Curran stepped in again to limit the scope of his questions. Again, Laughlin's attempt to expose the arbitrary nature of the government's treason prosecutions went nowhere. The court forbade him to address the issue of those American citizens (Zucca, Georgia von Richter, Constance Drexel, Jane Anderson, *et al.*) who broadcast for the Nazis but did not face trial in an American court.

In three and a half days of testimony, John Kelley rattled Mildred into several critical and damaging admissions. She acknowledged that the State Department asked all Americans on non-official business to leave Germany after the invasion of Belgium and Holland. She pleaded untruthfully for a thirty-day extension on her passport in order to raise funds for her passage to the United States. She also acknowledged that she had made no effort to ask the US Embassy for passage home after the Gestapo threatened her, just as she had made no effort to run into the arms of American forces liberating Paris in 1944. Asked why, she simply responded, "I didn't want to be separated from Professor Koischwitz by any troops, because I wanted to be with Professor Koischwitz."

> KELLEY: That meant more to you than anything in the world, did it?
>
> GILLARS: I believe that a man generally means more to a

woman than anything else. I would have died for him. Yes.

Legally, the most devastating discovery of the Government's case occurred when John Kelley introduced into evidence an expired passport found in the possession of Mildred's block leader in Berlin. Although Mildred testified that she had no passport or papers identifying her as an American citizen after the vice consul "snatched" it, the revelation of the passport's existence tore what was left of the defense's case apart. At the end, her tired attempts to limit her answers to saccharine, flag-waving recitals of love for America met with solemn derision by prosecutor Kelley:

> GILLARS: Mr. Kelley, why else do you think I risked my life to go to France to get those messages to send back to America?

> KELLEY: Why do you think the Germans were paying you to get those soldiers to go on the air with you?[437]

Exhausted and weeping, Axis Sally asked the judge for a recess. When the trial resumed, the intensity of the questioning did not let up. With eyes full of tears, she met the questioning with defiance. When the questions concerned the eldest daughter of Professor Koischwitz, the prosecutor hit the rawest of nerves. Stella Koischwitz was a teenager when Berlin fell to the Red Army, and Kelley claimed that the young girl cast her father's mistress out of her apartment.

Mildred replied, "Stella was not there. Professor Koischwitz's mother was there and she was frantic because Stella had disappeared. The streets of Berlin were strewn with naked corpses and dead horses—"

"Forget about the naked corpses," Kelley interrupted, "and answer my question."

Mildred straightened in her seat. "It was my own decision to leave."

"When did you last see Stella?" Kelley shot back.

Again, she became evasive "If you have the testimony of Stella, I'd prefer that you and her—"

Furious, Kelley shouted at the defendant. "Will you please answer my question?"

White as a sheet, she asked the Judge, "And what happens if I refuse?"

After the lawyers approached the bench, the prosecutor withdrew the question, moving on to even more sensitive subjects—the most embarrassing aspect of her love for her "man of destiny."

KELLEY: Isn't it a fact that when you and Professor Koischwitz declared your love for each other his wife was pregnant and bearing their fourth child?

GILLARS: I found out about it the day before the child was born.

KELLEY: You knew that he was married?

GILLARS: Are these *ad hominem* tactics going to be pursued? Is that the only kind of attack you have, Mr. Kelley?[438]

Her evasions ran so deep that she even attempted to deny that it was her voice on the recordings. Kelley read aloud from the transcript of the May 1943 *Home Sweet Home* program that made such an impression at the start of the trial. "I love America but I do not love Roosevelt and all his kike boyfriends who have thrown us into this awful turmoil."

"Did you say it?" Kelley pressed her again.

Flustered, she wavered, and once more, Judge Curran stepped in. "You heard the Government Exhibit #1 when it was played back? Is that your voice or not?"

Unbelievably, Mildred attempted to claim that she could not be sure. "But Your Honor, you can't always know. I have had so much experience with broadcasting, and the voice of a girl whom I know very, very well, I have listened to her voice five times now, and I swear to you that I do not recognize her voice. If I hadn't known that she had been in the studio ..."

Even John Kelley seemed taken aback by this stunning denial of reality. "Just a minute, Miss Gillars. My question to you is: is that your voice that was played back to you?"

"Well, it seemed to be my voice," she reluctantly admitted.[439]

What logic there was to her defense had been pummeled away by Kelley's deft cross-examination. Despite the obvious worldview behind her radio statements, she insisted that she never adhered to Nazi ideology and could not answer whether she had ever opposed Nazism or any of its measures, stating, "I don't know how to answer that question, because to act in opposition would have meant death."[440]

Then Kelley turned to the question of anti-Semitism. Reading from transcripts of her most virulent broadcasts, Mildred took the mantle of avid anti-Communist at the dawn of the Red Scare. "I have made many statements about Communism and fighting on the German side against Communism, and that is what I meant at all times."

Kelley did not retreat an inch. "You didn't use the word 'Communism' very much, did you?"

"I used the word 'Bolshevism' more than Communism," she shot back.

The prosecutor's eyes met hers. "Your specialty was the word 'Jew,' wasn't it?"

Quietly Mildred admitted, "I used it quite often."[441]

He challenged her assertion that she temporarily quit her job in January 1945 because of the presence of the convicted traitor, Lt. Martin James Monti.

"Just why wouldn't you have been glad to assist or help a spy—an American spy—in working for his country in Germany?"

She searched within herself for an answer.

"I don't like unclean people."[442]

When Mildred's testimony came to a close, John Kelley called Johannes Schmidt-Hansen as a rebuttal witness. Flown to the United States at government expense, Schmidt-Hansen was allegedly the man at Reichsradio who had demanded an oath of allegiance from Mildred in 1941. Laughlin requested that the former radio manager be brought in as a defense witness, but a lengthy interrogation by the FBI on his arrival from Germany changed that. Schmidt-Hansen took the stand and testified that he had no memory of requesting a written loyalty oath from his unruly American employee.

"Do you have any recollection of ever asking Miss Gillars to supply you with a statement or oath of allegiance to Germany?" the prosecutor asked.

Nervous and stammering, Schmidt-Hansen replied, "I do not recollect having asked—"

Kelley interrupted the witness and demanded a straight yes or no answer.

"No," the thin, shaking German replied.

Laughlin sensed that the witness had been intimidated. Under cross-examination, Schmidt-Hansen's certainty withered as he admitted that the incident might have indeed happened. It had been ten years since the event, he explained, and "it is impossible for any human to recall exactly such details. I do not deny that it might have been a matter of routine...a form letter for security reasons."[443] Schmidt-Hansen also claimed that he could not remember if he discussed the oath with Mildred's colleague, Erwin Christiani.

The defense recalled Erwin Christiani to the stand to rebut Schmidt-Hansen's testimony. A few days earlier, he had told the court of Mildred's fateful decision to remain in Germany: "She told me there was nothing to expect for her in America but she loves America and wanted to go home. But on the other hand, she loved her work in Germany and wanted to continue because so many people thought she was so good."

Christiani told her it was "impossible for German forces to enter the US, and Mr. Roosevelt had said that American soldiers would not fight in Europe, so I was sure there would be no war. I told her I thought she would have a better future in Germany."[444]

Her loyal friend confirmed without question that Schmidt-Hansen had demanded the oath and was certain that he had spoken to the manager about it in December 1941.

Laughlin asked the radio engineer one final question: "Could she have stopped broadcasting for German Radio if she wanted to?"

Solemnly, Christiani shook his head. "No, she couldn't."[445]

Several months after the end of the war, a German journalist and former RRG staff member named Hans König told American authorities that the imprisonment of Overseas Service employees for political crimes was not uncommon. "I have reason to believe that there was a high rate of convictions for political offenses with concentration camp sentences, as well as membership of resistance groups, among the foreign broadcasting staff. The wider horizons of the mainly non-Party staff members, subject as they were to draconian thought control and eavesdropping, bred a spirit of opposition among people of their intellectual training, especially when their professions and their life abroad had largely inclined them to liberal attitudes."[446] US officials knew that the danger of arrest and deportation was a real one faced by all Overseas Service employees—German and non-German alike. No witnesses were made available to testify to the fate of those unfortunate Reichsradio employees. When testimony about the danger of refusing to broadcast was given by the defendant's friends and colleagues, Judge Curran instructed the jury to disregard it.

James Laughlin made a valiant effort. In the face of Mildred's frustrating reluctance to follow his direction and the judge's active refusal to allow testimony favorable to his client, he pursued several arguments aimed at sowing seeds of doubt about her guilt. It became a defense built on shifting sands—torn between the stubborn pride of his client, the massive power and resources of the Federal government, and the rigidities of law and precedent. Disadvantaged by a lack of available witnesses, a Justice Department eager to provide incentives to German witnesses for their continued cooperation, and a lack of financial resources, Laughlin attempted to beat back a tidal wave of emotion-laden evidence with contradictory but fervent arguments.

His first core argument was that Mildred Gillars was always an American citizen during the time of her alleged treason. As a citizen of the United States, her constitutional rights were flagrantly violated by her arrest and three-year internment. At the same time, Laughlin argued that the oath of allegiance that his client allegedly signed after the Pearl Harbor attack was a legal renunciation of her citizenship in accordance with the 1940 Nationality Act. If the jury believed that Axis Sally was still an American citizen at the time of the broadcasts, then the Federal government did not treat her as one and violated her constitutional rights—rights including *habeas corpus*, unlawful search and seizure, self-incrimination and due process. If the jury believed that she had renounced her citizenship after December 7, 1941, then her arrest and incarceration were illegitimate—opening the door for an acquittal.

Either way, the *intent* of the accused was central to determining her guilt or innocence. Laughlin provided multiple witnesses who made it quite clear that she was never in a position to refuse her hosts. Ulrich Haupt, Emil Beckman and Erwin Christiani did everything possible to express the terror they had faced at the hands of a ruthless police state. Laughlin constantly tried to remind the jury that those dangers applied to Mildred Gillars as well. Daily survival depended on collaboration. If, for instance, she had the option that Georgia von Richter had—to either broadcast for Berlin Radio or work in a munitions factory—would one job be any less a form of treason than the other?

Laughlin insisted that Mildred had remained steadfastly loyal to America (notwithstanding her hatred and distrust of President Roosevelt) through the darkest days of the war, and never, at any time, intended to betray her nation. He pointed to her insistence on visiting the prisoner of war camps, her requests to American listeners that they inform the friends and families of the POWs about their safety, and her refusal to speak to the convicted traitor Martin James Monti as proof of her patriotism.

The clarity of these explanations was muddied by Axis Sally's adulterous affair with Koischwitz and her unapologetic love for the man. Laughlin's depiction of the Professor as a Svengali leading an American girl to ruin did not conform to the history and attitude of the worldly woman on the stand. She simply did not want to leave her man—even in 1944 as Allied armies closed in on Paris. She did not abandon him in the midst of Germany's defeat—not to save her own skin nor to plead her innocence before the Americans authorities. As she told John Kelley on the stand, no army would separate them—even unto death.

CHAPTER 11

Convicted

"Heavy hangs the head that plays the role of a traitor."
—John M. Kelley[447]

MARCH 1949–JUNE 1961

The first week of March 1949 brought the latest in a series of shocking Soviet espionage cases. Judith Coplon, a Justice Department analyst, was charged with providing classified national security documents to her Russian lover, an employee of the United Nations. Coplon was accused of providing the Soviets with FBI files detailing the investigation of possible Communist agents in the Federal government. As another lovestruck American woman took center stage, the trial of Axis Sally slowly ground to a close. The scores being settled in Mildred Gillars' Washington courtroom seemed out of sync with the times as the American public turned its attention to new dangers of subversion from within. In a matter of months, John Kelley would be tapped to lead the prosecutorial charge against Judith Coplon, but on March 8, 1949, the rising star in Attorney General Tom Clark's Justice Department began his closing argument for the conviction of Axis Sally.[24]

In a ninety-minute statement laced with bitter sarcasm, Kelley depicted the defendant as one of the most morally bankrupt characters in American history. Like a firebrand evangelist condemning the evils of sinful flesh, he lashed out at the "unholy traitor" who cast her lot with the Nazis. Calling her "a stupid woman" with "lovers aplenty," Kelley claimed that Axis Sally happily shared the exultation of Hitler's early wartime victories. Reminding the jury of the Führer clicking his heels in triumph at the French surrender, he drew a direct connection between Adolf Hitler and Axis Sally:

> She was on the winning side and all she cared about was her own selfish fame. She too absorbed the joy of conquest.... She believed the Nazis simply couldn't lose and she made up her mind which side to be on. She broadcast time and time again that she had chosen the German side and said it was the right side ...
>
> Lock stock and barrel, she sold herself to the Nazis for 3,000 Marks a month. She had a nice apartment, antiques, flowers, lovers aplenty, cocktail parties at the press club and the [Hotel] Adlon with traitors like Best and Chandler.... She sold out, that is all. She thought she was on the winning side and the only thing she cared about was her own selfish fame.[448]

Kelley resisted any effort to define Axis Sally as the innocent victim of a manipulative and controlling lover. He depicted Koischwitz not as a lonely matron's man of destiny, but a despicable adulterer who shamelessly carried on with the defendant while his doomed wife carried his child:

> Otto Koischwitz: the mountain gazer, the dynamic Mr. Koischwitz ...
>
> And who is this dynamic Mr. Koischwitz?
>
> So dynamic that he had to have his extra butter and his special food to keep his knees from buckling under him ...
>
> What a dynamic personality he was. And what a character we were told.... So much character that at the time he formed this unspeakable association with the defendant in the spring of 1943, it was at a time when his wife was carrying his fourth child ... *so* dynamic that he had to go to the mountains of Silesia and gaze into their vast beauties and have the spirits tell him that they blessed his whole affair, and he wrote his love

letters. What a special cad. Whether she was hypnotized or who was hypnotized, I don't know and I don't care.[449] What a stupid woman. She thought she could go over there and rub elbows with mountain-gazing Germans and get culture by the quart.[450]

Reading from one of Midge's *Medical Reports*, the prosecutor depicted Axis Sally as being as depraved and sadistic as any death camp guard:

Tell me, why in the name of humanity would any decent woman tell a mother of her son's death and then sadistically go into the details of his mortal injuries? In God's name, what can excuse that? Only one thing—Treason![451]

This was cruelty if ever I listened to it. And she got a sadistic joy out of it."[452]

Although Kelley admitted that Midge's prisoner-of-war interviews were propaganda-free, he maintained that she slyly waited for her moment to put the poison in:

Later, along came our Midge at 3,000 Nazi Marks a month to tack on the dirty propaganda in front of, and behind the recorded interviews, so that in order to listen to your boy, you had to listen to that rot ...

Of course, she was taking [the war] seriously, sashaying around with the hypnotic professor and getting him extra butter rations. But, of course, our boys weren't taking it seriously in the foxholes with all hell breaking loose around them while they listened to her tell them to lay down their guns and "toddle off home."

Why didn't she ask the Germans to lay down their guns and stop shooting our boys if she was a loyal American and taking it so seriously?[453]

In reality, this was her snide, stinking little way of torturing American boys in the foxholes. She knew the Nazis weren't paying her to entertain US troops.[454]

> If she didn't have a rotten conscience, why didn't she stay
> [in Paris] and be liberated? She knew what she had done as a
> traitor to her land…. Can there be any doubt in the minds of
> anyone what was in the traitorous heart of this woman?[455]

Mildred sat unmoving, her eyes darting about as Kelley's barrage went on. The prosecutor sat down and yielded the floor to James Laughlin. The urbane, silver-haired attorney rose and approached the jury box. Like an indulgent father defending the good intentions of a wayward daughter, he called his client "unjustly maligned and accused." "Horse manure about sums up the government's case," Laughlin said. "This lady never wanted to do anything against the United States [and] never wanted to betray her country."[456] The Government's response to her wartime activities was a gross overreaction. "Not a life was lost as a result of her broadcasts," Laughlin emphasized. "On the other hand, you can infer that many an American mother got comfort from the news of her son's whereabouts which came to her on those broadcasts."[457]

Ignoring the hours of testimony from former POWs, Laughlin insisted that there was "no evidence that the broadcasts were harmful to the country, or that they tended to undermine the morale of the armed forces."[458]

In the face of the mountain of damning evidence, Laughlin tried to exploit the racial composition of the jury. He pointed to the Justice Department's enthusiasm for prosecuting dangerous characters like Miss Gillars with a heavy hand, all the time refusing to lift a finger against lynch mobs and "those who persecute the Negro in the South":

> Are you going to condemn anti-Semitism in Hitler's Germany
> and uphold it in this country? I hope the Justice Department
> will be fair and punish those who persecute the colored man
> in the South by violating his civil liberties. The soul of the
> black man is just as precious in the sight of Almighty God as
> the wealthiest man in this country.[459]
>
> Let's be absolutely fair in this case. If you are going to
> crush race prejudice so it will never rise again, you can't per-

mit the violation of the colored man's civil liberties in the South, and the Justice Department should be prosecuting vigorously all those who violate them.[460]

Laughlin took aim at the questionable motives of the prosecution witnesses, condemning the government's slavish willingness to take the testimony of former Nazis at face value. The perks and advantages available to cooperating Germans should cast doubt on their testimony, he said. "The word of a Nazi should never be taken over that of an American citizen. Everyone knows that." He compared the meager five dollars per day that the jury received to the ten dollars a day stipend that former Nazi functionaries were paid for their cooperation. Moreover, the witnesses were given employment opportunities unheard of in war-wrecked Germany.

No matter how he tried to distract the jury from the facts of the case, Laughlin had to address his client's unsavory relationship with Koischwitz. "From the time of Sodom and Gomorrah," he told the jury, "married men have been carrying on affairs with women. That's wrong—but we are dealing with human beings." Testing the credulity of every person in the room, Laughlin inferred that the affair was not wholly consensual. "She didn't know his wife was pregnant," the attorney insisted. "Our laws allow females—in order to save their lives, to allow their bodies to be violated."[461] Despite his client's clear adoration of the Professor in her own sworn testimony, the defense blamed "coercion and enemy compulsion" in the figure of Otto Koischwitz as the main reason she remained on the Berlin airwaves:

> What would any of you have done? ... Suppose she had crossed him? He could have had her put away at any moment. ... She's only a human being and she's a woman. The law does not expect a woman to hold her ground to such an extent that she would have been sent away to a concentration camp or death. She's not supernatural. She's only human.

Not just a victim, a martyr; "Here is this lady—taking her chances with the bombs falling," ensuring that the soldiers' messages home get through to their families. She walked a tightrope between her desire to help the GIs and to meet the expectations of the dreaded Horst Cleinow. "Refusal meant death. Cleinow with a wave of his finger could have sent her to a concentration camp and death—not immediate perhaps—but slowly of starvation."[462]

Laughlin saved his most powerful assault for the United States government's violation of Mildred Gillars' constitutional rights. Arrested, released and rearrested without charges in a foreign land; imprisoned without a hearing or a speedy trial, her rights as an American citizen were trampled upon. The same American government that denied her those rights hypocritically sought to convict her subject to that very same Constitution. Laughlin charged that Mildred and the other radio traitors were all being held to a new and dangerous redefinition of the crime of treason. For over a hundred years, "mere words" were not enough to constitute treason, but this new conception of the crime made the speaking of words into a microphone a capital crime. Sidestepping the fact that the words were spoken on enemy territory, Laughlin charged ahead, warning that this redefinition could undermine the First Amendment and have a "destructive effect on free speech and thought" at home:

> The right of civil liberty—of personal liberty—is at stake in this trial. If this defendant is convicted, the right of free speech could not help but be impaired ...[463]
>
> The only way you can repudiate this tyranny is to acquit this defendant. To put your stamp of approval on such conduct means no one in this country would be safe. Freedom of speech would be wiped out and the writ of habeas corpus would be suspended.[464]

It took five hours for Laughlin to finish his plea for Axis Sally's acquittal. In a final gesture, he raised his arm like a master of ceremonies, swept it toward the defendant and closed with a final acclaim, "Ladies and Gentlemen, I give you Mildred Gillars."[465] As he sat down, the lawyer hesitated. He rose again to remind the jury of Mildred's oath of allegiance to Germany:

The testimony is further that she turned it over to Mr.

Schmidt-Hansen. His testimony is that he did not recall it, although on cross-examination he said that he did not deny it, it could have been a routine or something like that. However, Christiani testified that he did have a conversation about that, and as a result of that oath she was permitted to return to work. I ask you, therefore, to keep that in mind, as to whether she signed an oath, and the circumstances under which she signed it. If it conformed to the statute, she expatriated herself, and she should be acquitted on that count if no other.[466]

Despite his earlier agreement to the stipulation that Mildred was an American citizen who owed allegiance to the United States at all times, Laughlin pinned his hopes on a thin reed that he foolishly threw away at the beginning of the trial. Although her story about the oath was only confirmed by Erwin Christiani, no supporting documentation existed. Nevertheless, Laughlin used it in an attempt to invalidate the entire trial. If defense counsel had taken that position in the beginning and claimed that she had expatriated himself in 1941, acquittal might have been, at least, a possibility.

Her lips tightly pursed in nervous anticipation, Mildred listened closely as Judge Curran instructed the jury. Asking them to use "the same good common sense you apply to the problems of everyday life," Curran told the jurors that if the defendant gave "aid and comfort" to the enemy and acted with the intention to betray the nation, the verdict must be guilty. As the judge continued, he whisked away each one of the defense arguments, deeming them irrelevant to Axis Sally's guilt or innocence. It did not matter whether she lived in fear of arrest and internment in a concentration camp. It did not matter if she felt compelled to broadcast for the Nazis—*unless* she lived in fear of "imminent and impending death or bodily harm" at *all* times.[467]

Curran explained: "Force and fear must continue *all the time* [author's italics] in which the traitorous act or acts is performed."[468] To meet that standard, Axis Sally would have had to experience the imminent fear of death or torture every day from December 8, 1941 to May 8, 1945. "Fear that she might be sent to a concentration camp is not sufficient," he said, an unusual twist of logic in a world freshly acquainted with the horrors of Buchenwald, Dachau and Treblinka:

Fear of injury to one's property or of future bodily harm do not excuse an offense, and in order that compulsion may operate as a defense, one must be without fault or blame in causing it. That one commits a crime merely because he or she is ordered to do so by some superior authority is, in itself, no defense, for there is nothing in the mere relationship of the parties that justifies or excuses obedience to such commands.

Moreover, the force and fear, in order to constitute a defense in a case of treason, must continue during all the time of such service with the enemy, and one who makes force his defense must prove that he left the service as soon as he could. In other words, ladies and gentlemen of the jury, this coercion or compulsion that will excuse a criminal act must be present, immediate and impending, and of such a nature as to induce a well-grounded apprehension of death or serious bodily injury if the act is not done.[469]

The fact that the defendant was in love with Dr. Koischwitz, or that Dr. Koischwitz was in love with the defendant, is not sufficient, nor is the fact that Dr. Koischwitz was a man of dynamic personality, if you so find that he was, and that he asserted his influence over the defendant, is not sufficient. Nor is it sufficient that the defendant thought she might be sent to a concentration camp, if you so find, nor are threats to other persons sufficient. Nor is it sufficient that the defendant continued her employment with the German Broadcasting Company and committed these acts merely because she wanted to make a living.[470]

Finally, Curran reminded the jurors of the stipulation signed by Mildred herself affirming her American citizenship. The stipulation (and her acceptance of it) made her "oath of allegiance" insufficient to avoid conviction:

You are instructed that so vague and indefinite a statement as translated would be something to the effect that, "I swear allegiance to Germany and signed Mildred Gillars," which statement was handed by one person to another is not an oath, affirmation or other formal declaration of allegiance to a foreign state within the meaning of Section 401 of the Nationality Act of 1940.[471]

One by one, Curran eliminated every defense from the jury's consideration. Mildred despondently sank down into her chair. Laughlin reddened. With their options severely limited, the jury filed out to decide the fate of Axis Sally. It would be a long vigil. After several hours of deliberation, the jury adjourned to a nearby restaurant for dinner. At 10:30 p.m., with no verdict, Federal marshals transported the jurors to the Hotel Continental for the night.

The following morning, Mildred arrived at court in a bus packed with prisoners. Edna Mae Herrick and her husband Edward waited outside in the searing wind. The last to emerge from the coach, Mildred greeted her half-sister with a cheerful "Good morning, dear." Mildred appeared heartened by the lack of a quick decision. She was then led to a basement holding cell in the courthouse where she waited. Morning passed with no word, and when the jurors emerged at one o'clock to eat lunch at a 5th Street restaurant, reporters scanned their faces for some sign. The only indication of their discussions was a request for the transcripts of the 22 Axis Sally recordings entered into evidence.

Friday afternoon passed with no word from the jury room. With the weekend fast approaching, the jurors sent word at 4:28 p.m. that they had reached a verdict. Within minutes, Mildred was brought upstairs. At 4:45, the jury filed in. She intently eyed each one but not a single man or woman met her gaze. Judge Curran entered and asked her to stand. The bailiff asked the jury foreman, Henry G. Davis, if the panel had reached a decision. Without hesitation, Davis answered "Yes. Guilty." Mildred's face drained of color and Edna Mae began to sob. Laughlin demanded a poll of the jury. Barely audible above the din of spectators and press, each juror answered "Guilty." One spectator shouted "Ah, hell," as the slow procession dragged on. Print reporters swarmed out of the room to file their stories. Axis Sally was found guilty on only one of eight counts: #10—participation in the radio drama *Vision of Invasion*. After all the testimony by former prisoners of war, wounded servicemen and German collaborators,

Mildred was convicted for acting in a play—a work written by a man charged with treason in 1943 and whose indictment was signed by the judge who now held her life in his hands. Death removed any possibility that Otto Koischwitz would face justice, but Mildred Gillars would bear the penalty for both of them.

As promised, Laughlin motioned for a new trial—a considerable long shot since Judge Curran would make the decision. Sentencing was set for March 25. In the meantime, Axis Sally would remain in the District Jail. A Federal marshal stepped up behind the convicted woman and pulled out her chair as a signal to leave. She glanced once more at her distraught sister. Trembling, Edna Mae dropped a cup of water as Mildred was led away. A reporter waited by the holding cell for a comment. Unbowed, she said, "I wish those who judged me would be willing to risk their lives for America as I did."[472] She paced back and forth in the cell, drawing on a cigarette, until a black paneled van pulled up in front of the courthouse. "It looks like you are going to get your picture taken again," the marshal jocularly told her. "I shouldn't be surprised," she replied dryly as she stepped out into the crowd.[473]

Her face, taut and strained, peered out the van's narrow window. Nearby, Edna Mae was visibly bitter, telling one reporter, "I don't think they will sleep much tonight."[474] Leaving court, James Laughlin met the press. He called the judge's behavior an "outrageous and shocking violation of accepted judicial procedure." Curran swept away every one of his defenses, he claimed. "There [was] no basis for much of it. He excluded anything concerning concentration camps. We know concentration camps are tantamount to a death sentence," he said. In short, it was "an invitation to return a guilty verdict."[475]

That evening, Mildred was greeted by a surprise telegram from the attorney whose services she had disavowed publicly a year before. From the wilds of Alaska, John Holzworth reminded the convicted woman of his past warnings and attacked her choice of legal counsel:

DEEPLY REGRET YOUR CONVICTION PARTICULARLY IN VIEW SOLE AND UNASSAILABLE DEFENSE OF GERMAN CITIZENSHIP BASED ON FACTS FURNISHED ME. WARNED YOU AGAINST LAUGHLIN IN AUGUST CONFERENCES. NEWS DISPATCHES STRESSED HIS LEGAL SHORTCOM-

INGS. WAS MY JANUARY 27TH TELEGRAM RECEIVED STATING
LAUGHLIN NOTORIOUS FOR DOUBLE DEALING AND CROSSING?
YOUR SOLE HOPE FOR CONVICTION REVERSAL ON APPEAL IS VIO-
LATION [OF] CONSTITUTIONAL RIGHT TO COMPETENT, LOYAL
LEGAL REPRESENTATION BY COUNSEL. IN WASHINGTON SOON....

JOHN M. HOLZWORTH[476]

Confronted by the prospect of life in prison or even a death sentence, Holzworth's telegram was a bitter emotional blow. As her sentencing approached, her behavior became more erratic and difficult.
Mildred resisted Laughlin's attempts to launch an appeal; refusing to
sign necessary documents to proceed *in pauperis*. Penniless, she could
not hire and pay for any other legal representation. On appeal, there
would be no publicity bonanza for a lawyer in search of renown. It
would be James Laughlin or no one.

"I'll never be able to understand …"

On March 25, Mildred arrived for sentencing in the same black dress
she wore throughout the trial. Once again, Edna Mae dutifully stood
behind her. Curran immediately denied the motion for a new trial and
asked Mildred to stand and receive her sentence. He asked if she had
anything to say before he passed sentence. She looked down at the
defense table and stiffened. "I'll never be able to understand," she
began, "why I was found guilty in *Vision of Invasion*, which was written by Professor Koischwitz, who also directed and played in it. He
was indicted for treason in 1943, and he was exonerated by this government. You, as a U.S. District Attorney, signed the papers."[477] Curran cut in, "I'm told so. I have no recollection of it."

Determined to have her say, she continued her monologue: "If the
Vision of Invasion was so heinous and odious, why was an American
passport given to Mr. (Ulrich) Haupt?"

"Don't ask me," replied Curran.

"It interests me. It affects my fate," she replied.[478] "I shall never
be able to understand—"

Curran cut her off saying that her attorney had already argued her
case. Comparing her crimes with those of Douglas Chandler and

Robert H. Best (both of whom received life sentences), the judge acknowledged that Mildred did not participate in "conferences with high Nazi officials to formulate policy." Therefore, he sentenced Axis Sally to a 10-to-30-year sentence with a $10,000 fine. She raised her chin, turned quickly and walked out of the courtroom. Aware that her sister was playing the lead role in the greatest drama of her life, Edna Mae told reporters, "I don't think Ethel Barrymore could have done a better job of taking the verdict."[479]

Reaction to the sentence was swift and nearly unanimous. "She should have been strung up," one ex-soldier said in response to the verdict. "That's my opinion and every man in the Ninth Division would agree with me.... She knew where you were located and she'd tell us to expect a visit and then they'd come over and bomb the hell out of us."[480] Some residents of her former hometown felt she should be shot. The Herricks returned to Ashtabula, Ohio, to face years of both open discrimination and quiet disdain. Edna Mae's devotion to a half-sister she barely knew cost her family dearly. At the same time, Mildred became increasingly unappreciative of the sacrifices made for her.

"Gradually deteriorating"

She is an intelligent, clever, scheming, overbearing, demanding person with an intense hatred for American ideals and principals [sic]. She is thoroughly imbued and indoctrinated with racial and religious prejudices. She detests "Jews" and the "Technicolor" group which, of course, are the Negroes. She has an elevated opinion of her talents and abilities. When she isn't catered to, she gets belligerent and wants special treatment. She has a self-righteous attitude and now feels she is persecuted. The long periods of incarceration in jails and quarters have begun to have an obvious effect on her personality. She has become irritable and difficult to manage, although she is enjoying better treatment in the United States than she did in Continental Europe. She believes that she didn't get a fair trial or justice in her case. The Assignments Board, Department of Corrections DC, is of the opinion that she should be placed in a reformatory type of institution where specialized care is available because of length of sentence and her gradually deteriorating personality.[481]

In June of 1950, Jail Superintendent Colonel Curtis Reid wrote to the Director of the DC Department of Corrections about one of his most troublesome prisoners. Despite his dislike of Axis Sally, her emotional instability was of great concern. James Laughlin tried for weeks to get her to sign the necessary papers to launch her appeal, but she refused. With the deadline approaching, the attorney begged Colonel Reid to intercede. She suddenly changed her mind and sent a flurry of notes to Reid demanding to know when the documents would arrive for her signature. Only days after Laughlin argued her case before the United States Court of Appeals (the prosecution had meantime dropped two counts against her), Mildred reported crippling digestive problems to the jail's physician. Within a week, the doctor placed her on a strict diet of black coffee and buttered toast.[482]

Understandably fearful that the appeal was the last gasp of her legal hopes for freedom, Mildred sent several notes to Colonel Reid demanding a personal interview. On March 6, she "fainted" in front of the matron's office while working on the laundry detail. An injury report stated that Mildred "suddenly threw her hands in the air and fell to the floor in a sitting position."[483] She was uninjured, but the disturbing incident recalled previous fainting spells, as in 1928, when she swooned in the Camden jail for the press, and in 1949, when she passed out in court after the jury heard her call American forces "murderers" in a recorded broadcast. When the going got tough, Axis Sally tended to pass out.

At her own request, she was transferred to the Women's Division of the District of Columbia Workhouse at Occoquan, Virginia. But nine days later, she was returned without explanation to the District Jail at the request of authorities. Frustrated amid a seemingly endless wait for the decision of the Appeals Court, Mildred lashed out again. This time, she struck Edna Mae from her visitors list. Colonel Reid wrote a sympathetic note to Mrs. Herrick to inform her of Mildred's decision and "save [her] ... a trip to this city."[484] As the outlook for a favorable decision looked increasingly bleak, she cut her ties with her only living relatives. From late 1949 to the summer of 1950, Edna Mae kept in touch with Colonel Reid regularly. In one letter, she asked the superintendent if she could send shoes or a small chicken to Mildred for Christmas "if it wouldn't cause too much dissension [*sic*] among the prisoners."

On May 19, 1950, almost five months after Laughlin argued the case, the Court of Appeals upheld the jury's decision and the judge's conduct. Judge Charles Fahy wrote that the weight of the evidence was sufficient to convict her on the tenth count (participation in *Vision of Invasion*), even though she was found not guilty on the remaining seven. The three eyewitnesses who witnessed her actions (Ulrich Haupt, Georg Heinrich Schnell and Hans von Richter) were never challenged as to their competence in the original trial, so their testimony could not be disallowed.

The Best Years of Their Lives

In December 1949 at the request of the Office of Alien Property, the FBI dispatched agents to interview former German colleagues and friends of Max Otto Koischwitz. Their task was to determine whether the return of money and property belonging to the Koischwitz family and expropriated by the Federal government after their return to Germany in 1939 could be safely returned to the surviving daughters. Stella, the professor's eldest, was living in New York City, and the FBI was especially interested in the role she had played as a radio announcer during the war. Following Koischwitz's death, she worked as an announcer and news reader on Reichsradio to make ends meet, and the young girl's political leanings had to be determined before the property was returned.

Ironically, the United States was, at the same time, welcoming dyed-in-the-wool Nazis—some with blood on their hands—into the country because they were perceived to be valuable assets in the struggle against Communism. To determine whether the return of the property would harm the national interest, agents interviewed Horst Cleinow (the once-feared radio manager who threatened Mildred after he discovered that she had been broadcasting without a censor), Adelbert Houben, Hans von Richter (her former friend and manager) and, most importantly, Gerd Wagner.

Wagner was the head of the News Division for the USA Zone and a personal friend of Max Otto Koischwitz. Wagner met him on his return from America at the outbreak of war in September 1939. A frequent visitor to the Koischwitz home, the Professor revealed to Wagner a crucial fact about his time in America; one that sheds light on his decision to take US citizenship in 1935:

> MR WAGNER stated that he had talked with MAX OTTO KOISCHWITZ in Berlin, the exact date he could not recall, at which time KOISCHWITZ had stated to him that he, KOISCHWITZ, had been requested by the German government to secure his American citizenship for the purpose of carrying on German propaganda in the United States.... He advised that in conferences with MAX KOISCHWITZ, he was very anti-American in his views.[485]

As early as 1935, Max Otto Koischwitz took his orders from Berlin—and even assumed American citizenship so that his service to the Third Reich would not be interrupted. His yearly trips back to the Fatherland, dissatisfaction with the Hunter faculty's refusal to grant him a full professorship, and anger at those students who resisted his attempts at Nazi indoctrination make sense in this light. Wagner's revelation explains why the newly minted American was welcomed back to Germany with open arms and a Foreign Office job in September 1939. Moreover, it reveals a man capable of betraying those closest to him for the sake of the Reich, and shows how and why he pressured, cajoled and manipulated a lonely American to take actions that jeopardized her citizenship, her freedom, even her life.

Other former *Reichsradio* functionaries interviewed that December were not as forthcoming. Cleinow, von Richter and Houben portrayed Koischwitz as a dissenter, even anti-Nazi. Horst Cleinow was residing in Emmaus, Pennsylvania—another by-product of the treason trials, in which once-loyal minions of the Hitler regime were rewarded for their assistance to the Justice Department with new "temporary" homes in the United States. Despite his application for party membership in 1937, Cleinow denied ever being a Nazi:

[Cleinow] never received any indication that Koischwitz was a Nazi Party member. He said that the latter's employment in the Foreign Office did not necessarily mean that he was a Party member, although it was quite possible that his Party membership may have been concealed. He did not believe that this was the case, however, since Koischwitz was one of the few people with whom Cleinow freely discussed and criticized the German political situation. In these discussions, Koischwitz indicated his very sharp criticism concerning matters initiated by the Nazi Party. He said that if Koischwitz was a Nazi Party member, he was not a fanatical one.

Cleinow believed that Koischwitz enjoyed life in the United States much better than in Germany and did not feel at home in Berlin. He said that Koischwitz never expressed any positive or negative political statement toward the United States but that he was generally regarded in Berlin as favoring the mentality of the Anglo-Saxons.... According to Cleinow; Koischwitz was cautioned by the members of the German Foreign Office to remain silent and to retain to himself his pro-American admiration.[486]

Incredibly, Cleinow told the FBI that he "knew of no contributions, literary or financial, by Koischwitz to the Nazi cause," even as Mildred Gillars was beginning a ten- to thirty-year sentence for performing in one of his "literary contributions" to the cause.[487] He went further:

Since Koischwitz was a German citizen and radio was considered essential by the German government during wartime, Koischwitz would not have had the opportunity to discontinue his broadcasts even if he desired to do so.[488]

Cleinow asserted that Koischwitz, as a German citizen, could not discontinue his broadcasts even if he had wanted, at the same time that the Justice Department refused to accept that a friendless American woman was unable to stop *her* broadcasts. More than a double-standard, it was the cornerstone of the government's case against her. Cleinow addressed the case of the now-imprisoned American by further whitewashing his late colleague:

> Koischwitz associated with Mildred Gillars (Axis Sally) ... and he undoubtedly influenced her broadcasts. He said that Koischwitz entertained Gillars in his home and that she was very friendly with Koischwitz's wife.... Cleinow said Koischwitz went completely to pieces after his wife's death.[489]

With Axis Sally securely in jail, Cleinow's rewritten history went unchallenged. He wasn't a Nazi or even pro-Nazi, nor was Koischwitz. Instead, the two men were vocal critics of the party's actions and could rely on the confidence of each other when voicing their dissent. In Cleinow's fantastic telling, the Professor entertained Axis Sally in his home while his pregnant wife formed a warm friendship with the American.

Alderson

On August 10, 1950, a train stopped at daybreak in the small rural town of Alderson, West Virginia. Mildred Gillars and two other female prisoners emerged from a Pullman car into the bracing morning fog. For the first time in her long incarceration, no reporters or photographers awaited her arrival. An iron-barred prison wagon traversed the steep winding road that led from the train station to the main gate of the Federal Reformatory for Woman. As the sun rose over the mountains, a guard unlocked the gate. The three women were led to the Orientation Building, known to insiders as Cottage 26. Since the prison's founding in 1927, the experimental nature of the facility was reflected in the language used to describe its "cottages," "rooms" and the sprawling campus called the "Reservation."

In Cottage 26, Mildred began a sentence that could last 30 years. She filled out a long questionnaire that asked a slew of personal questions, including "Are you a lesbian?" A similar questionnaire was sent to Edna Mae asking for details on her sister's personality, preferences, character strengths and weaknesses. Elizabeth Gurley Flynn, a Communist jailed for violating the Smith Act, wrote a memoir of her

Alderson prison experience. Gurley Flynn resented the questionnaires and called them "a despicable form of petty spying on a prisoner and her family [that] gave the authorities private and personal information about her which they had no right or need to secure. Since there was no psychiatric treatment or occupational therapy at Alderson, it was not designed to help the prisoners."[490] Nevertheless, family members dutifully answered the questions, some fearing that a refusal might lead to revocation of their visiting privileges.

After fingerprinting and a mug shot, Mildred was ordered to strip down to be examined by a nurse. An enema was administered to ensure that no narcotics were being smuggled in. After the medical exam, she was allowed to shower and changed into a rayon night-gown and housecoat. Every incoming prisoner was locked in quarantine for three days in a private room. Cottage rooms were equipped with a bed, toilet, washbasin and radiator. The inmates' hair was dusted with DDT, for delousing, and prison officials ordered that the (now-outlawed) chemical not be washed out for 48 hours.[491] For 72 hours, the new inmates were allowed no human contact except when jail guards brought in meals. In their solitude, they could hear the whistle blow at the start of the workday and again ten minutes before its end (the latter signal ordered all males in the area to leave so that the "girls" could be returned to their cottages—eliminating the possibility of fraternization). Every morning at 2 a.m., a guard (usually a local resident working the night shift) opened the door to the sleeping inmate's room to shine a flashlight at the bed.

Alderson, the first Federal prison dedicated to housing female inmates, was an outgrowth of the woman's suffrage movement. The brutal treatment of women convicted of federal crimes and then pushed into the state prison systems was the prime impetus for reform. Championed by Eleanor Roosevelt, Florence Harding (widow of President Warren G. Harding) and Mrs. Henry Morgenthau, Alderson was dedicated to rehabilitation rather than punishment. The 105-acre site looked more like a college than a prison. Inmates were assigned tasks designed to teach a trade or skill associated with the home, such as crafts, ceramics, laundry, sewing, photography and gardening. Prisoners came from all walks of life, convicted of crimes ranging from prostitution to forgery, theft and narcotics—even the production and sale of moonshine. Some were unfortunates—illiterate women of all races who were tempted or forced into a life of crime by a man or abject poverty or both. Others were hardened criminals—gangsters' molls, grifters and murderers. A few were convicted of politically motivated crimes. Lolita Lebrón, the Puerto Rican nationalist who participated in a 1954 attack on the US House of Representatives, and Gurley Flynn were just a few of the prisoners serving sentences for politically-motivated crimes. In addition, Mildred's wartime counterpart in Japan, Iva Toguri D'Aquino, known as "Tokyo Rose," was resident in the prison.

On her fourth day at Alderson, Mildred was released from quarantine and allowed to join the population for three weeks of orientation. In orientation, the women memorized prison rules, received vaccinations and took intelligence and aptitude tests.[492] The prison staff was leery of bad publicity, especially from Walter Winchell and the newspaper columnist Westbrook Pegler (Winchell once made an embarrassing reference in his broadcast to rampant lesbian activity at the prison).[493] The new inmates washed and waxed the cottage floors on their hands and knees as part of their introduction to the prison's 6 a.m.–9 p.m. workday. Racial prejudice was ever-present (the facility was not desegregated until 1955), as "about half [of the inmates] were Negroes; a few were Spanish-speaking."[494] African-American guards were posted only at the maximum security cottages. Inmates were allowed to attend religious services twice a week, and a movie once a week. A Roman Catholic priest was on staff to conduct Mass and had a reputation for being helpful and compassionate to prisoners of all or no faith. The orientation period ended with a graduation ceremony attended by the warden, Nina Kinsella.[495]

Throughout orientation, Mildred's difficult manner was a matter of concern to prison officials. Her first days at Alderson are summed up in an October 1950 evaluation:

> She had a superior manner, was abrupt with the receiving officer and rude to the two girls admitted with her. She objected loudly to being committed under the name of Sisk rather than Gillars, was alert and observant but very uncooperative ...
> At first she was annoyed at everything, carried a chip on

her shoulder, could not be reasoned with, felt persecuted, and expected bad treatment. She smoked alone, retired to her room to read during all spare time rather than join the group, and at the table seldom said much [and] appeared to be day dreaming. She was annoyed because girls urged her to attend a ball game so that others could go. She consented reluctantly and sat with her back to the field.

Constant complaints were received because she could not get cascara (*an herbal laxative*) ... then complained because the order for cascara was not large enough. More and more was requested until she was called to the clinic for special attention and special medicine.

During the second week, she joined the group in the living room but declined to participate in activities, preferring to sew on her clothing, which she altered well but reluctantly. In some ways, she was most pleasant and interesting but, at times, was selfish, greedy, grasping, and asked for favors or disregarded regulations to suit her convenience. When annoyed, she always felt bad and retired to her room sometimes, requiring insistence to get her to meals which she ate heartily. She spoke appreciatively of the food and resisted any insinuations of insufficiency or quality from others—impressing upon them the suffering she had witnessed from "sheer starvation."

Other girls did not usually attempt to argue with her, were pleasant in her path, and did not impose themselves upon her. She declined to attend religious services and movies and was clever enough to avoid loss of privileges.[496]

One reason that other inmates avoided the aloof and condescending Axis Sally came from the Alderson gossip mill. Rumors swirled around the silent, silver-haired woman about her wartime activities. Elizabeth Gurley Flynn wrote that, as late as 1955, Axis Sally had a frightening reputation. "You know what she did? ... Made lampshades out of the skins of our soldiers," was only a sample of the gossip surrounding her.[497] Gurley Flynn politely informed the others that they had confused Mildred with "The Bitch of Buchenwald"—Ilse Koch. Koch (1906–1967) had been the wife of an SS camp commandant accused of collecting the tattooed skins of Jews and ordering inmates to participate in rapes and other sadistic sexual acts. Released by the American military, Koch was retried by a German court and sentenced to life in prison—a fate she avoided by hanging herself in 1967.

As Mildred entered the general population, she was transferred to Cottage 23, a maximum security facility. Political criminals were typically assigned to maximum security areas, whether or not the offense was violent in nature. Women convicted for treason, violation of the Smith Act (advocating the violent overthrow of the government), espionage or other politically motivated crimes were thoroughly monitored. Books and other reading material was evaluated for "subversive" content, and letters to and from inmates were opened and read by the FBI. It was not uncommon for the recipient of a letter from one of these prisoners to be visited by Federal agents and interrogated.

Clearly embarrassed by her sister's refusal to write or speak to her, Edna Mae nevertheless held out hope for reconciliation as she wrote to prison officials in October 1950:

> You may think it strange if she doesn't correspond with me. For some reason, she thinks I have failed her. But if the time comes she thinks she would like to write me again, I hope you might assure her I'll always want to hear from her. Our home and heart will always be open for her. We are building a fine big twelve roomed home on two acres of land and it is her home. What she doesn't know is that we have changed our building plans so we might build rooms just for her. There will even be a private entrance for her, if she prefers privacy.
>
> She knows she is innocent and I know it, but what I don't believe she realized is how cruel the people might be to her when she gets out, unless she has a sheltered home to come to and until she has time to prove her innocence.[498]

Loneliness and isolation characterized Mildred's first years in West Virginia. Assigned to Cottage 23, she never spoke to other inmates unless spoken to first. Moreover, she carried an unrelenting bitterness from her long incarceration and trial. Mildred's annual review for

1953 spoke plainly about her initial resistance: "Somehow she felt her-self to be a martyr and was never able to take any of the blame for her incarceration. Instead, she seemed to enjoy being bitter, and unwilling to conform to the usually accepted loyalties."[499] She was uniformly disliked by other inmates—a dangerous position considering the num-ber of violent and/or mentally ill or retarded women relegated to the prison.

"Most of the cottage members disliked Mildred because of her condescending manner, her greediness about food, and her general tactlessness," the report continued. "Usually, she managed to get along with the group by not mixing much, but there was some fric-tion when she disagreed with others as of positive opinions as her own."[500]

Slowly, she warmed to her cottagemates. Assigned to the craft room, Mildred became a skilled weaver and seamstress. The craft area housed a kiln for ceramics, looms and an array of sewing tables. Inmates assembled bedspreads and quilts, dresses and nightgowns for fellow prisoners. They knitted sweaters, hats and scarves to be put on sale for visitors to purchase. Her room, filled with various projects, won the admiration of her guards. Eventually, she began to attend Roman Catholic mass. Her accomplishments in the craft room led her to teach her skills to the other "girls."

In January, 1952 she moved to Cottage 7, where she would spend the rest of her prison term. Although her housemates found her to be "pleasant, courteous, sometimes officious," she remained difficult and remote. She "wears an arrogant, superior manner like a cloak, is lone-ly and aloof ... bitter and sarcastic at times.... Her attitude was hos-tile and uncooperative. She always upheld girls against officers, no matter how bad their behavior."[501] In her new home, she tended to the garden at the rear of the building. Fanatical in her maintenance of the flowers and plants, she was widely suspected of hoarding garden implements for her own use and "continually looking about the grounds for plants she could appropriate."[502] Locked into her room at the end of the workday, her nights were filled with reading and, even-tually, she was allowed to practice the piano. Eventually, her cloak of self-imposed isolation gradually slipped away as she joined her cot-tagemates at occasional parties and get-togethers.

Mildred's isolation from her family ended in June 1952, when Edna Mae and her young son Thomas made the long trip from Ashtabula, Ohio to the West Virginia hills. The silence ended when Mildred sent a Christmas wire to the Herrick family in December 1951, followed by another in March 1952. Inmate visits were held in a separate cottage fitted with comfortable armchairs and tables designed to evoke a living room atmosphere. Relatives had a difficult time finding suitable accommodations in Alderson proper. Boarding houses were few, usually "whites only" establishments that tended to be unclean and unfriendly to prisoners' kin. The families of "colored" inmates were forced to find lodging in nearby towns.

The warden, Nina Kinsella, granted a two-hour extension to the visit. Kinsella hoped that Mildred's reunion with her only living relative would help her cope with prison life and relieve her isolation. In the 1950s, mental health professionals in prisons were few and far between, and Axis Sally's clear psychological disintegration continued to trouble Alderson officials: "She can be charming and gracious if she puts her mind to it.... She is not a leader for her manner repels, her opinions often are biased, and she has no interest or sympathy for, in her judgment, the common, ordinary inmate.... [She] seemed to feel far superior to other inmates and to officers."[503] Her air of superiority extended to her assignments, where she rejected all criticism and considered herself "infallible in her work, thinking, ideas and opinions."[504]

At times, her behavior bordered on the bizarre. When a German doctor visited Alderson for a tour of the facility, Mildred told the guard that someone of her status could not be seen performing "menial work" for it would make a "very bad impression" of the prison.

Edna Mae visited once a year, usually in the summer months. The relationship, as always, was rocky. Guards noted in a report to the warden that a July 1956 visit was almost cut short by an argument shortly after Mildred arrived in the visiting area. Mrs. Herrick was "indignant" about the long delay she experienced waiting for her sister. "Immediately after Mildred came," an account of the visit noted, "they became involved in an argument and Mrs. Herrick refused to speak for about 20 minutes. From then on, most of the visit was pleasant, but frequently there were harsh words and injured feelings between them."[505]

"Accept your fate for it is sealed"

The years of bitterness and anger slowly gave way to acceptance. By 1953, authorities noticed a pronounced change in the attitude of their difficult prisoner. Mildred slowly adapted to the reformatory's lifestyle and became a productive member of the population, but more than that, discovered some fulfillment and spiritual peace in Catholicism. A discontented life filled with great disappointment evolved into one determined to serve God and others in the time left to her. She began to direct the Protestant choir in 1957 and was responsible for assembling the music for the Catholic Mass. In the absence of a "civilian" music teacher, she enthusiastically coached the singers and sought to teach them the meaning of the lyrics. Although some found her imperious attitude grating, other inmates benefited from her contagious commitment to the sacred music. Her 1957–58 progress report stated:

> She makes a real effort to show the choir members the meaning of music in worship and the necessity for it being well-done.... Although she has some difficulty with the Latin, she studies it diligently and tries very hard to have the members of the Catholic Choir pronounce it correctly. She also interprets to the best of her ability, so that they may appreciate the meanings involved.

Proving to be a talented teacher with a broad background of experience and knowledge, Mildred earned the admiration and respect of the Catholic Chaplain, Father Thomas Kerrigan, and prison officers. Befriended by the priest, she became deeply attached to the Church and its liturgy. She found some measure of solace in the deep meaning of its rituals and, although Episcopalian by birth, she eventually converted to Roman Catholicism. In 1960, she was baptized and confirmed in the Church by the Coadjutor Bishop Thomas J. McDonnell in Wheeling.[506]

Assigned to work in the craft room, she was also responsible for the management of the ceramics kiln. Elizabeth Gurley Flynn warmly recalled the beautiful blue Bavarian beer steins that Mildred made, emblazoned with words in German that translated to *"Accept your fate, for it is sealed."* In reality, Axis Sally had accepted her fate. As early as 1956, her fellow prisoners encouraged her to seek a pardon or commutation. Mildred was not eligible for parole until 1959, but the release of several other Nazi-era prisoners—some convicted of the bloodiest of crimes—caught the attention of the other inmates. Gurley Flynn wrote:

> I showed her news of similar cases. Constance Drexel, a Philadelphia socialite, was held on the same charge but never brought to trial. I told her of Ezra Pound, who was then held without trial at St. Elizabeth's. I called her attention to cases of German war criminals who were being released. One, Joachim Peiper, commander of the Nazi Elite Guardsmen, had been found guilty of responsibility for the Malamedy forest massacre of Christmas 1944, when 142 Americans were killed. His sentence of 35 years was commuted in December 1956. He had served less than one-third of it. This was by order of the Parole and Clemency Board of six—American, British, French and West German. Reading all this, I could not be enthusiastic about keeping this woman in jail.[507]

When Iva Toguri D'Aquino was freed from Alderson in January 1956, it was evident to all that American public opinion was moving ever so slowly toward tolerance, if not forgiveness of former collaborators. Fearing the bitterness and reproach of the outside world, Axis Sally was not eager to leave the confinement of prison. Iva had been hounded by immigration authorities upon her release, and a similar deportation order was waiting for Axis Sally. The Justice Department was determined to send the two women back to the country where they committed their crimes. If that were to occur, Mildred would be forsaken in her own land and probably unwanted in the new Federal Republic of Germany.

In March 1959 she waived her right to apply for parole. Fifty-eight years old and looking at least ten years older, she could not face the prospect of survival in the outside world. The circumstances of her last release in Christmas 1946 were still fresh in her memory. Penniless, homeless and totally dependent on the good graces of friends for survival, she was rearrested within a month to be sent to America for trial. She certainly did not want to go through it all again at almost sixty years of age.

Nevertheless, Mildred eventually changed her mind and applied for parole with the encouragement and support of Father Kerrigan. With no employment prospects, she was denied parole in February 1960. In May 1960, she was baptized in the Roman Catholic Church and, two weeks later, received her first Holy Communion and Confirmation. Sister Mary Assumpta P.C.J. (Order of the Poor Child Jesus) was present and described the ceremonies as "rare, successive and beautiful."[508] Then Kerrigan actively enlisted sisters from the Our Lady of Bethlehem convent to help him develop a release plan for Axis Sally. Sister Mary Assumpta and Sister Mary Magdalen, P.C.J. visited Mildred in prison and offered her a job upon release "doing general work, including coaching."[509] With an offer of employment and the support of individuals whom she trusted in the Church, she reapplied for parole. The convent agreed to provide "room and board plus thirty dollars a month." Mildred would teach music and other subjects to the girls in the convent school, but the offer was contingent on there being no reporters or photographers on the convent grounds when she arrived.

Warden Nina Kinsella was greatly concerned about Mildred's life on parole. In a letter to the Director of the Bureau of Prisons, Kinsella expressed her concerns that unwanted publicity and government harassment would scuttle the release plan:

> Mildred is now sixty years old and as the years go on she will have less and less opportunity to get employment. The plan suggested for her is an excellent one. In addition to being assured of board and room and a small allowance, she can get such pupils and she can keep any income thereby derived. Naturally, the school would not want publicity covering this assignment.

Miss Cottrill, Supervisor of Classification and Parole, has called to my attention that at the time Iva D'Aquino was released, the Immigration authorities placed a detainer against her which they claimed was under an old law which they had the right to apply. At that time, the Immigration Officer asked to review Mildred Sisk's file and indicated that the Immigration authorities intended to place a warrant against her. This would be most unfortunate and would result in some publicity.[510]

On January 12, 1961, the Parole Board approved the release of Axis Sally to the Our Lady of Bethlehem Convent in Columbus, Ohio. Mildred was scheduled to be released on July 10, but Sister Mary Assumpta, who was traveling through the summer months, encouraged her to arrive after Labor Day. Once again, Edna Mae would be called on to aid Mildred and fulfill the promises she made so many years before. The Parole Board determined that "Mildred can go to the home of her sister in Ashtabula, Ohio for the summer months."[511] That summer would prove to be the final episode in the stormy relationship between two strong-willed but very different women.

CHAPTER 12

Penitent

"The great irony of her adult life was that she spent the first thirty years of it seeking publicity in the public eye—and then spent the last forty years trying to avoid it."

—Robert Boyer[512]

JUNE 1961–JULY 1988

On a rainy Monday morning in July 1961, a group of twenty newsmen waited at daybreak to get their first glimpse of Axis Sally. Twelve years earlier, the 48-year-old convicted traitor with rouged lips and arrogant manner had walked into the women's reformatory at Alderson, West Virginia. No photographs had emerged since that day, and the cameramen were eager to get a shot of her. A De Soto carried Edna Mae and her latest husband, Edwin Niemenen, up to the gate. Scheduled for release at 6 a.m., Axis Sally was running late. The newsmen huddled in the fog and rain for more than 25 minutes. Finally, at 6:26 a.m., a guard heard a car coming down the hill.

"Here she comes," he called.

A black sedan with the words "Department of Justice, Bureau of Prisons" emblazoned on its doors pulled up to the far side of the entrance. Every bit the actress, Mildred Gillars gestured excitedly to her driver, Lt. Helen England. For over a minute, the crowd waited for her entrance. Edna Mae emerged from the automobile and hurriedly crossed under the gate. One of the three guards on duty tried to stop them, but let them through when another sentry recognized the family.

234

"It's all right. It's her people," he said.

Impatiently, Edna Mae swung open the car door and Mildred burst out of the car into her arms.

She had aged dramatically in prison. "She did not show her 60 years and it was hard to tell if her hair was blond or gray,"[513] one observer noted, perhaps trying to breathe some life into an image of mystery long faded. Others were not so kind:

> To one reporter, she looked like an aging and forgotten actress who had been rediscovered for a moment and who enjoyed the attention she had been receiving. To another, she looked like the social leader of a small town who had called a press conference to announce winners in the garden club contest, and, after the reporters got there, learned that her husband had absconded with $20,000 of the firm's money and his secretary.
>
> If that was the case, she should have been satisfied. It was painful, but she pulled it off.[514]

Wearing a grandmotherly black hat and shoes, beige suit and dark coat, she hurried past the press. As the family walked toward the car in the drizzle, a reporter asked Mildred if she had anything to say.

"Well, after some 15 years in prison," she responded testily, "what am I supposed to say?[515] I don't feel like making much of a statement this morning."[516]

One reporter wanted to know where she would be working.

"I can't tell you that," she smiled evasively. Noting the tape recorder that one of the radio men carried, she suddenly became engaged, saying, "Oh, I see this is also being recorded."[517]

Interrupting, Edna Mae pointed to her running car and Mildred cut off the interview. She slid into in the center seat as the press shouted questions after her.

"Where are you going?"

"We're going north," Mildred said.

"To Ashtabula ...?"

"Yes. To Ashtabula," she replied. "After 15 years, you don't feel like having much to say."

"Will you talk to us later?"

The car sped off.

Enjoying her first hours of freedom, it took a leisurely six hours for the DeSoto to travel the 110 miles to Charlestown, West Virginia. She savored the moment, telling waiting reporters, "I was drinking lots and lots of coffee. And believe me, if there had been flowers in the bottom of the cup, I'm sure I could have seen them. It's mighty weak."[518]

Asked about her plans for the future, she expected to "rest not more than six or seven weeks at the most," and then leave Ashtabula for her new post in Columbus.

The following day, Mildred spoke to reporters. Dressed conservatively befitting her 60 years, her only jewelry was a handmade brooch and earrings from Alderson's craft room. Holding a dog named Rajah and a duck name Cleo in the bright July sun, she spoke from Edna Mae's yard. Fielding questions, she was unapologetic about her actions during the war.

"When I did the broadcasting, I thought I was doing the right thing. Would I do it again? Certainly, given the same knowledge and the same circumstances ..."[519]

"After all, I was a professional broadcaster in Germany when the U.S. entered the war. It was my job. Besides I was very much in love with a German and hoped to marry him. At the time I felt I could love the United States and still serve the Berlin Broadcasting Corporation."[520]

Yet she admitted that she would not have made the broadcasts if she had known at the beginning of the war what she now knew about the crimes of the Nazi state. Once more, she pointed to the long-forgotten Rome Axis Sally, Rita Louisa Zucca, as the source of so many of the scurrilous legends about her.

"It is a great pity that everything said by any woman on the radio in Europe was attributed to me."[521] She still believed that she was incapable of treason: "I certainly think it is strange that a person who signed an oath of allegiance to Germany could be convicted of treason. It is true no matter what the circumstances under which a person must sign an oath."[522]

Was she bitter?

"I wouldn't say exactly bitter. I'm just not the kind of person to be bitter. If I were, my bitterness at the injustice and perjury I have suffered would have destroyed me by now."

Despite the excitement surrounding her release, her mind was still with the women she met at Alderson: "Instead of being concerned about me, I wish you newspapers would give some attention to the tremendous unused potentialities and talents of some of those women in the prison. Their loyalty is terrific and their sense of honor is something you would be lucky to find in a church."[523]

The following Sunday, Edna Mae arranged for her neighbor, Mary Lou Sespico, to take Mildred to a Catholic Mass at a nearby church. After the service, she joined the Sespico family for dinner. The young woman likened her to "someone's maiden aunt" who was "real straight, very neat ... and well-mannered." At dinner, she carried a small tin around to catch her cigarette ashes—a habit she developed in prison. She remembered Mildred warmly. "I really liked her. I wanted to get to know her better," but time in Ashtabula was running out.[524]

A few weeks before leaving for Columbus, she rang up Sespico and donated some expensive black lace underwear to the Bishop's clothing drive—items she clearly would not need within the confines of a convent.

After a month with the Niemenens, Mildred traveled to Columbus to take up her teaching position at Our Lady of Bethlehem Convent. It would be the final time that Edna Mae would see her sister. After all the years of her sibling standing by her, and all the whispers and ostracism she had endured for being Axis Sally's kin, Mildred never maintained correspondence with Edna Mae and her family.

"That was the last time I saw her, when she went out that door, and that was that," Edna Mae said in 1995.[525]

The Olentangy River Road School of the Sisters of the Poor Child Jesus had a convent school devoted to teaching high school subjects to girls with an interest in entering the Order. Accustomed to prison rules, Mildred quickly adjusted to the disciplined and rigorous lifestyle.

Shortly after beginning her employment in September 1961, she was interviewed by Associated Press reporter Mary McGarey about her conversion to Catholicism, her love of teaching, and her focus on the future. In the simple convent parlor, Mildred spoke somewhat ambivalently about her newfound freedom. Now 60 years of age, she clearly felt that her time behind Alderson's gates and almost twenty years of probation amounted to a life sentence:

> I've served 12 years, a life sentence for many. I'm free, but you're not really free when you have to report to a parole officer regularly until 1979. I've paid my debt to society. [I'm] old and unattractive and no longer news ...

She was opaque about the origins of her conversion to Catholicism; insisting that the reasons were "too personal" to reveal. She referred to the cataclysmic year of 1944 as the beginning of her spiritual rebirth:

> I had thought about [conversion] as early as 1944. I was confirmed in 1960. I might have been raised a Catholic—it was in my family, I just collected my legacy a little late.[526]

Although she acknowledged the support and guidance of Father Thomas Kerrigan, Mildred gave thanks for her salvation to God alone, quoting St. Augustine: "You would not have found me if I had not been seeking you first."[527] Wary of questions that delved too deeply into her past, she was visibly animated and relaxed when discussing her happy days directing the Protestant and Catholic Choirs at Alderson.

"Just the idea of working with people appeals to me, in a convent or wherever," she told McGarey.[528]

Sister Mary Assumpta asked the press to let Mildred teach "without further fanfare or publicity." She explained the convent's decision to accept Axis Sally to the local Catholic press:

> Her background in languages, music and cultural art will be put to good use at the convent.... [Mildred] requested that she be afforded the opportunity to devote the remaining years of her life in the Lord's service. We decided to take Miss Gillars because we felt it was the Christ-like thing to do.[529]

"Who Am I to Talk About Wars?"

Her moral and professional failures had been public ones. She was determined that her successes remain between herself, her friends and God. For several years, Axis Sally faded from public view. Her circle of friends was small, mostly nuns from the convent and occasionally a parent or two of the students entrusted to her care. Her days were filled with teaching, reading and eventually returning to the college education she had abandoned forty years before. She had indeed changed, as her 1965 probation report revealed. Perhaps she had mellowed and grown, perhaps her faith transformed her volatile personality into one dedicated to service and learning.

The Mildred Gillars of 1949 would never have been described as having an "excellent attitude toward authority."[530] She seemed to find in the Catholic Church the same approbation and sense of purpose that she received as *"Midge at the Mike"* decades before. Gradually, her list of friends increased to include a handful of former schoolmates who remembered her from Ohio Wesleyan. One former classmate, however, was hesitant to reacquaint herself with Axis Sally. Dorothy Long explained her reluctance in 1966:

> So far as I know, Mildred is still teaching in the Columbus convent. I have never seen her, I feel that I was never close enough to be a welcome visitor; that she would feel my visit was motivated only by curiosity, and the poor soul has had enough of that sort of thing. I do feel she has been the victim of her own desire for limelight and that possibly she wasn't really intelligent enough to realize what a terrible thing she was doing as Axis Sally—or that the Nazis had flattered her enough that she thoroughly enjoyed her position.... Some people that I know have gone to see her, and say she is quite content ...

In the early 1960s, Mildred brought students from Columbus to Ohio Wesleyan for classical music concerts. In later years, she performed in a local dramatic group that specialized in readings of

Shakespeare. In the way that Charles Newcomb opened her eyes to the dramatic arts and Otto Koischwitz introduced her to German literature and philosophy, Mildred took on the role of mentor—advocating the importance of arts and letters in the lives of the young girls in her care. In her latest and final role, she was respected, needed, valued—even beloved.

In January 1967, a young UPI reporter named Helene Anne Spicer was given an assignment: to find and interview Axis Sally. In a phone interview in 2009, Spicer remarked that it was a common "joke" in the Columbus press corps to assign a cub reporter to track down the reclusive legend of World War II. A Roman Catholic with contacts in the Columbus diocese, Spicer located Axis Sally at the convent school and, to the surprise of her editors, was granted an interview. Knowing only Axis Sally's reputation as a reviled traitor, Spicer found "a sweet, little old lady ... nothing like what I expected." The dignified and convincing woman before her seemed worlds away from the vicious propagandist of legend.

In a sparse living room with only two chairs and a fireplace, Spicer asked Axis Sally's opinion on America's latest foreign war: Vietnam. At a time when the conflict was tearing at the fabric of the nation's body politic, any comment would have scuttled the intensely private life she had built since leaving prison and almost certainly jeopardize her parole.

Before Alderson, Mildred would not have hesitated to voice her opinion. Now, older and wiser as one who had felt the full brunt of the government's ire, she replied, "Who am I to talk about wars? No one would be interested in what I have to say."[531]

She limited her comments to another declaration of her innocence: "There is no doubt in my mind that I received an unfair trial," she said. Her voice trailed off as if she finally recognized the futility of her protests. "It all happened so long ago ..." she mused.[532] Nevertheless, the 66-year-old seemed content with her obscurity:

> Miss Gillars appeared at peace with the world. The tiny lines around her eyes were scars of laughter. She was dressed simply—a black skirt with a three-buttoned over jacket and white

blouse. She wore just a touch of makeup and her grey, upswept hair was kept in place with a comb. She asked that no picture be taken of her.[533]

The school's principal, Sister Mary Assumpta, told Spicer of the positive influence her infamous employee had on her students, remarking "She is definitely a good influence on the girls. She has developed their taste for art and literature."[534]

In her first seven years at the convent, her salary had increased from $30 to $100 per month. Her duties expanded as well. By the late 1960s, Mildred was teaching English, German and French, piano, drama and choral music. On Saturdays, she taught piano at the Cathedral to inner city children. But the convent and the Order were facing challenging times. In 1961, the convent had an average of 30 high school-age girls in attendance, but the reforms of the Second Vatican Council and the loosening morality of American life took its toll on the Order of the Poor Child Jesus. By 1968, the number of high school girls interested in religious life attending the school fell to 11.

That year, Mildred suffered a detached retina and her doctor recommended immediate surgery. As local surgeons could only promise a 66% chance of success, she requested to see a California doctor who reattached retinas through a new method—laser technology. The doctor, profiled in *National Geographic* magazine, claimed a 90% success rate with the technique.

Her finances, precarious as always, got a much needed boost when her probation officer secured her Maine birth certificate and encouraged her to apply for Social Security and Medicare. A visit to the benefits office revealed that she had $450 in retroactive benefits coming—money that would be essential for her trip to the West Coast. In June 1968, she traveled to Palo Alto, California where she underwent successful laser surgery. She recovered in San Francisco, staying with a longtime friend, Sister Mary Clarice. Through that summer, she earned extra money babysitting or tutoring students recommended by the local nuns.[535] In the autumn she returned to Columbus for the new school year but first stopped in Beckley, West Virginia to see her prison chaplain, Father Thomas Kerrigan.

Redemption

Sunday, June 10 1973 was commencement day at Ohio Wesleyan
University. The audience was startled to see a 72-year-old woman with
a deeply lined face and serene smile dressed in cap and gown. When
her name was announced, she grinned broadly as she walked up to
receive her degree at long last. It was an education that had an inter-
regnum of fifty years, broken when a headstrong girl dashed off to
Cleveland to begin what she hoped would be a stellar career as a stage
actress.

That Sunday, most did not recognize the name of the scorned traitor of yesteryear. After the discord of the Vietnam and Watergate eras,
it might not have mattered. University President Tom Wenzlau shook
her hand and smiled. The University did not formally announce her
graduation, but the wire services and the evening newscasts covered
it uncritically. There was no public outcry. Walter Winchell had died
the year before—a shell of the Red-baiting, flag-waving columnist
who had flagellated Axis Sally, Tokyo Rose and countless others on a
weekly basis. Drew Pearson, the columnist who supplied prosecutor
Lamar Caudle with former POWs to testify against Axis Sally,
passed away in 1969. After the graduation ceremony, one editorial
writer wrote charitably of Axis Sally's "redemption": "Hers is a story
of penance, reparation, and now, deserved joy and forgiveness from
others."[536]

Mildred attended classes at several local institutions in order to
complete her degree. One of her teachers at Otterbein College was
Senior Lecturer Robert Boyer, who gradually became aware of his
senior student's checkered past:

> It was a rather slow process. At first, there were just some
> hints that she had been in Berlin when Americans were not in
> Berlin for the most part. That she had served some time in
> what she called the "ladies finishing school," which I found
> later, was Alderson prison for women in West Virginia. Then
> finally, she told me one day she was being given a degree from
> Ohio Wesleyan—it was then that she got a little bit of public-
> ity. I actually saw her on the Walter Cronkite evening news

and was quite surprised, although, as I say, there had been hints.[537]

For the most part, the old woman was unapologetic about her past actions in Germany. In time, Mildred explained to Boyer the factors that led to her decision to remain in Germany:

[Mildred] lived apparently rather an impoverished life. I think it is important to know that at the middle of the war perhaps 1942, 1943, she was making the equivalent of $1,000 a month from foreign broadcasting for her work. She lived in a very elegant apartment and had many, what we would consider luxuries. And so to get out from under what she had started. She was being threatened by the Gestapo, so I never got the idea that she was ideologically a Nazi—a hardened Nazi, if you will.[538]

At the age of 74, she moved out of the convent to an apartment house on Broadmeadows Boulevard near Ohio State University. Mildred tutored language students from nearby Bishop Watterson High School.

Jim Dury was teaching German, American History and French in the 1980s when it came to his attention that a local woman was offering her services as a language tutor. At first, he did not know the true identity of the "nice old lady" providing a service to his students, but eventually a colleague pulled him aside:

A fellow teacher with whom I worked with as coach of the school's inter-scholastic quiz team told me that she had run across Miss Gillars name in a question: "By what better name do we know Mildred Gillars? Axis Sally—needless to say, we were astounded.

The tutoring was a major help to my students—bringing them from D's to A's. She was also a very cultured and intellectual woman. She exposed my students to German music and culture. I remember one student being amazed that she did crosswords in German.[539]

After a number of chats about her tutoring, Dury discreetly asked about her years in Germany and posed what likely was the most uncomfortable question of all:

> Once I uncovered her past, I did on one occasion that I remember ask her how she happened to be in Germany during the war and she responded vaguely about a man she was involved with at the time—I believe a German officer.
>
> I also once obliquely asked how the Germans could not have known what was happening to their Jewish (and other) neighbors and fellow citizens. I remember only a short, and somewhat rueful, "we didn't know" answer.[540]

With no car or telephone at first, she surrounded herself with books and keepsakes, and regularly tended to a small flower garden. Colleen Wiley and her daughter Iris lived in the same apartment building and eventually became friends with Mildred in the 1980s. Neither mother nor daughter knew of their elderly neighbor's notorious reputation until after her death. Iris recalled that Miss Gillars was generous with her time, helping the high school students raise money for school activities through paper drives. Once, Mildred brought the Wiley family a gift—a homemade chocolate cake made with sauerkraut. She told them that the ground sauerkraut kept the cake moist—a baking tip she likely picked up in Germany.[541] Her apartment was "book lined ... crowded with knickknacks and old drawings," one visitor noted, reminding Iris of "a little European flat" full of books and art.[542] Unlike Iva Toguri D'Aquino (Tokyo Rose), who publicly and successfully obtained a Presidential pardon in 1977, Axis Sally never sought one. As she always believed in her innocence, she saw no reason to request clemency or express remorse. Closed to questions, each inquiry was met with the same refrain: "No questions at all."[543] Her refusal to talk was legend in the local media. One of her parole officers said in 1977, "[It] has been a running battle for 15 years. She's never given an interview that I know of. Even to give her side."[544] One Ohio columnist, Mike Harden, said that although Axis Sally refused his repeated interview requests, she did make a book recommendation in 1983: "She suggested that I read a certain book about a woman who shoots a journalist who keeps hounding her."[545]

In 1979, Axis Sally was released from parole—bringing more than thirty years of internment, incarceration and probation to an end. Her friend Robert Boyer recalled that day:

> She received a letter from the State Department stating that her parole was over and that they no longer had any interest in her and so forth. She was rather amused—one of the lines in the letter stated that given the fact that they believed she probably would not repeat her offense, they were releasing her from parole and also from the fine. She was rather amused by that.
>
> She asked a strange question at that point. She said, "Do you think I am a citizen again?" And I said I don't know whether you ever really lost your citizenship. I said why don't you call the State Department or someone who would know that kind of law? She never did as far as I know.[546]

In 1988, Mildred Gillars was diagnosed with metastatic colon cancer. Admitted to Grant Medical Center for inpatient treatment, she eventually demanded to return to her apartment. Her neighbor Colleen Wiley checked on her regularly but she was so troubled by Mildred's weak and frail state that she phoned the doctor. The physician admitted that Mildred was much too ill to be left alone.[547] Shortly after, she took a turn for the worse and returned to the hospital.

At 3 a.m. on June 25, 1988, Mildred Gillars passed away. Her death certificate listed her occupation simply as "Teacher."[548] A friend, James Sauer, announced that there would be no public funeral service for the woman the world knew as Axis Sally. On June 28, a small group of friends attended her burial at St. Joseph's Cemetery. "She was a charity case," the cemetery caretaker recalled.[549] Impoverished most of her life, she remained so at its end. All of her earthly possessions (furniture, clothes, books, etc.) amounted to an estate worth only $3,194.16. All money from the estate was used to pay for her eight doctors, rent and hospital care.[550]

To this day, no head or footstone marks her grave. Even in death, the woman who drank from fame's bitterest cup demanded privacy.

* * *

A week after Mildred's death, her obituary appeared in *The New York Times*, the *Washington Post*, and on the wire services. After the turmoil of the Vietnam War, Jane Fonda's 1972 propaganda broadcasts from Hanoi, and the student movement's overt support of the Viet Cong as American forces fought, the crime and punishment meted out to Axis Sally seemed like a quaint relic of a bygone national morality. The *Times* chose to focus on the style of the woman rather than the substance of her crimes:

> Her 1949 trial attracted enormous public attention as much for the soap opera quality of Miss Gillars' life as for her crime. At her trial, Miss Gillars fascinated the public and the press with her flamboyance and cool self-possession. She cut a theatrical figure in tight fitting black dress, long silver hair and a deep tan. She had scarlet lips and nails.... She sent a frisson through the trial when she described her obsessive love with Mr. Koischwitz, who was married.[551]

The "newspaper of record" repeated the false assertion that Mildred moved to Berlin "to marry a German citizen," who it misidentified as Otto Koischwitz, "a former professor at Hunter College in New York."[552]

Back in Ohio, Colleen and Iris Wiley were shocked to learn that their elderly neighbor was one of the most infamous women of World War II. Interviewed by the *Columbus Dispatch* shortly after Mildred's death, Mrs. Wiley was effusive about her friend. "She was brilliant. She spoke and taught French and German. She was a great reader. She loved to go to the Ohio Theatre and see the old movies. She was interested in about everything. We thought the world of her."[553]

In Ashtabula, another woman who thought the world of Mildred Gillars opened the local newspaper to discover that her half-sister had died. Edna Mae had neither seen nor heard from Mildred since 1961.

In 1995, Edna Mae gave an interview to Carl Feather of the Ashtabula *Star-Beacon*. The still mentally agile former dance teacher had not come to terms with the passing of her sister: "It doesn't seem possible that she could be dead," she told Feather. One final time, the elderly woman came to Mildred's defense and tried to explain why the government, the judge, the jury and the press treated her with so much malice compared to other "radio traitors" of the day: "I think perhaps it could have been the hotsy-totsy air she had. She just thought she was a perfect person."[554]

"The story should be told ..."

Within weeks, former students and friends of Axis Sally began to share their memories and reveal what they were told about her days in Hitler's Germany. Most friends and acquaintances did not pry into her past, but over the years, a story emerged that was part fact, part fiction, and tailor-made for American consumption. A letter to the editors of the *Columbus Dispatch* from Mary M. Badders of Lawrence, Ohio shed some light on the tale she told. Starkly different from a trial testimony that few were likely to research and even more unlikely to find, the story tied up the loose, embarrassing ends of her life; and made her past actions and beliefs somewhat palatable to those who discovered or knew about her past. Collaborationists in Vichy France, the Nazi conquered lands of Eastern Europe, and German war criminals constructed such exculpatory stories to argue their innocence or ignorance, insist on their doubts and even opposition to Hitlerism, in an attempt to make each day "livable" in a world haunted by the deaths of six million Jews and countless dead and wounded. Mrs. Badders' letter gives a summary of Axis Sally's story:

> Recently, Mildred Gillars, aka Axis Sally, died. As one who knew her, I would like to share a brief portion of her story.
> When World War II broke out in Europe, Gillars had been living in Europe for a number of years and was engaged to be married to an officer in the German army. This man opposed Adolf Hitler and was imprisoned. Gillars was also arrested and instructed that unless she cooperated with the Nazis, her

fiancé would be shot. Unknown to her, he had already been killed.

Thinking she was buying his life, she did as she was told. I am not trying to justify what she did. It was terribly wrong. But it does point out, though, that without absolutes of right and wrong firmly established in our minds, we listen to our hearts, we practice situational ethics and we make horrible mistakes.

The beautiful part of this story, however, is that during the same time in Germany, there was an order of Catholic nuns who were also persecuted by the Nazis. Some of the nuns escaped to France. From there, they traveled to England and later to the United States. When Gillars was in prison, these same nuns, who should have hated anyone associated with the Nazis, faithfully visited her and prayed for her.

When she was released from prison, they gave her a job at their convent school (I was a student at that school). Through their efforts, she was converted to Christ because they loved their Lord enough to forgive, to pray for an enemy, and to do good to those who persecuted them.

I do not justify Gillars' actions, but I do feel the story should be told.[555]

Robert Boyer spent many hours with Mildred in the last years of her life. He recalled one instance where the subject of the extermination of Europe's Jews came up. It was met with an uncharacteristic and uncomfortable defensiveness:

I can only remember one occasion in which we were riding in the car and the radio was on and there must have been something about the Holocaust or the Nazi period on and she turned to me and rather emphatically said, "You know, we didn't know about all of that," meaning apparently the destruction of the Jews and the extermination camps and so forth. And I was rather taken aback by it, and she went on to say, "When the news is controlled you don't know what's really going on." Now I don't particularly buy that argument—

but that's the only time I heard her give a defense for what she had done.

It's the excuse that I have heard from many, many Germans who lived through that period in Germany and that is they claim not to have known it is difficult to understand how they could not know just from the evidence of their eyes, when all the Jews disappear from your town you must make certain conclusions, but I'm sure there was a certain amount of intentional blindness. [556]

Nevertheless, Robert Boyer explained that his friend displayed a certain pride in surviving the many misfortunes of her life and took comfort in friends and faith:

She lived a simple life, but a good life. She had many friends, I think, all of whom knew her situation and I think she was quite proud of the fact that she had come through it all—and was not broken.[557]

Epilogue

On a grassy hillside in Lockbourne, Ohio is the unmarked grave of one of the most reviled names in American history. Surrounded by veterans of that struggle, she maintains her privacy in death. Not even a simple number marks the lot where she lies. Only a gusting wind breaks the silence of that common ground where a statue of the Holy Family keeps watch over the victors and the vanquished. In Ohio, Mildred Gillars came full circle—back to the land where her rootless childhood finally settled into a few happy, hopeful years. As a young lady, her thirst for notoriety and the stage set her on a path that led to desperation and poverty.

In Berlin, she finally found rewarding employment—first, as a film critic and then as a radio announcer for the Nazi state. Willfully blind to the suffering of Berlin's Jews and the approaching clouds of war, she chose to remain in Germany. When she experienced success unlike anything she had ever known in America, that good fortune reinforced her belief in the wisdom of her decision to stay. When the war claimed the life of her German fiancé, she descended into an adulterous affair with her radio manager—a naturalized American indicted for treason. His death in 1944 snuffed out her last chance to become a German citizen by marriage. At the war's end, she was unmarried, impoverished, alone and without a country.

With most of her adult life spent either under Nazi rule, in Allied prison camps or US jails, her insatiable desire for fame was supplanted by the desire to live out her life in peaceful obscurity. Always seeking to avoid the inevitable, unanswerable questions about her personal racial and political beliefs, Mildred Gillars kept her views to herself. Axis Sally was on the run long after leaving prison. Nevertheless, close friends like Robert Boyer, as well as acquaintances such as Jim Dury, eventually posed the most difficult question: How could she and her German friends and colleagues not have known what was happening to the Jews? Thousands of Berlin's men, women and children were rounded up and transported to the East during the eleven years she lived there. Her paramour, a Foreign Office official welcomed as Ribbentrop's guest to the *Wolfsschanze*, had to be aware of the rumors that came back from Poland and the Reich's other occupied territories. It was *that* question, always answered with an insistent and final "we just didn't know," that would always keep Mildred Gillars at an uncomfortable distance from her fellow Americans.

She left America for Europe in 1934 when isolationism was still in vogue, and repeated those beliefs in her broadcasts as an employee of Berlin Radio. By the late 1930s, isolationist policy was challenged by FDR's desire to take action against the Fascist dictatorships; but Mildred had been away too long to sense the changing temper of the times in the United States. Unaware of the signal change in American public opinion after Hitler's broken agreements, and disinterested in politics, she became the mouthpiece for the beliefs of a man she admired, respected and loved. When the worm turned on December 7, 1941, there was no going back.

Axis Sally believed that she could love America and still do her job for Reichsradio. It was that belief that went to the question of intent, and played a central role in the jury's decision to convict her on only one count: participation in *Vision of Invasion*. The only charge that specifically accused her of directly subverting the war aims of the United States, it was at the same time the work of an actress who neither wrote nor edited the material. The rest of the Justice Department's charges—the interviews with prisoners of war, the medical reports on wounded soldiers, *et al.*—could be construed as the actions of a woman behind enemy lines doing what she could do to help imprisoned American servicemen. It was *Vision of Invasion*—an overacted, overwrought, barely audible radio play—that tipped the scales toward

treason. Clearly, its only aim was to sow doubt and despair among soldiers slated to fight and die on the beaches of France.

Mildred's inability to admit her own errors of judgment, her stubborn insistence on remaining in the limelight, and her enthusiastic parroting of the Nazi propaganda line long after Germany's defeat, were
all factors that led to her tragic end. Long after it was clear that the
Nazi experiment led only to war and starvation, Mildred still could
enthusiastically lecture newsmen on the "correctness" of Hitler's ideas
regarding Communism, and tell her CIC interrogators that the war for
her was against England and the International Jewry ("I just couldn't
get the Jews out of my mind...", she claimed in one memorable statement). She accepted the Nazi worldview, believed her own propaganda, and paid a heavy price for that delusion.

Suicide Note to the
Camden Evening Courier

Following is the supposed suicide note that "Barbara Elliott" (a.k.a. Mildred Gillars) sent to the *Evening Courier* in Camden, NJ. Gillars' performance as a love-struck, abandoned mother was the first to gain her notoriety, but by no means the last.

To Whom It May Concern,

It is more than humanly possible to continue any longer this bitter agony of bringing into this poor, deluded world another unwelcome child. The few who may give my sorry act any thought at all will probably think only in a conventional way, saying, 'What a weak thing she must have been.' Who will ever have the perception to realize that I am taking this step because I have an intelligence and soul that are sensitized to the nth degree?

What have all our great reformers and philosophers ever done to bring serene harmony to the universe? Nothing. We cringe with horror when we contemplate ruthless destruction – wars and murders. We wish stupidly for human peace but make no effort to achieve it. If it were actually possible to estimate the percentage of really welcome children, what would it be? Good God – probably not more than one percent. And yet I am supposed to bring this poor soul into what Milton called 'a vale of woe.'

Ah, my dear, dear Charles, if you ever hear of my fate – remember that there was nothing else left for me. I know so bitterly the awful loneliness of a child's life without parental love. I have visualized completely the arrival of this baby of ours. I have seen myself watching through the years. I know the agony I would suffer each time I would catch that wistful gleam in his eye when he saw another child happy in his father's love.

It would be a constant misery to see that look in his eyes. All the dreams I have ever had would come back to my heart and stay there like ghosts. I would remember the plans I had cherished of a mate, such as I thought you would be – of dear, delicate souls that I would create and then understand. Create them because I wanted them – because they were welcome.

Tonight in the dining room they played Schubert's famous Serenade and I remembered the times when I had played it for you. My heart was so heavy. You know, my dear one that the only creed I have is to fill life completely with beauty – never to do an unlovely thing – that is the only sin in life. If only people could see that. Isn't it strange that life is full of so many ugly impulses for most people?

My darling – life could only hold for me now, an aching, dull bewilderment. You were my absolute complement. I should never get over it, and it would hang like a shadow over my child.

I am leaving, dear soul, on an adventure far greater than your days in the heart of the Orient. I wish I could make a plea to the poor, unseeing people of this world to give and receive only loveliness. The ultimate end comes so swiftly. I want everyone to try to understand my last human act. Perhaps I am the only person in the world's history to have died for beauty in its most comprehensive meaning.

It is the greatest maternal tenderness I can bestow upon my dear child that I end my life with his that he may not be numbered among the host of unwelcome children.

Barbara Elliott

(*Source:* The Evening Courier, *Camden NJ, October 19, 1928, p. 28*)

APPENDIX II

Selected Transcripts of Axis Sally Broadcasts

MIDGE AT THE MIKE
May 1943

This is Berlin calling. Berlin calling the American mothers, wives and sweethearts. And I'd just like to say, girls, that when Berlin calls it pays to listen. When Berlin calls it pays to listen in because there is an American girl sitting at the microphone every Tuesday evening at the same time with a few words of truth to her countrywomen back home. Girls, you all know, of course, by now that it's a very serious situation and there must be some reason for my being here in Berlin, some reason why I'm not sitting at home with you at the little sewing bees knitting socks for our men in French North Africa.

Yes, girls, there is a reason and it is this: it's because I am not on the side of Roosevelt and his Jewish friends and his British friends; because I've been brought up to be a 100 per cent American girl: conscious of everything American, conscious of her friends, conscious of her enemies. And the enemies are precisely those people who are fighting against Germany today and in case you don't know it, indirectly against America too, because a defeat for Germany would mean a defeat for America. Believe me, it would be the very beginning of the end of America and all of her civilization and that's why girls, I'm staying over here and having these little heart-to-heart talks with you once a week. I know they're awfully short and there's not much one can say, but at least I'm so convinced that it's the truth and I'm sure the truth will win. And besides that, you know I'm in constant touch with your men over here interned in

Germany as prisoners of war and I'm sure you'll be very happy to get some news of them from time to time. And I'll do my best to transmit that to you just as often as I can.

And now girls, just last week in speaking to one American boy, he told us then about the films which he had seen in America - films which dealt with the barbarism of Germany, and of the treatment which she deals out to American prisoners and all of that sort of thing. He said he realizes today that that's only Jewish propaganda, that whereas he was told at home, before donning the American uniform, that he would be beaten and knocked around by the Germans if he ever got into a prisoner of war camp. That has not been the case. He's never been beaten. He's only had the most ideal treatment, and even said 'I can only say to you that I'm happy here in this German prisoner-of-war camp' and receives just the same treatment that the Germans also receive, and said, 'well, that was just Jewish propaganda. I realize it now. I did not realize it when I was at home, but I'd just like to say that today I have my own opinion.' Well, girls, and one day you're going to have your own opinion too. The only thing I'm afraid of is that perhaps it will be too late. And that's why I'm just going to put all the energy I can into these few moments I have with you each week and try to get you to see the light of day and to let you realize that you're on the wrong side of the fence."

Gee, girls, isn't it a darn shame; all the sweet old American summer atmosphere which the boys are missing now. Just imagine sitting out on the old back porch in a sweet old rocking chair listening to the birds at twilight. Instead of that, the boys are over there in the hot, sunny desert longing for home and for what? Fighting for our friends? Well, well, well, since when are the British our friends? Now, girls, come on, be honest. As one American to another, do you love the British? Why, of course the answer is 'no'. Do the British love us? Well, I should say not! But we are fighting for them. We are shedding our good young blood for this 'kike' war, for this British war. Oh, girls, why don't you wake up? I mean, after all, the women can do something, can't they? Have you tried to realize where the situation's leading us to? Because it is the downfall of civilization if it goes on like that. After all, let God save the King. If he's worthy of it, I'm sure God can. At least there's no reason for we Americans to get mixed up in British messes.

Well, girls, you can put American uniforms on our boys; you can put a rifle in their hands; you can send them across with orders to destroy Germany; to bombard the women and children; to fight side by side with the British soldiers and, as the old homily adage goes, 'You can bring a horse to water but you can't make it drink.' And you can force the American soldiers to fight side by side with the British soldiers, but you can never bring understanding between the Americans and the British. Thank God, and I hope it never will happen. But I don't have to hope because it never will. But the basis for a healthy, sane friendship and understanding always has been and always will be there between Germany and America, and that's the thing I'm going to fight for. And I say, damn Roosevelt, damn Churchill and damn all of their Jews who have made this war possible. And I as an American girl will stay over here on this side of the fence, on Germany's side because it is the right side, as I've told you many, many times before."

(Source: Appellate Brief, United States v. Mildred E. Gillars (Sisk), December 1949, US Court of Appeals for the District of Columbia, Washington DC: National Archives)

* * *

HOME SWEET HOME
June 24, 1943

(Mildred Gillars as MIDGE, *Frederick W. Kaltenbach as* FRED, *Max Otto Koischwitz as* FRITZ)

MIDGE: I never let myself get roped into Mr. Churchill and Mr. Roosevelt's war business. We Americans don't have to bother about it. Well, folks, because life is really so sad and I'd like to cheer you up a little bit, because I'm pretty sure you're down in the dumps over there. Well, we're going to have a half and hour of nonsense, just as silly as can be, because the sillier the better. Don't you think so, kids...?

FRED: Well, I see you here at the microphone.

FRITZ: And listen to you.

FRED: It's really touching the way you entertain those boys in Africa

MIDGE: Ah, sweet of you, Fred.

FRED: Well, there's so much feeling in what you say, and in how you say it. Sometimes it makes a man's heart...

MIDGE: Yes, I know and I feel it myself. I'm sure the boys in Africa would like to express their appreciation if there only was a way to show it to you.

FRITZ: Yes, how those boys would like to touch you?

MIDGE: I beg your pardon.

FRITZ: I mean, just as you're touching them.

MIDGE: Oh, that's just fine.

FRITZ: You see, they can hear you, but you can't hear them, and yet you've got so many admirers among them.

MIDGE: Really, how do you know?

FRITZ: I happen to know, because well, you know, I wouldn't be surprised if some of the boys have actually fallen in love with you...I mean with your voice. As I was just saying, I've proof of it right here in my pocket. One of the boys actually managed to get a kind of fan letter from Africa to Berlin for you.

MIDGE: No, Fritz.

FRITZ: And mailed from Africa, just imagine from the A.E.F.... It reached its destination finally. You see, the true admirer, the lover, always finds ways and means to get a letter to the girls in wartime through all the offices of military censors

MIDGE: Let me see the letter.

FRITZ: Of course. Now don't get impassionate. I mean impatient.

MIDGE: Well, now, listen Fritz, the letter was meant for me.

FRITZ: Well, there weren't any secrets in it. You see, he couldn't write any secrets in letters that have to pass now in wartime.

MIDGE: Well, I'm so excited.

FRITZ: A sort of open letter. This admirer of yours who wrote it sent the letter to an American newspaper, see. And the editor of that paper printed it. And then the newspaper was sent to Portugal by clipper. And someone in Lisbon picked it up and forwarded it to this station. That's the way I got hold of it....I told you there wasn't any secret in it. But wait till you hear it.

FRED: You couldn't read it right now, it's much too long.

MIDGE: Oh, do tell me what it says, I'm very curious.

FRITZ: No, no, well, it says the boys like your voice.

MIDGE: How sweet of them.

FRITZ: It's sounds to them like the girl next door, just like back home in the States. And it makes them feel kind of homesick.

MIDGE: Oh, gee, the poor kids.

FRITZ: But they enjoy it so much. And they'd like to know your name.

MIDGE: Oh, I see. What difference would that make? You know, Shakespeare once said: 'A rose by any other name would smell just as sweet', remember? I'm not calling myself a rose...

FRED: But if the boys were able to see you. If they could see you, I know you'd be the biggest success on the air.

MIDGE: Well, thanks for the compliment, Fred.

FRED: I don't want anything. I know it's a fact.

FRITZ: Yes, our Midge at the mike is the most charming girl that ever sat to a microphone.

FRED: Yes, I know. Would you like to know what she looks like?

FRITZ: Too charming for words.

MIDGE: Oh, now, Fritz, really I'm getting embarrassed.

FRITZ: We're telling the truth. Now listen, boys. I'll give you a description of what my eyes see in front of me, right here - a word picture of your announcer. Full of good looks, if that's possible – you see with your ears. Charm, prettiness, attractiveness: Midge at the mike. I told you boys. Midge at the mike presents a sort of charm. And the figure: very slender, in fact.

MIDGE: Now, Fritz, listen. You know you asked my permission to say something over the mike tonight, but if you're going to talk about me all the time.

FRITZ: But I really do think the boys ought to know something about you. Now, listen boys, I'll be perfectly objective. I'll give you a description of your girl in our service, a description that sounds like a passport: Color of hair, color of eyes, size, weight, place of birth.

MIDGE: And no birthmark? Well, I think we'd better let those go.

FRED: What else is on a passport?

MIDGE: Well, something about age. You'd leave that out, wouldn't you?

FRITZ: Well, with that schoolgirl complexion you couldn't conceal the recent date of your birth anyway.

FRED: With the compliments of Palmolive soap.

MIDGE: No, I'm not keeping anything back on you, Fritz. Well, you know, I think you've been drinking whiskey, or gin or something.

FRITZ: Honest, Midge, I haven't been drinking for ages. There just isn't enough to drink now to get inspiration. You know that as well as I. Inspiration comes from your presence.

MIDGE: Oh, drink to me only with thine eyes!

* * *

MIDGE AT THE MIKE
July 27, 1943

"Good evening, women of America. This is Midge speaking. As you know, as time goes on, I think of you more and more. I can't seem to get you out of my head, you women in America, waiting for the one you love, waiting and weeping in the secrecy of your own room, thinking of the husband, son or brother who is being sacrificed by Franklin D. Roosevelt – perishing on the fringes of Europe.

Perishing, losing their lives. At best, coming back home crippled – useless for the rest of their lives. For whom? - For Franklin D. Roosevelt and Churchill and their Jewish cohorts.

First of all, I'd like to take the British angle of the subject tonight. I've got a very nice, interesting article here by Mrs. Franklin D. Roosevelt herself. This appeared in the American Collier's magazine, February 27, 1943. I'll even give you the page. Its page 18 – you can check on it yourself. And it says as follows – this is by Mrs. Franklin D. Roosevelt. I don't like her myself, girls. She's no friend of mine for allowing your husbands, fathers, sons and brothers to perish on the fringes of Europe for Mr. Roosevelt. So I suppose you have a certain amount of sympathy for Eleanor. Well, this is what she said on the 27th of February, 1943 on page 18 of Collier's Magazine.

'While we have a few people whose conditions tie them closely to Britain, we have a considerable number who are critical of the British people and who find their mannerism and the way they talk and act not only arrogant but highly objectionable.'

I repeat that: 'not only arrogant but highly objectionable'.... Who are these people? All of them of America who help these people – your sons, fathers, brothers and husbands are perishing on the fringes of Europe. And yet, the British are not only arrogant but highly objectionable, according to Eleanor Roosevelt. It's interesting, isn't it? Oh, I find it highly interesting, I must say....

'The British government is inferior and the British are wily and see only the good of the Empire. The British have conquered many countries and while it is acknowledged that they colonize very well, it is also accepted that the rule has meant the exploitation of the conquered areas rather than development for the sake of the conquered people. This gives us the opportunity to point with pride to the attractive achievements of the United States in their colonial possessions. Consequently, the average American has developed a dislike for Britain.'

Well, that was said to you by Mrs. Franklin D. Roosevelt. If I had such a dislike for a country certainly I wouldn't sacrifice those I love most of all for their interest. Would you, girls? I'm sure you wouldn't if you thought it over before. But it all came overnight and somehow you trusted Franklin D. Roosevelt when he said to you that no American boy will be sacrificed on foreign battlefields. And it all then came so suddenly before you knew what was happening. I'm sure that's the way it was.

Well, women in America, thousands and thousands of your men now going from French North Africa via Sicily to Europe are on their last roundup. *(Music: The Last Roundup)*

Do you know, women of America, since I'm over here in Europe I think I've got a better perspective than you have. I come in touch with your men and also with some great German officers. It is very interesting. I'm sure you would like to hear this little story – a few evenings ago, I was at a party where there was a German war correspondent and he told me about a combat experience over in French South Africa where your men and the Germans were engaged in a fierce battle. Afterwards, he came to a sort of field hospital. It was rather makeshift, of course, and lying in this field hospital there was an American officer and he decided he'd like to have a little chat with him and went up to the bed and sat down and they conversed for a little while. Then, the American officer opened up his heart, and told him just how he felt when he got over to French North Africa and first entered into this fierce combat. He'd been told, of course, when leaving America that he'd find no resistance on the part of the German soldiers, that the Germans were tired – tired of battle – that they'd give no resistance. It would be a walk away for the American soldier, that's what he said.

They gave all they had and still couldn't drive the Germans back and then (unintelligible) most of all in the world was killed in action. His pal standing next to him and saw him depart from this life and he said 'In that moment, I hated the Germans more than I had ever hated them in all my life.' They'd taken the life of five pals, and he went on and all the intensity and fierceness he had in his being and then he was wounded. He became unconscious. It was much later that he regained consciousness and found himself, as I said, in this makeshift field hospital. And the quote sentence which made an impression upon his dazed was the following (in German, but he could understand German, having been in Germany himself sometime before the war – if I'm not mistaken during the Olympic Games. And he heard this German boy say to the doctor 'No, take care of him first. He needs it much more than I.' - a thought of what a German soldier said to the doctor in charge: 'Take care of the American soldier; he's wounded worse than I am." Then, the German doctor came over then to the cot of the American officer and said to him, 'Well, old fellow, let's see what we can do for you.' And at that moment, he heard his own language spoken to him by a man who showed sympathy for him. All of a sudden, he said to himself, 'Why, why, why is Germany and America against each other.'

Well women, I think I have to leave you with that. I'm sorry the time is so short. Why? I'll tell you – for the Jews. The Jews are in this war – have got us into this war – for an ideal, not for the love of humanity, but for money. They had no feeble concern for America and no feeling for the sons of the Whippoorwill, for the beautiful maple trees in summer – all of these things which are America. No, the Jews are sending our men over to Europe to fight so that their money bags will get filled. Well women, I'm sorry I haven't got time for you, but I hope this little story by an American officer to the German officer will be an eye opener for you.

* * *

HOME SWEET HOME
September 19, 1943

While you are over in French North Africa fighting for Franklin D. Roosevelt and all his Jewish cohorts, I do hope that way back in your hometown nobody will be making eyes at honey.

* * *

MIDGE AT THE MIKE
October 5, 1943

"You know, after all, Franklin D. Roosevelt promised you that none of your boys would be sacrificed on foreign battlefields, didn't he? Well, your president did not keep his word. And I remember at the beginning of the war, how the upper circles, we might say, in England and America just laughed to scorn the idea that Germany, for example, at the beginning of the war, got ration cards. Sometimes we remember that, at the very beginning, everyone got his usual quantities of soap, and butter and eggs and sugar and cream and so on and so on. Everything was rationed beautifully, and England and American threw up their arms and laughed and said: 'Well, that's the downfall of Germany already.'

Quite the contrary, you see now in Germany, we're getting extra butter rations. You probably heard the speech, last week, in which the harvest was discussed – such a marvellous wheat harvest – and so much food. We're going to have plenty of butter and plenty of bread and even more meat.

Well, you see, Germany has rationed the food right from the very beginning, and so has guaranteed a better food situation for all of the Germans and all of the foreigners who are now in Germany for the duration of the war. It's not going to be a repetition of the state of affairs that the German people had to endure from 1914 to 1918. I think in the last year of the last war, it was pretty sad. I've heard that from many sources.

My dear listeners in America, that's not happening in this war. And I've even heard that in America, you're having some difficulty now with your rationing. You've got your ration books already; well, you're getting them rather late. In the meantime, all of the Jews they have confiscated the lovely things which you have in time over in America, your Heinz 57 Varieties and such things. So between the Black Market and the (*unintelligible*), you have a much worse time than the people in Germany.

Mark my words! I'm living here; I have been living here ever since before the war and I know how beautifully everything is regulated; as if you need a new pair of shoes, you get a new pair of shoes and you don't have to swindle about it or tell any silly stories, you simply get anything that you need, but everything is honest and everything is under control and checked on.

This you have not yet had in America and I doubt that you'll ever be able to do it, with the flair for organization which the Germans always have had and always will have. Be careful, Gentile women in America, that the Jews don't hoard all the things now, so that in a year or two, you really will be feeling the pangs of hunger. I told you before it's my firm conviction that, in reality, this is no war between Germany and America, in that sense of the word, but a war between the Jews and the Gentiles."

(Source: Transcript of Shortwave Broadcast "Comment", October 5, 1943, FBI HQ Axis Sally files. College Park MD: NARA.)

* * *

HOME SWEET HOME
October 14, 1943

"Don't forget kids, that Midge is just ticked to death to be at the microphone every night with her gang over in French North Africa. I'd just like to know if you could count on the fingers of one hand the Jewish boys who are fighting along with you. I doubt it very much. Well, think it over, gang, and don't forget how many times I have pointed out it's a Jewish war with good honest-to-God American Gentile blood being shed for it. Do you want to be on that side of the fence? Well, I don't kids. Do think it over, will you?"

(Source: Transcript of Shortwave Broadcast "Home Sweet Home," October 14, 1943, FBI HQ Axis Sally files. College Park MD: NARA.)

* * *

HOME SWEET HOME
November 26, 1943

"Well, boys, I guess all of you have felt the same about some girl. Well, you've parted now, and you may dislike my repeating this to you, but it's the truth, especially if you boys get all mutilated and do not return in one piece. I think then you'll have a pretty tough time with your girl. Any girl likes to have her man in one piece, so I think in any case, you've got a pretty hard future ahead of you."

(Source: Berlin Calling by John Carver Edwards. New York: Praeger, 1991, p. 91)

* * *

MEDICAL REPORTS
February 26, 1944

"And now folks, please standby for some medical reports giving you some information as to the present condition of wounded American fliers, shot down over Germany or German-occupied territory. I regret very much to have to inform two families in America at the beginning of this broadcast that I have two death messages. I regret also that I was unable to broadcast them sooner. In both cases, there was no home address given. The first concerns Sergeant Gene H. Munson, M-U-N-S-O-N. I have no service number, no personal details about Sgt. Munson whatever, and I can only beg all of my American listeners to be good enough to see what they can do about getting this word... to the nearest of kin of Mr. Gene H. Munson, M-U-N-S-O-N. He had received injuries—had been shot as a matter of fact in the left knee and the right lower leg. He was admitted to hospital on New Year's Eve, the 31st of December 1943, and died on the 2nd of January 1944, as a result of a malignant embolie.

And now, my second death message concerns Pilot George E. Jones. I fortunately have his service number – that may help somewhat in identifying him – it is 13022168T43. Mr. Jones was brought to hospital on the 26th of November 1943. His left upper leg had been completely crushed; he had received severe injuries to the right leg and his left hand was also totally crushed. He died on the 27th of November, 1943 and this report was made out by the doctors and went through on the 28th of November. Of course, you know that....ah....among flyers the pilot is the last one to bail out and so, of course, naturally the machine can be in....a terrible state by the time he gets his parachute on and is ready to make what in this case was a fatal jump. I'm sorry, very sorry that I haven't the address of his parents and I do hope that they'll get the news soon, although perhaps it's better for them if the news is somewhat delayed.

Well folks, that's what comes of this war of course....they're coming in by the hundreds, these American boys, who day after day are flying over Germany in their terror raids trying to extinguish a whole race, killing ruthlessly helpless women and children. I ask you American women if you brought your boys up to be murderers? - Have you? - Because that's what they are becoming. And, of course, if I have these death messages for you that's....a quite necessary. I mean in general, I get only those reports which concern boys who are lying in hospital at the moment but sometimes some of these messages creep in and then, of course, I read them to you.

Well, I must continue with this broadcast now, and get in touch with Middletown, New York. Calling Mrs. A.N. Kernochan, her name is spelled K-E-R-N-O-C-H-A-N, Rural Delivery #3, in Middletown NY. I have some word for her about her son, John D. Kernochan whose rank is that of Second Lieutenant. He was born on the 19th of September 1921, in Saranac Lake, New York. His service number is 0464657. Mrs. Kernochan, your son had a fracture of the right ankle and his left ankles were sprained. Well, you see, he was very lucky, as a matter of fact, most of these boys have some kind of injuries to their legs you see because, of course, bailing out and making a parachute landing is a very strenuous affair and....in most cases, they injure their legs, when touching the *(unintelligible).*

I should now like to get in touch with Milwaukee, in Wisconsin. Milwaukee, Wisconsin. I have word concerning Louis C. Koch, spelled K-O-C-H. He was born also in Milwaukee, Wisconsin, where his folks seem to be living today at 1327 W. Harrison Avenue, Harrison, H-A-R-R-I-S-O-N, and his date of birth was 29th of April, 1923. Now, I have two reports here concerning his condition. The first, from the 19th of December, states that he had a crushing fracture of the right arm, which was so bad that the doctors had to amputate part of the arm. His condition was unchanged at that moment, and a month later on the 29th...of December the doctors stated the wound was healing well and that the patient was doing quite nicely.

Well folks, that's the end of this little broadcast I'm afraid and tune in every night with the exception of Sunday. This is Midge signing off and wishing you all good night."

(Source: Written Transcription of Federal Communications Commission Memovox Recording #07684, Recorded at Silver Hill, Maryland, between the hours of 23:00 o'clock E.W.T., and 00:00 o'clock E.W.T. on February 26, 1944. Washington DC: John Bartlow Martin Papers, Library of Congress Manuscript Division)

* * *

MEDICAL REPORTS
1944

"Here is word now for Johnsonburg, Pennsylvania. Johnsonburg…The report is about Lieutenant William H. Kupole or Lupole, L-U-P-O-L-E; I believe it is, born on the 14th of February 1922 in Johnsburg, Pennsylvania. Well, that was a nice little Valentine for his mother at that time. And how little did she ever dream that she'd be asked to sacrifice him for Roosevelt and his Jewish cohorts. Well, he's going to remember the American Government for the rest of his life, for his right leg had to be amputated below the knee, and the ankle bone in his left leg was broken. The left leg already has been placed in a walking cast and the patient is doing exercises with an artificial limb fitted to the right leg. Now, his mother lives at 235 West Center Street in Johns…. Johnsonburg, Pennsylvania. Well, Mrs. Lupole, you've seen nothing of this war. You only read Jewish propaganda in your newspaper. But if you've been listening to this broadcast then you know that for many weeks I went from war hospital to war hospital, from one prisoner of war camp to another prison-of-war camp in France and I saw your boys, saw the pitiful state of untold thousands of them. Ah yes…only that is to say thousands, I talk of.

There are hundreds and hundreds of thousands of them, scattered all over Europe, asked to sacrifice their youth, asked to sacrifice their future, because when they get back they will be in no state to take up a job of any consequence. And you people are so short-sighted. You know so little about politics, about history, about what is going on in Europe, about the great role which Germany is playing in the future of the Western Continent. Well, if you folks want to fight to aid and abet, the decline of the West… well, you are certainly taking the right action. Germany has vision. Germany has culture. Germany has supplied all of Europe, to say nothing of America and other western countries with culture. I ask you Americans, 'What have you done for posterity? Can you answer me? Here are the three things for which you people are known all over the world: money, jazz and Hollywood. Compare your three contributions with the contributions of Germany to the world throughout the ages…And so you want to sacrifice your sons to try to destroy that great country, Germany. Folks, it's a responsibility which you should have never taken on your shoulders. It's the blackest page in the world's history. America should hang her head in shame. Think it over America, will you? This is Midge signing off, so goodnight everybody..."

(Source: Appellate Brief, United States v. Mildred E. Gillars (Sisk), December 1949, US Court of Appeals for the District of Columbia, Washington DC: National Archives)

*   *   *

MEDICAL REPORTS
1944

"The first town on my list tonight is Greenville, Alabama. I have word for Mr. H.E. Jernigan Sr. about his son, Second Lieutenant Henry E. Jernigan, J-E-R-N-I-G-A-N, who was born on the 24th of June 1922. His service number I should like to give you, for assistance of identification, 0710286T43-44. Now, Mr. Jernigan, your son Henry got his left leg broken above the knee. He also is suffering from flesh wounds on the left leg above the knee and has also had a general collapse and considerable loss of blood. The doctor states that hospital treatment will be necessary for a period of somewhere around 3 or 4 months. So it seems that the case is rather serious because it seldom happens that one has to stay so long in hospital.

Well, after all you American parents wanted it, didn't you? And so day after day your boys have to pile through showers of flak....thousands and thousands of feet up in the air....sometimes the ship explodes...they're burned alive in the airplane....or they bail out....and only break their legs and arms and so on. Well, you seem to think you've got a grudge against Germany....you prefer perhaps the Jews? You'd like to crony around with them? You prefer Communism. You prefer Bolshevism. Well, that's no America for me, I must say, and I'd rather die for Germany than live one hundred years on milk and honey in the Jewish America of today."

(Source: Appellate Brief, United States v. Mildred E. Gillars (Sisk),

December 1949, US Court of Appeals for the District of Columbia, Washington DC: National Archives)

* * *

SURVIVORS OF THE INVASION FRONT
1944

"Mothers and Dads in America, you've no idea what hell your boys have been through. And to thank....they've got Franklin D. Roosevelt, who promised you American mothers that no American boy would be sacrificed on foreign battlefields. I only wish you would get a little glimpse at the conflict going on in Normandy. Well, Roosevelt asked you to do it for him and you did. Wait until some of these human wrecks get back to you once again. You won't even be able to recognize some of them. Believe me....I've seen them. Well, this is Midge signing off."

* * *

SURVIVORS OF THE INVASION FRONT
September 1944

MIDGE: All right, where are we calling?
KENNETH HEALY: Chicago
MIDGE: Oh Chicago. Calling Chicago that toddling town/
HEALY: If anyone can get a hold of Mildred Healy in Chicago tell her, tell her that her son Kenneth is ok and all well.
MIDGE: Chicago's a big town. Better have a street address, you know?
HEALY: I don't know where she is.
MIDGE: Your mother?
HEALY: Well, She moves around quite a bit. You know, Well, I just don't know. Someone will know there. Mildred Healy...is all right *(unintelligible)*
MIDGE: Well, uh
HEALY: And uh, I expect to be home very soon.
MIDGE: Well, let's hope so for your mother's sake. Thank you, Mr. Healy. All right now, we've finished with that little message for Chicago.

I do hope it gets to her, since we have no street address for Mrs. Healy. And now, where this little message going to?

PRISONER 2: Philadelphia

MIDGE: Oh, Philadelphia. The good old Quaker town...

PRISONER 2: That's right

MIDGE: Street and Name

POW: Tucker St.

MIDGE: And who are you calling over in Philadelphia?

PRISONER 2: Mrs. John P——. 5051 West Tucker St....

MIDGE: Is that your mother?

PRISONER 2: My mother

MIDGE: And now you have the microphone all to yourself.

PRISONER 2: Mom, I'm ok. Don't' worry about me, I'll be home pretty soon. I'm in the best of health. Well, when I get home, I'll be asking for the little baby.

MIDGE: And whose little baby is that?

PRISONER 2: That's my sister's.

MIDGE: Oh your sister. Never saw the little baby, hmm?

PRISONER 2: A little girl.

MIDGE: Yeah, I'll bet you do...it must have been tough for you to take part in the invasion...Bet you're glad to have a little rest then....

PRISONER 2: Yeah, in a way.

MIDGE: Well, I'm going to give another boy a chance then, shall we? It's your turn, is it not? Where to?

PRISONER 3: Iowa

MIDGE: What town in Iowa?

PRISONER 3: Albia, Iowa

MIDGE: How do you spell that?

PRISONER 3: A-L-B-I-A.

MIDGE: Albia, oh yes. Quite a small place, isn't it?

PRISONER 3: Yeah, about 10,000.

MIDGE: Well, I like little American small towns. They're sweet aren't they? Nice and cozy. Everybody knows everybody else. All the corny cousins.... The drug store.... Sipping cider out of a bottle with the girl you love.

PRISONER 3: Well, not quite cider.

MIDGE: (laughs) who have you got over there?

PRISONER 3: My mother. Mrs. Margaret Blanton

MIDGE: Mrs. Margaret Blanton, Northeast Street, St. Albia, Iowa.

PRISONER 3: Come through the invasion all right, mom. In a little I'll be back eating them pancakes for breakfast

MIDGE: And maple syrup. Mmm....Grand! Aunt Jemima pancakes. I'm sorry I haven't got any over here. I'd make some for you myself. I'd help you eat them too. Heh, heh....

PRISONER 3: I'm ok. And I've come through all right without a scratch. Just waiting for the day when I'll be back

MIDGE: It must have been pretty hard for your mother, hmmm?

PRISONER 3: Well I supposed she expected it.

MIDGE: Any brothers or sisters over there?

PRISONER 3: Yes, I have two brothers and a sister.

MIDGE: Ah ha. So your mother's not quite alone.

PRISONER 3: No, she's not alone.

MIDGE: Well, that's a big relief for her. Because mothers always have the hardest time, don't they?

PRISONER 3: Hmmm.

MIDGE: Well, anyway, I'm awfully glad to have been able to give this little message to your mother. And hope it will cheer her up a lot.

PRISONER 3: Well, so do I.... Bye, bye mom!

* * *

SURVIVORS OF THE INVASION FRONT
September 20, 1944

"Hello America....this is Midge talking to the American families once again tonight and this time from this invasion front. You know for many years, I have been the go-between between your men in Germany and you, the beloved ones, way back home. Well folks, I've gone to quite a bit of trouble now to get next to the latest prisoners of war taken along the coast of Normandy. Because I can just put myself in your place and know how very, very worried you are. And so now, I've seen some of your boys, talked to them, realized their great, great disillusionment and how practically to a man they've said to me 'we would never, never fight another war'. Well, folks tonight first of all I present to you one of these soldiers, a paratrooper who left England on D-Day and was, he claimed, to be perhaps the first man to have been captured by the Germans in the invasion. I happened to have a little chat with him in the officers' barracks not very far from Paris. I'd now like to give you the little recording which is for Mr. EVANICK, the relatives in New York City. Now be good enough all you folks to drop a postcard to those concerned, in case they themselves were not sitting at the radio set. And now, here is Mr. Evanick:

MIDGE: So I think we are calling New York City.
EVANICK: Yes,
MIDGE: Is that right?
EVANICK: Yes.
MIDGE: And if you'd give the name of the person or persons to whom you'd like to greet and so they'll be very surprised to know that you are fine.
EVANICK: I'd like to greet my sister-in-law in New York City, 500 East 13th Street in New York City.
MIDGE: 500
EVANICK: East 13th Street, New York City
MIDGE: East 13th Street you said, 500 did you? Not 503?
EVANICK: 500
MIDGE: 500 East 13th Street, and your sister-in-law's name is…
EVANICK: (*unintelligible*)
MIDGE: Alva?
EVANICK: (*unintelligible*)
MIDGE: Evanick and would you please spell Evanick?
EVANICK: E-V-A-N-I-C-K
MIDGE: E-V-A-N-I-C-K is that right? Well I think that's very clear. And I suppose they have no idea that you're over in a prisoner of war camp in France at the moment.
EVANICK: I don't know.
MIDGE: (*unintelligible*)
EVANICK: Well… (*unintelligible*) she's knows I came here from England.
MIDGE: Some time ago.
EVANICK: Short time ago.
MIDGE: Well, when did you leave England?
EVANICK: Well, I couldn't tell you that, well on D-Day …
MIDGE: Oh, on D-Day…of course, (*laughs*) and where did you go from

there?

EVANICK: I went in France

MIDGE: Into France...as what?

EVANICK: As a paratrooper, a fighting man.

MIDGE: Do you want to tell your sister-in-law something about it, about your adventures getting over here?

EVANICK: Well, I can tell her, you know, I'm all right and a prisoner of war, Say hello to everybody over in New York , all my friends and...

MIDGE: The Great White Way...

EVANICK: That's right

MIDGE: Uh huh.

(unintelligible)

MIDGE: That's his son?

MIDGE: He's quite a favourite of yours, apparently.

EVANICK: I've got his picture with me.

MIDGE: Oh have you really? Well you might show it to me afterwards. Well, have you got any special little thing to tell her? She might be awfully interested to hear about your experiences, I think you've had a very vivid life, haven't you?

EVANICK: Well, yes, but the only thing I have to tell her now...

MIDGE: Anything to tell her about the treatment you are getting over here? To put her mind at ease perhaps....in case she's worried about you?

EVANICK: The treatment...Not too good, not too great....

MIDGE: You're satisfied then.

EVANICK: Satisfied.

MIDGE: After all, a prisoner isn't living in a castle, is he?

EVANICK: That's right

MIDGE: Prisoner of war. So you're leading a soldier's life and taking it as it comes.

EVANICK: Yes.

MIDGE: You told me a little while ago, before we began speaking here, that all the boys wanted to get back home?

EVANICK: Well yes, we'd like to finish the war and go back home.

MIDGE: Well is there anything else you'd like to say way back to New York from Gay Pareè, not very far from us?

EVANICK: Well, I'd just like to say hello to everybody and I'll be seeing you.

MIDGE: I hope it won't be too long...Well, I hope I've made you a little happy with this message back home?
EVANICK: Yes. Appreciate it very much.
MIDGE: (unintelligible)
EVANICK: (unintelligible)
MIDGE: Well, goodbye New York!
EVANICK: Goodbye, New York!

(Source: Author's Transcription of NARA tape recording of Survivor's of the Invasion Front, September 20, 1944. College Park MD: Archives II)

* * *

MEDICAL REPORTS
October 6, 1944

"And now folks, I hope that you still have your paper and pencil there....and that you'll cooperate with me by jotting down these medical reports....which will give you some information as to the present physical condition of wounded American, and in some cases Canadian, fliers shot down over Germany or German-occupied territory and lucky enough to have escaped alive. Now, tonight, I have one report for Canada....which I'll read to you first. It's from Toronto, Ontario...for Mrs. G. Prisupa, P-R-I-S-U-P-A, of 959 College Street, Toronto, Ontario, Canada. The report is about her son Gustav Prisupa....whose rank is that of Sergeant....the date of birth.....the 16th of August, 1922, and her Serial Number, 654758.

Now Mrs. Prisupa should you be listening I hope that you have reception there is Toronto....your son....got his right shoulder blade broken. He is suffering from multiple abrasions. I can't tell you anymore tonight, but I suppose [since] you have a son in the Air Service that you'll keep in touch with this broadcast.

Now, standby, Evansville, Indiana....Calling Evansville, Indiana with word for Mrs. Anlie, A-N-L-I-E, of 1104 First Avenue, Evansville, Indiana, a report about her son Sergeant Robert T. Mitnet, M-I-T-N-E-T, born on the 9th of April 1918. His service number is 205322859. Now he's got a bullet wound in the left knee joint. The doctors say that if no complications develop he'll have to stay in hospital anywhere from 2 to 3 months. Now of course that always means getting a bullet in one of the joints and there [are] generally very unpleasant complications in afterlife, but he'll be very happy in any case.

How many....very badly mutilated boys have I seen and they've said to me..."I don't care how I get back....just so I get back." You see, that's the way they think now. What do you suppose they'll think in later years when there are no jobs for cripples? That's the question.

Well now, I should like to contact Santa Monica, in California. I have word there for Sylvia Edinger, E-D-I-N-G-E-R, of 938 Marco Place, Santa Monica, California – a report about her brother, Staff Sergeant Manuel Rosen, R-O-S-E-N, born on the 19th of May 1911. Here is his service number 33037982T42-43. Ah.....Miss Edinger, your brother got his left leg crushed below the knee and the right leg broken below the knee. Well, that's pretty bad if he got both of his legs so....badly....ah....wounded. Of course, the left one sounds bad where the doctors say that it was crushed below the knee. Let's hope he won't have to lose it, but I suppose it's quite probable. But anyway, otherwise he seems to be getting along all right, so I suppose you'll be very happy to have got this news about him anyway.

And now, I have a message for the West. This is for Tillamook, in Oregon, T-I-L-L-A-M-O-O-K, for Mrs. Emile Schofield, S-C-H-O-F-I-E-L-D, of 1008 East 6th Street, Tillamook, Oregon, word about her son. Staff Sergeant Denny Schofield got a bullet in his left arm above the elbow which caused a fracture. The muscle is paralyzed. In addition, he got superficial bullet wounds and fractures. Also, his left ankle was sprained may be fractured, the doctors have taken an X-ray....ah....pictures in the meantime and perhaps at a subsequent broadcast I'll have more news for you.

Now—Calling Narberth, Pennsylvania, N-A-R-B-E-R-T-H, with word for W.R. O'Sullivan - 85 Windsor Avenue, Narberth, Pennsylvania - about Lieutenant Walter Robert O'Sullivan - born on the 11th of April

1921, in Narberth, Pennsylvania. Here is his service number: 0805104. The right leg was fractured above the knee. The fracture was caused by a bullet. The doctors say that from 5 to 6 months hospital treatment will be necessary, so as harmless as this wound may sound, it must be pretty complicated because we hardly ever get cases where the boys have to stay in hospital for nearly half a year. So Mr. O'Sullivan, or whoever happens to be the nearest of kin, please watch out for this broadcast and I hope to have more word for you about Walter O'Sullivan.

Now, my concluding report tonight unfortunately has no exact address. It's only New York City, New York, which you know as well as I, is most vague. It concerns Staff Sergeant Francis H. Cousins C-O-U-S-I-N-S, born on the 1st of June 1916 in New York. I have his service number, which should of course help in identifying him 33288676. He was hit by a bullet causing a fracture to the right leg above the knee and, unfortunately, splintered the bone. However, his chances of complete recovery are good, the doctors say. Well, folks, I see now that my time is up, but please watch out....ah....for this broadcast which comes to you each and every evening with the exception of Sunday. This is Midge signing off. Thank you for your attention."

(Source: Written Transcription of Federal Communications Commission Memovox Recording #10097, Recorded at Silver Hill, Maryland, between the hours of 22:15 o'clock E.W.T., and 23:15 o'clock E.W.T. on October 6, 1944. Washington DC: John Bartlow Martin Papers, Library of Congress Manuscript Division)

Notes

1. An Unwelcome Child

[1] *Evening Courier*, Camden, NJ, October 18, 1928, p. 3.

[2] Ibid.

[3] Ibid.

[4] Ibid.

[5] *Evening Courier*, Camden, NJ, October 19, 1928, p. 1.

[6] Ibid.

[7] Ibid., p. 1

[8] *The Evening Courier*, Camden NJ, October 20, 1928, p. 1.

[9] Ibid.

[10] Ibid., p. 8.

[11] Ibid.

[12] Ibid.

[13] Ibid., p.1

[14] Ibid.

[15] Ibid.

[16] *Evening Courier*, Camden, NJ, October 21, 1928, p. 1.

[17] "Companionate Tragedy Exposed as Movie Stunt," *New York World*, op. cit., p. 24.

[18] Ibid.

[19] Ibid.

[20] *Sisk v. Sisk*, Supreme Judicial Court of Maine. Portland, Maine. Docket Record #29782 #419, October Term 1907, May 31, 1907. Courtesy: Maine State Archives.

[21] *The Washington Post*, February 24, 1949, p. 4.

[22] Admissions Summary for Mildred E. Gillars, Federal Reformatory for Women at Alderson, West Virginia, October 12, 1950. College Park MD: National Archives and Records Administration (NARA), p. 4.

Vincent Sisk remarried soon after the divorce and moved to Baltimore, where he worked on the railroad. As of 1930, according to that year's U.S. Census, Sisk was still married to his second wife and was the father of five children.

[23] FBI File 61-117. Report to Director regarding Mildred Gillars birth and citizen-

ship, College Park, MD: National Archives and Records Administration (NARA), p. 2.

24 US Department of Justice Memorandum, Campbell to J. Edgar Hoover, August 17, 1948. College Park MD: National Archives and Records Administration (NARA).

25 *Star Beacon*, Ashtabula, Ohio, November 20, 1995, p. B1. Courtesy: Conneaut Public Library.

26 News-Herald, Conneaut, Ohio, April 8, 1961, p. 1. Courtesy: Conneaut Public Library.

27 *Star Beacon*, Ashtabula, Ohio, November 20, 1995, op. cit.

28 *Star Beacon*, Ashtabula, Ohio, December 20, 1998. Courtesy: Conneaut Public Library.

29 *The Tattler*, St. Patrick's Number, 1917, Conneaut, Ohio: Conneaut High School. Courtesy: Conneaut Public Library.

30 *The Tattler*, Senior Number, June 1917, Conneaut, Ohio: Conneaut High School. Courtesy: Conneaut Public Library.

31 Abridged transcript of *U.S. v. Gillars (Sisk)*. John Bartlow Martin Papers. Washington, DC: Library of Congress Manuscript Division, p. 18.

32 Handwritten notes by John Bartlow Martin from interview of Edna Mae Herrick, undated (c. September 1948), John Bartlow Martin Papers, Washington DC: Library of Congress Manuscript Division.

33 Ibid.

34 Ibid.

35 Ibid.

36 *Chronicle-Telegram* Elyria, OH, July 25, 1919, p. 30.

37 Letter and outline from John Bartlow Martin to Editor, *McCall's*. September 18, 1948. John Bartlow Martin Papers. Washington DC: Library of Congress Manuscript Division.

38 John Bartlow Martin, "The Trials of Axis Sally," *McCall's*, p. 25.

39 Admissions Summary for Mildred E. Gillars, op. cit., p. 5.

40 Ibid.

2. In Front of the Footlights

41 Letter from Mrs. Allen C. Long (Ohio Wesleyan Magazine) to John Nelson, March 30, 1966. Delaware, Ohio: Ohio Wesleyan Historical Collection.

42 Ibid.

43 Ibid.

44 Ibid.

45 Ibid.

46 Admissions Summary of Mildred E. Gillars, op. cit. p. 5.

47 FBI File 61-180. FBI Interview with Richard R. Shipley, January 4, 1949. College Park MD: National Archives and Records Administration (NARA), p. 2.

48 Ibid.

49 *Mansfield News-Journal*, Mansfield, Ohio.

[50] Ibid.

[51] Program of *Mrs. Dane's Defense*, December 10, 1920, Delaware OH: Ohio Wesleyan University Historical Collection

[52] Abridged Transcript of *U.S. v. Gillars (Sisk)*. John Bartlow Martin Papers. Washington DC: Library of Congress Manuscript Division, p. 18.

[53] Ibid.

[54] Ibid., p. 19.

[55] Admissions Summary for Mildred E. Gillars, op. cit., p. 6.

[56] Ibid., p. 3.

[57] Ibid., p. 4.

[58] Letter of Mrs. Allan C. Long to John Nelson, March 30, 1966, op. cit.

[59] Abridged transcript of *U.S. v. Gillars (Sisk)*, op. cit., p. 19.

[60] Ibid. p. 20.

[61] Michael Kantor and Laurence Maslon (2004) *Broadway: The American Musical.* New York: Bulfinch Press, pp. 69.

[62] Research notes for *The Trials of Axis Sally*, condensation of *US v. Gillars (Sisk)* trial transcript. John Bartlow Martin Papers, Washington DC: Library of Congress Manuscript Division, p. 21.

[63] *The New York Times* November 17, 1917

[64] IBDB (www.ibdb.com).

[65] IBDB (www.ibdb.com).

[66] Letter from Mrs. Allan C. Long to John Nelson dated March 30, 1966. Delaware, Ohio: Ohio Wesleyan University Archives.

No legal record of such a marriage has been located, so Mildred may have considered herself a common-law wife. Later in life, she claimed to have never married.

[67] *The Port Arthur News*, Port Arthur, TX, January 17, 1926, p. 10.

[68] Research notes for *The Trials of Axis Sally*, op. cit., p. 23.

[69] Ibid.

[70] Ibid., p. 24.

[71] *The Port Arthur News* Port Arthur, TX, January 17, 1926, op. cit.

[72] Ibid., p. 25.

[73] Inez Robb (1950) "Remember when Millie Dived under the Bed?" *The Lima News* Lima, OH, April 18, p. 6.

[74] Ibid.

3. Expatriate

[75] FBI Report on interview of Mario Korbel, November 25, 1943, FBI HQ Files, College Park MD: NARA p 1.

During her 1949 trial, the prosecution would intimate that Korbel gave her the money in exchange for a liaison. Mildred angrily insisted that the money was a loan.

[76] Ronald Weber (2006) *News of Paris.* Chicago: Ivan R. Dee, p. 5.

[77] Passenger List of United States Citizens for the SS *Majestic* voyage from Cherbourg to New York, 16 October 1929, p. 22.

[78] Robert VanGiezen and Albert E Schwenk (2001) "Compensation from before

World War I through the Great Depression," Washington DC: Bureau of Labor Statistics (originally printed in *Compensation and Working Conditions*, US Department of Labor—Bureau of Labor Statistics, Fall 2001).

[79] Author's transcript of "Midge at the Mike" recording, dated July 1943. Washington DC: Library of Congress.

[80] Paul Beekman Taylor (2004) *Gurdjieff's America*. Lighthouse Editions Ltd, p. 215.

[81] Paul Beekman Taylor (1998) *Shadows of Heaven: Gurdjieff and Toomer*. San Francisco: Samuel Weiser, p. 70.

[82] James Carruthers Young (1998) "An Experiment at Fontainebleau: A Personal Reminiscence," *Gurdjieff International Review*, Summer, p. 42.

[83] Taylor, op. cit., p. 23.

[84] *Syracuse Herald*, February 17, 1924, p. 1.

[85] Abridged transcript of *U.S. v. Gillars (Sisk)*, op. cit., p. 26.

[86] Charles K. McClatchy (1929) "Algiers: the Beautiful also the Most Filthy," *Fresno Bee*, March 8, p. 1.

[87] Abridged transcript of *U.S. v. Gillars (Sisk)*, op. cit., p. 27.

[88] Diplomatic List of the British Foreign Office (1944), courtesy British Foreign and Commonwealth Office.

Bernard Metz later advised in the planning of the US and British invasion of North Africa and joined the American Military Civil Affairs Administration after the Allies regained North Africa in 1942. Paul Beekman Taylor recalls his mother Edith telling him in 1945–46 that Metz had to leave Algiers "in a hurry" because he was engaged in "some sort of espionage." (Taylor, *Gurdjieff's America*, p. 215.) He later changed his name to Bernard Mayne and immigrated to the United States. He died in Florida in 1981.

[89] *Star-Beacon*, Ashtabula, Ohio, November 20, 1995, p. B1

[90] William R. Shirer (1941) *Berlin Diary: The Journal of a Foreign Correspondent 1934-41*. New York: Black Dog & Leventhal (2005 edition), p. 13.

[91] Abridged transcript of *U.S. v. Gillars (Sisk)*, op. cit., p. 28.

[92] Ibid.

[93] *New York Times*, June 7, 1933.

[94] Abridged transcript of *U.S. v. Gillars (Sisk)*, op. cit. p. 29.

[95] Ibid., p. 30.

[96] Ibid.

[97] Abridged transcript of *U.S. v. Gillars (Sisk)*, op. cit., p. 30.

[98] Claire Trask (1934) "And Turbulently Flows the Rhine," *New York Times*, December 30.

[99] Claire Trask (1934) "A Jewish Playhouse in Berlin," *New York Times*, April 8. Hans Hinkel was later transferred to the Propaganda Ministry where Goebbels eventually appointed him responsible for film.

[100] Claire Trask (1935) "Berlin Ends the Drama Season," *New York Times*, July 28.

[101] Author's transcript of "Midge at the Mike" recording, dated July 1943. Washington DC: Library of Congress.

[102] Ibid.

[103] Claire Trask (1936) "Broadway Melody Echoes in Berlin," *New York Times*, April 26.

[104] Klaus Kreimeier (1996) *The UFA Story: A History of Germany's Greatest Film Company 1918–1945*. NewYork: Hill & Wang, p. 246.

[105] Ibid., pp. 256–7.

[106] "Unhalting Nazis," *Time*, December 7, 1936.

[107] Claire Trask, "The Screen in Germany," *New York Times*, March 13, 1937

[108] *Variety*, January 19, 1938, p. 19.

[109] Abridged transcript of U.S v. Gillars (Sisk), op. cit. p. 30.

Ironically, many of these favored "Aryans" in Nazi-sponsored cinema were not German. Zarah Leander and Kristina Söderbaum were Swedish, Lilian Harvey was born in England.

[110] *Variety*, January 12, 1938, p. 27.

[111] *Variety*, January 26, 1938, p. 23.

[112] *Variety*, June 1, 1938, p. 37.

[113] Martin Gilbert (2006) *Kristallnacht*, New York: HarperCollins, p. 124.

[114] *Star-Beacon*, Ashtabula, Ohio, November 20, 1995, p. B1

[115] Ibid.

4. Wolves at the Door

[116] Research notes for "The Trials of Axis Sally," condensation of *US v. Gillars (Sisk)* Trial Transcript, p. 48.

[117] Ibid., p. 33.

[118] Peter Martland, *Lord Haw Haw: The English Voice of Nazi Germany*, Latham, Maryland: The Scarecrow Press, 2003, p. 38.

[119] Tom Hickman, *What Did You Do in the War, Auntie? The BBC at War, 1939–1945*, London: BBC Publishing, 1996, p. 16.

[120] Ibid., p. 16.

[121] Radio Station PCJ (Hilversum) and Radio Luxembourg were two of the most powerful and popular shortwave stations of the 1930s.

[122] Transcription of "The Broadcasts of Lord Haw Haw" audio, May 1940, Courtesy: Earthstation One.

[123] Ibid.

[124] The USA Zone was the department responsible for programming to the United States and Canada.

[125] Ralf Georg Reuth, trans.: Krishna Winston. *Goebbels*, Orlando: Harcourt Inc. 1993, p. 257.

[126] Ibid.

[127] Ibid. p. 283.

[128] Memorandum from Dr Markus Timmler, Radio and Culture Department of the German Foreign Office, dated 20 March 1940. Archive of the German Foreign Office—Political Radio Department. Bundesarchiv, Berlin, Germany.

[129] Research notes for "The Trials of Axis Sally," op. cit., p. 34.

[130] Statement of Erwin Christiani to the FBI at US Department of Justice Interrogation Center at Holminden, Germany, 1 October 1948. National Archives and Records Administration.

[131] Statement of Mario Balto at US Department of Justice Interrogation Center at Holminden, Germany, National Archives and Records Administration.

[132] Statement of Werner Berger taken at the Department of Justice Interrogation Center at Holminden, Germany. 22 April 1948, National Archives and Records Administration, p. 2.

[133] Ibid.

[134] John Bartlow Martin, "The Trials of Axis Sally," McCall's, June 1949, p. 112.

[135] US Department of Justice Press Release on the Indictment of Max Otto Koischwitz, Edward Delaney, Constance Drexel, Ezra Pound, Robert H. Best, Frederick W. Kaltenbach, Jane Anderson and Douglas Chandler, 26 July 1943. Francis Biddle Papers, Georgetown University, p. 13.

[136] Ibid., pp. 111–12.

[137] John Carver Edwards. Berlin Calling, New York: Praeger Publishing 1991, p. 68.

[138] Ibid., p. 72.

[139] Horst J.P. Bergmeier and Rainer E. Lots Hitler's Airwaves New Haven: Yale University Press, 1997, pp. 56

[140] "Koischwitz Broadcasts Nazi Propaganda to America," The Hour, 20 July 1940, no. 54, p. 4.

[141] Ibid., p. 73.

[142] Ibid., p. 75.

[143] Research notes for "The Trials of Axis Sally." op. cit., p. 43.

[144] New York Times, 24 February 1949, p. 5.

[145] John Bartlow Martin, op. cit., p. 111.

[146] New York Times. 24 February 1949, p. 5.

[147] William Russell, Berlin Embassy, London: Elliott & Thompson, 2003, pp. 27–8. Reprinted from the 1941 edition published by E.P. Dutton.

[148] Leni Yahil, The Holocaust: The Fate of European Jewry. New York: Oxford University Press, 1990, p. 292.

[149] Ibid.

[150] Although the story would be later discounted as concocted to assist her defense, the timing of this interview coincides with the beginning of the German effort to infiltrate the United States with saboteurs known as "Operation Pastorius." Hitler had been pressuring Admiral Wilhelm Canaris, the head of the Abwehr (German military foreign information and counterintelligence) as early as the autumn of 1941 to initiate sabotage efforts aimed at crippling the industrial might of America. Walter Kappe, head of the German-American Bund until 1937 and Abwehr agent, was responsible for recruiting English-speaking agents who had previously resided in the United States. The Germans eventually ferried agents via U-boat to the coast of the United States and deposited them on the beaches of Long Island and Florida. The agents' mission was to find work in critical war-related industries and plan sab-

otage attacks that would cripple the production effort for weeks or months. The eight were arrested in June 1942 and tried by a secret tribunal at the Justice Department in Washington DC. Six went to the electric chair in August of that year. It is not unreasonable to assume that the German government would have an interest in recruiting a woman who could blend into American society so easily.

[151] Statement of Erwin Christiani, op. cit.

c[152] Ibid.

[153] Ibid.

[154] In fact, Mildred's half-sister Edna Mae Herrick resided in Ohio at that time.

[155] *New York Times*, 24 February 1949, p. 5 and *Washington Post*, 24 February 1949, p. 4.

[156] Ibid.

[157] *US v. Mildred Sisk (Gillars)*. US Court of Appeals for the District of Columbia. Case 10,187. October Term, 1949. Washington DC: National Archives and Records Administration, p. 35.

[158] Research notes for "The Trials of Axis Sally," op. cit., p. 39.

[159] *US v. Mildred Sisk (Gillars)*. US Court of Appeals for the District of Columbia, op. cit., p. 36.

5. Smiling Through

[160] William L. Shirer. "The American Radio Traitors," *Harper's*, vol. 187, October 1943, p. 400.

[161] Research notes for "The Trials of Axis Sally," John Bartlow Martin Papers, Library of Congress Manuscript Collection, Washington DC, p. 43.

[162] Gerhard Keiper and Martin Kroger (eds), *Biographisches Handbuch des deutschen äuswartigan Dienstes 1871-1945*, Band 2, 2005, p. 596.

[163] John Bartlow Martin, "The Trials of Axis Sally," *McCall's*, June 1949, p. 112.

[164] *Washington Post*, January 28, 1948, p. 11.

[165] Research notes for "The Trials of Axis Sally," John Bartlow Martin Papers; condensation of *U.S. v. Gillars (Sisk)* Trial Transcript, Library of Congress Manuscripts Collection, Washington DC.

[166] United States Court of Appeals. *Gillars v US*. October term, 1949. No. 10,187. pp. 9–10.

[167] Ibid., p. 47.

[168] Ibid.

[169] Shirer, op. cit., p. 398.

[170] *Gillars v US*, United States Court of Appeals decision, pp. 9–11.

[171] *Washington Post*, January 28, 1949, p. 11.

[172] Ibid.

[173] Ibid.

[174] Research notes for "The Trials of Axis Sally," John Bartlow Martin Papers, Library of Congress Manuscript Collection, Washington DC, p. 42.

[175] Ibid.

[176] Ibid.

[177] Research Notes for "The Trials of Axis Sally," op. cit., p. 53.

[178] Joseph Goebbels, "Nation, Rise Up, and Let the Storm Break Loose," translated from "Nun, Volk steh auf, und Sturm brich los! Rede im Berliner Sportpalast," *Der steile Aufstieg* (Munich: Zentralverlag der NSDAP, 1944), pp. 167–204. Courtesy: German Propaganda Archive, Calvin College.

[179] David Clay Large, *Berlin.* New York: Basic Books, p. 344.

[180] Research notes for "The Trials of Axis Sally," condensation of *US v Gillars (Sisk)* trial transcript, op. cit., p. 48.

[181] Ibid.

[182] Ibid.

[183] Department of Corrections, District of Columbia Jail, Memorandum from Supt. Curtis Reid to the Director, June 17, 1950, p. 1.

[184] John Bartlow-Martin, "The Trials of Axis Sally," op. cit., p. 111.

[185] Research notes for "The Trials of Axis Sally," op. cit., p. 42.

[186] Ibid., p. 56.

[187] Ibid., p. 55.

[188] Ibid.

[189] Horst J.P. Bergmeier and Rainer E. Lotz, *Hitler's Airwaves*, New Haven: Yale University Press, 1997, p 44

[190] Department of Justice Press Release, Francis Biddle Papers, Georgetown University Library, Washington DC, August 26, 1943, p. 3.

[191] Statement of Erwin Christiani, Memorandum from US Army European Command Intelligence Division to the Director of Intelligence, General Staff, US Army, October 6, 1948, p. 2.

[192] John Carver Edwards, *Berlin Calling,* New York: Praeger Publishing, 1991, p. 205.

6. Did You Raise Your Sons To Be Murderers?

[193] Transcription by author of "Medical Reports" broadcast, February 24, 1944, College Park MD: Archives II, National Archives and Records Administration (NARA).

[194] Ibid. p. 57.

[195] Bergmeier and Lotz (1997), pp. 82–3.

[196] Research Notes for "The Trials of Axis Sally," Abridged transcript of *US v. Gillars (Sisk)*, John Bartlow Martin Papers, Washington DC: Library of Congress Manuscript Division, p. 44.

[197] Research Notes for "The Trials of Axis Sally," John Bartlow Martin Papers, op. cit., p 59.

[198] Ibid. p.63.

[199] Ibid.

[200] "American Prisoners of War in Germany," Washington DC: Military Intelligence Service, US War Department, November 1, 1945.

[201] Ibid.

[202] FBI File #61-811, Statement of James Capparell, April 26, 1948, College Park

MD: NARA, p. 5.

[203] FBI File #61-811. Statement of Robert Ehalt, April 26, 1948, College Park MD: NARA p. 3.

[204] Ibid.

[205] Transcription by Author of "Medical Reports" audiotape, February 24, 1944, College Park MD: NARA.

[206] Transcript of "Medical Reports" broadcast, Federal Communications Commission, Silver Hill, MD, October 6, 1944. John Bartlow Martin Papers. Washington DC: Library of Congress Manuscript Division.

[207] US Court of Appeals Decision, *Gillars v. U.S.*, October Term, 1949, No. 10,187, p. 14.

[208] Ibid.

[209] Transcript of William Scofield audio interview from "Berlin Calling" radio program, National Public Radio, produced by WUGA-FM, Athens, GA.

[210] "Axis Sally Remembered" by Paul F. Mosher, *100th Infantry Division Association* magazine, November 2000, p. 53.

[211] Ibid.

[212] John Bartlow Martin. "The Trials of Axis Sally," *McCall's* , June 1949 p. 112.

[213] Ibid.

[214] Cpl. Edward Van Dyne. "There's No Other Gal Like Axis Sal." *Saturday Evening Post*, January 15, 1944.

[215] Bergmeier and Lotz (1997), p 128.

[216] Ibid.

7. Survivors of the Invasion Front

[217] Research Notes for "The Trials of Axis Sally," John Bartlow Martin Papers, op. cit., p. 71.

[218] FBI Bureau File No. 100-232559. Statement of Michael Evanick to FBI, April 24, 1948, p. 9.

[219] Ibid., p. 11.

[220] United States Court of Appeals. *Gillars v. United States*. October Term, 1949. No. 10,187, p. 12.

[221] Ibid., p. 13.

[222] FBI Bureau File No. 61-44. FBI interview with Clarence Marion Gale, April 21, 1948, p. 8.

[223] Ibid., p. 9.

[224] FBI interview with Donald Rutter, May 4, 1948, p. 4.

[225] FBI File No. 61-44. FBI interview with Clarence Marion Gale, April 21, 1948, p. 8.

[226] FBI File No. 61-222. MCG. Statement of Carl Zimmerman to FBI, May 27, 1948, p. 2.

[227] Ibid., p. 5.

[228] *Survivors of the Invasion Front* broadcast, August 22, 1944, NARA. Zimmerman did not recall Gillars identifying herself in his statements to the FBI;

however, it is clear from the broadcast that he calls her "Midge."

[229] FBI File No. 61-222. MCG. Statement of Carl Zimmerman to FBI, May 27, 1948, p. 4.

[230] *Survivors of the Invasion Front* broadcast, August 22, 1944, NARA.

[231] FBI File No. 61-35. FBI Interview with Seaborn Warren. College Park MD, NARA, p. 4.

[232] FBI File No. 61-63. FBI Interview with Paul Kestel, April 22, 1948, p. 6.

[233] Bergmeier and Lotz (1997), p. 58.

[234] John Carver Edwards, *Berlin Calling*, p. 97.

[235] Washington Post, March 1, 1949.

[236] Ibid.

[237] Edwards, op cit., p. 98.

[238] Ibid.

[239] Ibid.

[240] Ibid., p. 61.

8. Alone

[241] Cpl. Edward Van Dyne, "There's No Gal Like Axis Sal," *Saturday Evening Post*, January 15, 1944.

[242] Anonymous (2005) *A Woman in Berlin: Eight Weeks in the Conquered City.* New York: Metropolitan Books, p. 2.

[243] Edward Davidson and Dale Manning (1999) *Chronology of World War Two*, London: Cassell, p. 219.

[244] Research notes for *The Trials of Axis Sally*, condensation of *US v. Gillars (Sisk)* trial transcript. John Bartlow Martin Papers, Washington DC: Library of Congress Manuscript Division, pp. 104–5.

[245] Ibid.

[246] Ibid.

[247] Bergmeier and Lotz (1997) , op cit. , p. 80.

[248] *Washington Post*, February 27, 1949.

[249] Ibid.

[250] Ibid.

[251] Ibid.

[252] Research notes for *The Trials of Axis Sally*, condensation of *US v. Gillars (Sisk)* trial transcript, op. cit., pp. 73–4.

[253] Ibid. p. 12.

[254] "Chancellor Hitler's Orders for a Last Stand in the East," *New York Times*, April 16, 1945.

[255] Statement of Walter Leschetizky to US Military Interrogators. College Park, MD: National Archives and Research Administration (NARA).

[256] Statement of WAC Catherine Samaha to FBI, College Park MD: National Archives and Research Administration (NARA).

[257] Oral History Interview of Oscar R. Ewing, April 30, 1969. Independence MO: Truman Presidential Library.

[258] Ibid.

[259] Gregor Dallas (2005) *1945: The War That Never Ended.* New Haven: Yale University Press, p. 7.

[260] *A Woman in Berlin,* op. cit. (Foreword by Antony Beevor), p. xx.

[261] Antony Beevor (2002) *The Fall of Berlin—1945.* New York: Penguin, p. 282.

[262] John Bartlow Martin (1949) "The Trials of Axis Sally," *McCall's,* June, p. 114

[263] "Hunt 22 Americans for Aiding the Foe," *New York Times,* February 20, 1946, p. 6.

[264] Counterintelligence Corps Memorandum from John P. Hogan to Special Agent Thomas McCabe, June 14, 1944. College Park MD: US Military Records Collection, National Archives and Records Administration (NARA).

[265] Interrogation of Rita Luisa Zucca, CIC Rome Detachment, Zone 5, July 5, 1945. College Park MD: US Military Records Collection, National Archives and Records Administration (NARA).

[266] *Washington Times-Herald,* Washington DC, June 4, 1945.

[267] *Ibid.*

[268] Interrogation of Rita Luisa Zucca. op. cit.

[269] Bergmier and Lotz, op. cit., p. 129 (quoted from *Der Spiegel,* September 1949, Seltsamer Haufe).

[270] "Americans Seize Axis Sally in Italy; Fascist Broadcaster Born Here," *New York Times,* June 8, 1945.

[271] *Washington Times-Herald,* Washington DC, June 4, 1945.

[272] FBI Memorandum from J Edgar Hoover to Assistant Attorney General Criminal Division July 3, 1945, p 2 (NARA).

[273] Letter of Raymond W. Kurtz to the Commanding Officer of the 50th Troop Carrier Group, August 20, 1945, College Park, MD: Military Records Division, National Archives and Records Administration.

[274] FBI Memorandum from Alexander M. Campbell, Asst. Attorney General, Criminal Division to J. Edgar Hoover dated October 6, 1948. College Park, MD: National Archives and Records Administration (NARA).

[275] "The Mildred Gillars Case," Synopsis of Case Against Mildred Gillars, dated March 11, 1948. US Counter-Intelligence Corps papers, College Park MD: US Military Records, National Archives and Records Administration.

[276] Ibid.

[277] Research notes for "The Trials of Axis Sally," condensation of *US v. Gillars (Sisk)* trial transcript, op. cit., p. 75.

[278] Ibid. p. 76.

[279] Ibid.

[280] "The Mildred Gillars Case," Synopsis of Case Against Mildred Gillars, dated March 11, 1948. US Counter Intelligence Corps papers, op. cit.

[281] "Axis Sally Admits Guilt; Ready for Consequences," United Press wire story datelined March 22, 1946, unidentified newspaper. Counter Intelligence Corps (CIC) files. College Park, MD: US Military Records Division, National Archives and Records Administration.

[282] "Axis Sally to Face Treason Trial in the US," *New York Times*, March 22, 1946.

[283] Ibid.

[284] Research notes for "The Trials of Axis Sally," condensation of *US v. Gillars (Sisk)* trial transcript, op. cit., p. 77.

[285] Ibid.

[286] Counter Intelligence Corps Interrogation of Mildred Gillars, Berlin, April 2, 1946, p. 2. College Park MD: Military Records Division, National Archives and Records Administration.

[287] Ibid.

[288] Ibid.

[289] Research notes for "The Trials of Axis Sally," condensation of *US v. Gillars (Sisk)* trial transcript, op. cit., p. 76.

[290] "Axis Sally is Recalled at OWU," Associated Press report in the Times-Recorder, Zanesville, Ohio, March 28, 1946.

[291] Research notes for "The Trials of Axis Sally," condensation of *US v. Gillars (Sisk)* trial transcript, op. cit., p. 78.

[292] Ibid.

[293] Ibid.

[294] Ibid. p. 79.

[295] "Axis Sally Calls Art Her Motive", *New York Herald-Tribune*, December 26, 1946.

[296] "Axis Sally Tells Why She Broadcast," *New York Times*, December 26, 1946.

[297] "Axis Sally Still on German Soil," Associated Press report, *Portland Press Herald*, Portland, ME, January 18, 1947.

[298] Referral Memorandum to President Truman on Letter to the President, December 30, 1946. Independence MO: Truman Presidential Library.

[299] Referral Memorandum to President on Letter to the President from Joseph Filner of Pittsburgh PA, January 5, 1947. Independence MO: Truman Presidential Library.

[300] FBI Memo from K.C. Howe to D.M. Ladd, January 13, 1947. College Park, MD: National Archives and Records Administration (NARA).

[301] Ibid.

[302] Research notes for "The Trials of Axis Sally," condensation of *US v. Gillars (Sisk)* trial transcript, op. cit., p. 79.

[303] "Axis Sally Seized in Germany," *New York Times,* January 23, 1947.

[304] "Pro-German Attitude Grows as US Troops Fraternize—Survey Shows Many GIs Have Less Regard for Allies than for Former Enemies—One Major Doubts Dachau Crimes," *New York Times*, September 29, 1945.

9. The Stage is Set

[305] *The Fresno Bee*, Fresno, CA, August 20, 1948 p. 7.

[306] *Oakland Tribune*, Oakland, CA, August 20, 1948, p. D3.

[307] Oscar R. Ewing Oral History Interview, April 30, 1969. Independence, Missouri: Harry S. Truman Presidential Library (NARA) pp. 156–8. The statute, enacted on April 30, 1790, stated that "The trial of all offenses committed on the high seas or

elsewhere, out of the jurisdiction of any particular State of district, shall be in the district where the offender is found, or into which he is first brought." (Quoted from *Chandler v. United States of America*, United States Court of Appeals, First Circuit, December 3, 1948, p. 8.)

[308] *Chandler v. United States of America*, United States Court of Appeals, First Circuit decision, December 3, 1948, p. 4.

[309] Oscar R. Ewing Oral History Interview, April 30, 1969. Independence, Missouri: Harry S. Truman Presidential Library (NARA), op. cit.

[310] Memorandum from SA Guy Hottel FBI File 61–116, undated, August 19, 1948.

[311] Ibid.

[312] Ibid.

[313] Memorandum to J. Edgar Hoover from Special Agent Guy Hottel on Interview of Warrant Officer Catherine Samaha, August 23, 1948. College Park MD: National Archives and Records Administration (NARA). p. 4.

[314] Ibid.

[315] Ibid.

There is no corresponding documentation or trial testimony supporting Samaha's assertion that Mildred visited Algiers during the Nazi occupation of North Africa. Allied forces liberated Algiers in June of 1943. Gillars neither had a German passport at the time (she did not receive one until 1944 after an appeal by Koischwitz to Horst Cleinow) nor a sponsor to accompany her for such a long period to North Africa. It is indeed possible that Samaha mistakenly referred to her travels to Algiers in 1933–34 as part of Mildred's wartime exploits.

[316] Ibid.

[317] Ibid.

[318] Edwards, John Carver (1991) *Berlin Calling*, p. 5.

[319] Memorandum to J. Edgar Hoover from Special Agent Guy Hottel on Interview of Warrant Officer Catherine Samaha, op. cit. p. 3.

[320] Ibid.

[321] Ibid.

[322] *The New York Times*, August 22, 1948, p. 16.

[323] *Oakland Tribune*, Oakland CA, August 22, 1948, p. 1.

[324] *The Fresno Bee*, Fresno CA, August 24, 1948, p. 6.

[325] Ibid.

[326] *Oakland Tribune*, Oakland CA, August 22, 1948, p. 1.

[327] Ibid.

[328] *The Fresno Bee* Fresno CA, op. cit.

[329] District of Columbia Jail Commitment Card #78526, August 21, 1948 (NARA).

[330] *The Fresno Bee* Fresno CA op. cit.

[331] Handwritten note from Edna Mae Herrick to J. Edgar Hoover, FBI HQ files, College Park MD: National Archives.

[332] *Star-Beacon*, Ashtabula Ohio, November 24, 1995.

[333] Interrogation of Mildred Gillars at the office US Counterintelligence Corps in Berlin, April 2, 1946, p. 1, US Army Records, Archives II, College Park MD.

[334] District of Columbia Jail Commitment Card #78526, op. cit.

[335] FBI File Boston Field Office 61–222. Report of Interview with Joseph and William Hewitson, August 19, 1948, p. 3 (NARA).

[336] Photocopy of article in the *New York Daily Mirror*, July 16, 1961, Drew Pearson Papers, Austin TX: Lyndon B. Johnson Presidential Library (NARA).

[337] FBI File #62-31615-568—photocopy of Walter Winchell column in the *New York Daily Mirror*, April 23, 1947, p. 6 (NARA).

[338] Letter from Albert J. Lawlor to Drew Pearson, February 2, 1947. Drew Pearson Papers, Austin TX: Lyndon B. Johnson Presidential Library (NARA).

[339] *The Daily Register*, Harrisburg, Illinois, June 6, 1947. Pearson was not as sure about the Federal case against Iva Toguri D'Aquino (Tokyo Rose). Although the columnist was aware that there were two Axis Sallys; he noted that Tokyo Rose's case was substantially different: "There were four different Tokyo Roses, all broadcasting at various intervals to American troops in the Pacific.... We had no witnesses who saw any of the four Tokyo Roses broadcast. No Americans were in Japanese broadcasting stations where they could witness Jap radio. Furthermore, Tokyo Rose did not visit prisoner-of-war camps in Japan, as did Axis Sally in Germany." Nevertheless, Iva Toguri D'Aquino was convicted of treason on September 29, 1949. She was released on parole in January 1956. President Gerald R. Ford pardoned her in 1977.

[340] Drew Pearson Broadcast Script, undated. Drew Pearson Papers, Austin, TX: Lyndon B Johnson Presidential Library (NARA).

[341] Ibid.

[342] FBI File 61-39 FBI Interview with Homer Charles McNamara (NARA) August 23, 1948, p. 9.

[343] FBI File Philadelphia Field Office #61-180 Statement of John Patrick Butler August 24, 1948, pp. 5–6.

[344] FBI Internal Memorandum f from Special Agent in Charge Philadelphia to Special Agent in Charge Savannah October 26, 1948 (NARA).

[345] Ibid.

[346] Memorandum from Assistant Attorney General Alexander Campbell to FBI Director Hoover, December 20, 1948 (NARA).

[347] Memorandum from Acting Assistant Attorney General Alexander Campbell to FBI Director Hoover, August 9, 1948, p. 3 (NARA).

[348] Ibid.

[349] Ibid.

[350] FBI File 61-39 FBI Interview with Homer Charles McNamara (NARA) *op cit* p. 7.

[351] Memorandum from Acting Assistant Attorney General Alexander Campbell to FBI Director Hoover, August 9, 1948, op. cit.

[352] FBI Internal Memorandum, F. J. Baumgardner to H. B. Fletcher, undated (NARA).

[353] Ibid.

[354] 7970th CIC Group, Region VI, Sub-Region Passau Summary of Information,

January 12, 1949. US Military Records, College Park MD: NARA.

355 FBI Internal Memorandum, F. J. Baumgardner to H. B. Fletcher, undated (NARA). op. cit.

356 "Big Bad Bear," *Time*, January 11, 1932.

357 Glacier Bay Administrative History (US National Park Service website— www.nps.gov).

358 "No Sale," *Time*, September 22, 1947.

359 *The New York Times*, August 25, 1948.

360 *Conneaut News-Herald*, Conneaut, OH August 30, 1948.

361 Memorandum from SAC Guy Hottel to FBI Director J. Edgar Hoover, August 31, 1948, p. 1.

362 *Conneaut News-Herald*, Conneaut, OH. September 7, 1948.

363 Handwritten note of Mildred Gillars, August 24, 1948, DC District Jail records (NARA).

364 Letter from Mildred Gillars to Chief Justice of the US District Court for the District of Columbia, August 26, 1948 (NARA).

365 *Star-Beacon*, Ashtabula, Ohio, November 24, 1995.

366 Trial's End, *Time*, December 11, 1944.

367 Letter from Mildred Gillars to Judge Richmond B. Keech, August 30, 1948, FBI Files (NARA).

368 Letter from Mildred Gillars to John Holzworth, August 30, 1948, FBI Files (NARA).

369 *Conneaut News-Herald*, Conneaut, OH August 31, 1948.

370 Ibid.

371 *Chronicle-Telegram*, Elyria, Ohio September 7, 1948, p 10.

372 Ibid.

373 Ibid.

374 Ibid.

10. Destiny

375 *Burlington Daily Telegraph*, Burlington NC, February 7, 1949, p. 4.

376 Notes from Washington by Richard H. Rovere *The New Yorker*, February 26, 1949, pp. 80-81.

377 Andrew Tully, "Static Axis Sally of Nazi Radio Waves is Quiet Now," *El Paso Herald-Post*, El Paso TX, January 26, 1949, p. 3.

378 John Bartlow Martin, "The Trials of Axis Sally," *McCall's*, June 1949, p. 24.

379 Ibid.

380 *The New York Times*, January 25, 1949.

381 *Chicago Daily Tribune*, Chicago, IL January 25, 1949, p. 9.

382 "The Trials of Axis Sally," op. cit., p. 24.

383 Ibid., p. 114.

384 *Lima News*, Lima, OH, January 25, 1949.

385 *Lowell Sun*, Lowell, MA, January 25, 1949.

386 Schofield, William G., *Treason Trail*, Chicago: Rand McNally & Co. 1964,

pp. 149–50.

[387] Ibid.

[388] *Chicago Daily Tribune*, Chicago IL January 26, 1949.

[389] *The Evening Star*, Washington DC, January 26, 1949, p. A5.

[390] *The Evening Star*, Washington DC, January 26, 1949, p. A5.

[391] *The Evening Star*, Washington DC, January 26, 1949, p. A5.

[392] Schofield, op. cit., p. 155.

[393] *The Evening Star*, Washington DC, January 31, 1949, p. A1.

[394] *The New York Times*, February 1, 1949.

[395] Big Role, *Time*, February 7, 1949.

[396] Gillars v. United States, US Court of Appeals for the District of Columbia, October Term, 1949, No. 10.187, pp. 11–13.

[397] *The Stars and Stripes*, Darmstadt, Hesse, Germany, January 29, 1949, pp. 11.

[398] Written transcription of Federal Communication Commission Acetate Recordings made at Silver Hill, MD, on July 27, 1944. Washington DC: Manuscript Division, Library of Congress.

[399] *The Evening Star*, Washington DC, January 28, 1949, p. A5.

[400] *The Evening Star*, Washington DC, February 9, 1949, p. B1.

[401] Ibid.

[402] *The Evening Star*, Washington DC, February 11, 1949, p. B1.

[403] Edwards, John Carver. *Berlin Calling*, New York: Praeger, 1991, p. 94.

[404] United States Court of Appeals District of Columbia Circuit—Gillars v. United States, 182 F. 2d 962, Washington DC: NARA.

[405] Ibid. p. 95

[406] Ibid.

[407] Schofield, op. cit., p. 154.

[408] Ibid.

[409] *Cumberland Evening Times*, Cumberland, MD, February 9, 1949.

[410] *The Evening Star*, Washington DC, February 1, 1949, p. A1.

[411] *The Evening Star*, Washington DC, February 1, 1949, p. A1.

[412] Research notes for *The Trials of Axis Sally*, condensation of *US v. Gillars (Sisk)* trial transcript. John Bartlow Martin Papers, Washington DC: Library of Congress Manuscript Division, pp. 12-2.

[413] Research notes for *The Trials of Axis Sally*, condensation of *US v. Gillars (Sisk)* trial transcript pp. 15-2—16-2.

[414] Ibid. pp 17-2

[415] Ibid., pp. 22-2—23-2.

Ruth S. Montgomery achieved notoriety in 1965 as the best selling author of *A Gift of Prophecy*, the story of psychic Jeanne Dixon.

[416] Ibid.

[417] *New York Daily News*, New York, NY, February 9, 1949.

When the trials were not in session, the US government advised witnesses to find employment or face repatriation to Germany after the completion of their testimony. If the Justice Department required their services in a future trial, they would be brought back to the United States at government expense. For instance, Inga Doman found work as a governess in South Carolina and Adelbert Houben, who testified in the Chandler and Best trials as well, worked in a factory.

[418] Ibid.

[419] *Mansfield News Journal*, Mansfield OH, January 28, 1949, p. 12.

[420] *Mansfield News Journal*, Mansfield OH, January 31, 1949.

[421] *Charleston Daily Mail*, Charleston, WV, February 9, 1949.

[422] Ibid.

[423] Ibid.

[424] Ibid.

[425] Ibid.

[426] *Chicago Daily Tribune*, February 18, 1949.

[427] Scholield. op. cit., p. 162.

[428] Ibid.

[429] *The New York Times*, February 22, 1949.

[430] *The Star Beacon*, Ashtabula, OH, November 22, 1995, p. C1.

[431] Research notes for *The Trials of Axis Sally*, condensation of *US v. Gillars (Sisk)* trial transcript, op. cit. p. 38.

[432] Ibid p. 40

[433] Ibid pp. 44–5.

[434] Ibid p. 53

[435] Ibid p. 49

[436] Ibid. p. 57

[437] Ibid.

[438] *New York Daily News*, New York, NY, February 25, 1949, p. 40.

[439] *New York Daily News*, New York, NY, February 25, 1949, p. 3.

[440] Ibid. p. 40

[441] Research notes for *The Trials of Axis Sally*, condensation of *US v. Gillars (Sisk)* trial transcript, op. cit., p. 66.

[442] Ibid.

[443] *The Evening Star*, Washington DC, February 24, 1949, p. A1.

[444] Research notes for *The Trials of Axis Sally*, condensation of *US v. Gillars (Sisk)* trial transcript, op. cit., p. 38.

[445] *The Evening Star*, Washington DC, March 2, 1949, p. A3.

[446] *Chicago Daily Tribune*, Chicago IL, March 3, 1949, p. 2 & *The Evening Star*, Washington DC, March 2, 1949, p. A1.

[447] Research notes for *The Trials of Axis Sally*, condensation of *US v. Gillars (Sisk)* trial transcript, op. cit. pp. 60, 7-3.

[448] Ibid. p. 7

[449] Ibid. p. 10

[450] Ibid. p. 12

[451] *The Washington Post*, Washington DC, March 5, 1949, p. 4.

[452] *The Evening Star*, Washington DC, March 2, 1949, p. A6.

[453] *Chicago Daily Tribune*, Chicago IL, March 3, 1949, p. A2.

[454] Bergmeier and Lotz (1997), p 34.

11. Convicted
[455] Research notes for *The Trials of Axis Sally*, condensation of *US v. Gillars (Sisk)* trial transcript, p. 32-2.
[456] *The Evening Star*, Washington DC, March 8, 1949, pp. A1.
[457] Research notes for *The Trials of Axis Sally*, condensation of *US v. Gillars (Sisk)* trial transcript, p. 31-2.
[458] *The Evening Star*, Washington DC. March 8, 1949 op. cit.
[459] Schofield, William G., *Treason Trail*, Chicago: Rand McNally & Co. 1964, pp. 170.
[460] Ibid.
[461] *The Evening Star*, Washington DC, March 8, 1949, pp.A1.
[462] *Washington Times-Herald*, Washington DC, March 8, 1949, pp. 2.
[463] *The Washington Post*, Washington DC, March 8, 1949 pp. 2.
[464] *Washington Times-Herald*, Washington DC March 9, 1949 p 1.
[465] *The Evening Star*, Washington DC, March 8, 1949 pp. A4.
[466] Schofield, William G., *Treason Trail*, op. cit. pp 171.
   Although Coplon was convicted twice in Federal Court, both verdicts were overturned on appeal.
[467] Ibid.
[468] *The Evening Star*, Washington DC, March 8, 1949 pp. 4.
[469] *Washington Times-Herald*, Washington DC, March 8, 1949 pp. 2.
[470] *The Washington Post,* Washington DC, March 8, 1949 pp.2
[471] *The Evening Star*, Washington DC, March 8, 1949, pp. 4.
[472] Ibid.
[473] Schofield, William G., *Treason Trail,* op. cit. pp 171.
[474] Statement of the Case, *US v Gillars,* November 22, 1949, Washington DC: Charles Fahy Papers. Manuscript Division, Charles Fahy Papers, pp 42.
[475] *The Evening Star* Washington DC March 8 1949 pp. 4.
[476] Ibid.
[477] Statement of the Case, *US v Gillars,* November 22, 1949, Washington DC: Charles Fahy Papers. Manuscript Division, Charles Fahy Papers, pp 32.
[478] Ibid.
[479] Statement of the Case, *US v Gillars,* November 22, 1949, Washington DC: Charles Fahy Papers. Manuscript Division, Charles Fahy Papers, pp 31.
[480] *Nashua Telegraph,* Nashua, NH March 11, 1949 p. 4.
[481] "Shock for Sally", Newsweek, March 21, 1949, p 32.
[482] *Conneaut News-Herald*, Conneaut, OH March 11, 1949 p 1.
[483] *Lima News*, Lima OH, March 11, 1949, p 1.
[484] Ibid.
[485] Western Union telegram John M. Holzworth to Mildred Gillars, March 10, 1949, College Park MD: NARA.
[486] Schofield, William G., *Treason Trail,* op. cit., p. 172.

487 *Star-Beacon*, Ashtabula, OH, November 24, 1995 p. B1.

488 *Conneaut News-Herald,* Conneaut, OH March 25, 1949 p. 1.

489 *Star-Beacon*, Ashtabula, OH, November 24, 1995 p. B1.

490 Letter from Curtis Reid to Director, Department of Corrections DC, June 17, 1950 p. 3, Department of Justice files, NARA.

491 Note from the Chief Medical Officer to the Steward, DC District Jail, January 11, 1950, Department of Justice files, NARA.

492 Report of Injury to Inmates on Detail, DC District Jail, March 10, 1950, Department of Justice Files, NARA.

493 Letter from Col. Curtis Reid to Edna Mae Herrick, May 9, 1950, Department of Justice Files, College Park: NARA.

494 FBI File 114-1 report on Alien Property Custodian Matter RE: Stella Beatrice Irmgard Koischwitz, Renata Martha Gertrude Koischwitz and Helene Elizabeth Nina Koischwitz, Harry Eisenbrown. December 20, 1949, p. 3 College Park MD: NARA.

495 FBI File 114-24 report on Alien Property Custodian Matter RE: Stella Beatrice Irmgard Koischwitz, Renata Martha Gertrude Koischwitz and Helene Elizabeth Nina Koischwitz, Harry Eisenbrown, December 15, 1949, p 4, College Park MD: NARA.

496 Ibid.

497 Ibid.

498 Ibid. p 6.

499 Flynn, Elizabeth Gurley. *My Life as a Political Prisoner.* New York: International Publishers, 1963. p. 28.

500 Ibid. p 26.

501 Ibid. p 30.

502 Ibid. p 33.

503 Ibid. pp 36–37.

504 Ibid. p 83.

505 Admission Summary for Mildred Elizabeth Sisk, Federal Reformatory for Women at Alderson, WV. October 12, 1950, pp 2-3. Department of Justice Files, College Park MD: National Archives.

506 Elizabeth Gurley Flynn. op. cit., p 146.

507 Admission Summary for Mildred Elizabeth Sisk, Federal Reformatory for Women at Alderson, WV. October 12, 1950, pp 5-7 Department of Justice Files. College Park MD: National Archives.

508 Annual Review, Federal Reformatory for Women, Reg. No. 9711_W, March 27, 1953. Department of Justice Files, College Park MD: National Archives.

509 Ibid.

510 Ibid.

511 Ibid. p. 3.

512 Ibid.

513 Ibid.

514 Federal Reformatory for Women, Alderson, WV Prisoner's Visitor's form with

attached note, dated July 26, 1956. College Park MD: NARA.

[515] Letter from Mrs. Allan C. Long to John Nelson, Delaware OH: Ohio Wesleyan University Archives, March 30, 1966.

[516] Ibid. p 148.

[517] *Catholic University Bulletin*, Cleveland OH, July 21, 1961 Courtesy: Ohio Wesleyan University Historical Collection, Delaware OH.

[518] Letter from Mary L. Cottrill, Supervisor, Classification and Parole, Federal Reformatory for Women to Elbert H. Williams, Chief US Probation Officer, Columbus Ohio, December 19, 1960. US Department of Justice Files, College Park: NARA.

[519] Letter from Nina Kinsella, Warden, Alderson Prison to James V. Bennett, Director, Bureau of Prisons. March 13, 1961, Department of Justice Papers, College Park: NARA.

[520] Letter from Mary L. Cottrill, Supervisor Classification and Parole to Elbert Williams, Chief United States Probation Officer, Columbus OH, May 10, 1961, College Park: NARA.

12. Penitent

[521] *Berlin Calling* radio program, National Public Radio, produced by WUGA-FM, Athens GA.

[522] *Charleston Gazette*, Charleston, WV, July 11, 1961, p. 1.

[523] Ibid.

[524] *The Bridgeport Telegram*, Bridgeport, CT, July 11, 1961, p. 9.

[525] *The Star-News*, Pasadena, CA, July 10, 1961, p. 1.

The Roman Catholic religious order, the Sisters of the Poor Child Jesus, was founded in the Prussian town of Aachen in 1844. At the height of its missionary work, the order founded orphanages, seminaries, boarding houses and convents in Austria, Belgium, Holland, England and eventually the United States.

[526] *Charleston Gazette*, Charleston, WV, July 11, 1961, p. 1.

[527] Schofield, William G., *Treason Trail*, Chicago: Rand McNally & Co. 1964, p. 173.

[528] "Thought I Was Right, Says Sally," *Cleveland Plain-Dealer*, Cleveland OH, July 12, 1961. Courtesy: Ohio Wesleyan University Historical Collection.

[529] Ibid.

[530] Ibid.

[531] *Star-Beacon*, Ashtabula, OH, November 24, 1995, p. B1.

[532] Ibid.

[533] *Star-Beacon*, Ashtabula, OH, November 24, 1995, p. B1.

[534] Ibid.

[535] *Galveston Daily News*, Galveston, TX, September 10, 1961, p. 22.

[536] Ibid.

[537] Ibid.

[538] *Catholic University Bulletin*, Cleveland, OH, July 21, 1961. Courtesy: Ohio

Wesleyan University Historical Collection, Delaware OH.

[539] 1966 Probation Report of Mildred Gillars (Sisk), August 5, 1966, US Department of Justice Files, College Park MD: NARA.

[540] *Fresno Bee*, Fresno, CA March 5, 1967, p. 13 W.

Spicer's success brought a series of telephone calls from reporters at *Look, Life* and other national magazines who were trying to locate Axis Sally.

[541] Ibid.

[542] Ibid.

Jim Dury left Bishop Watterson in 1988, shortly before Mildred's death. He eventually returned to the school and teaches French there as of this writing.

One wonders if any of the drawings that adorned her apartment were in the hand of Otto Koischwitz, although it is doubtful that any of the Professor's works survived the war.

[543] Ibid.

[544] Letter from Wm. Merritt Miller, Probation Officer to Albert Wuhl, Chief Probation Officer, San Francisco, June 7, 1968, US Department of Justice Files, College Park MD: NARA.

[545] *The Bee*, Danville, VA, June 30, 1973, p. 4A.

[546] *Berlin Calling* radio program, National Public Radio, produced by WUGA-FM, Athens GA, Courtesy: John Carver Edwards.

[547] Ibid.

[548] Letter from Jim Dury to Author, March 22, 2009.

[549] Ibid.

[550] *Berlin Calling* radio program, National Public Radio, produced by WUGA-FM, Athens GA, Courtesy: John Carver Edwards.

[551] Author's interview with Iris Wiley, February 26, 2009.

[552] *Greeley Tribune*, Greeley, CO, January 19, 1977, p. 35.

[553] Ibid.

[554] "Infamous Nazi Ally Rests Amid Area Vets", *Columbus Dispatch*, Columbus OH, August 24, 2008, p. 1B.

[555] *Berlin Calling* radio program, National Public Radio, produced by WUGA-FM, Athens GA, Courtesy: John Carver Edwards.

[556] Author's interview with Iris Wiley, February 26, 2009.

[557] Mildred Gillars Death Certificate, Ohio Department of Health.

[558] "Infamous Nazi Ally Rests Amid Area Vets", *Columbus Dispatch*, Columbus OH, August 24, 2008, p. 1B.

[559] *Star-Beacon*, Ashtabula, OH, November 24, 1988, p. B3.

[560] *The New York Times*, New York, NY, July 2, 1988.

[561] Ibid.

[562] "World War II's 'Axis Sally' is Dead at 87," *Columbus Dispatch*, Columbus, OH, July 1, 1988, p. 1C.

[563] *Star-Beacon*, Ashtabula, OH, November 24, 1995, p. B1.

[564] "Life of 'Axis Sally' Changed When She Met Up With Nuns', *Columbus*

Dispatch, Columbus OH, July 21, 1988, p. 6A.
[565] *Berlin Calling radio program*, National Public Radio, produced by WUGA-FM, Athens GA, Courtesy: John Carver Edwards.
[566] Ibid.
[567] Ibid.

Bibliography

Primary sources

Author's interviews: Jim Dury, James Sauer, Helene Anne Spicer, Iris Wiley

Birth Certificate of Mildred Elizabeth Sisk, State of Maine

College Transcript of Mildred Elizabeth Gillars, Ohio Wesleyan University

Death Certificate of Mildred Elizabeth Gillars, State of Ohio

Death Certificate of Robert B. Gillars, State of Ohio

Diplomatic List of the British Foreign Office (1944), courtesy British Foreign and Commonwealth Office

Divorce Decree *Sisk v. Sisk*, State of Maine, Maine State Archives, May 1, 1907

The Evening Star Photo Archives, District of Columbia Library, Washingtoniana Division, Washington DC

German Foreign Office Archives: Political Radio Department at the Bundesarchiv, Berlin, Germany. Memorandum from Dr Markus Timmler, Radio and Culture Department of the German Foreign Office, March 20, 1940 *(BA Bln R 901 Nr. 73166 Handakte Dr. Timmler (1940–1941) Bl. 34-42 Durschlag einer Stellungnahme AA Kult. R vom 20.3.1940 fur Dr. Timmler, Verbindungsstelle der Abt. Kult R des AA im Funkhaus zu Sprecherfragen)*

Joseph Goebbels, "Nation, Rise Up, and Let the Storm Break Loose," translated from "Nun, Volk steh auf, und Sturm brich los! Rede im Berliner Sportpalast," *Der steile Aufstieg* (Munich: Zentralverlag der NSDAP, 1944) Courtesy: German Propaganda Archive, Calvin College.

Le Bijou, 1922/1923 Ohio Wesleyan University Historical Collection, Delaware OH: Ohio Wesleyan University

Letter of Mrs. Dorothy Long (Ohio Wesleyan Magazine) to John Nelson, March 30, 1966. Delaware Ohio: Ohio Wesleyan University Historical Collection.

Memoranda to President Harry S. Truman, January 1947 regarding "Axis Sally," Independence MO: Truman Presidential Library.

Ohio Wesleyan Alumni Journal, 1922 Delaware OH: Ohio Wesleyan University Historical Collection

Oscar R. Ewing Oral History Interview, April 30, 1969. Independence MO: Truman Presidential Library.

Charles Fahy papers, Associate Judge of the United States Court of Appeals for the District of Columbia, Library of Congress Manuscript Division, Washington DC: Library of Congress.

Research Notes for "The Trials of Axis Sally," John Bartlow Martin Papers, Washington DC: Library of Congress Manuscript Division.

The Tattler, Conneaut High School, Conneaut, Ohio 1917, Courtesy: Conneaut Public Library

The Telegraph, Ohio Wesleyan University newspaper, Ohio Wesleyan Historical Collection, Delaware, OH: Ohio Wesleyan University, 1949

United States Court of Appeals for the District of Columbia decision. *Gillars v US*. October Term: 1949, No. 10,187, Washington DC: National Archives and Records Administration.

United States Department of Justice, FBI Files Released by Interagency Working Group Class #061, File #10988, Section 001, Box #008— Treason. College Park MD: National Archives and Records Administration.

United States Department of Justice, FBI Files Released by Interagency Working Group Class #065, File #55501, Section 001, Box #169— Espionage. College Park MD: National Archives and Records Administration.

United States Department of Justice FBI Files Released by Interagency Working Group; Walter Winchell from the National Archives

United States Department of Justice Press Release on the Indictment of Max Otto Koischwicz, Edward Delaney, Constance Drexel, Ezra Pound, Robert H. Best, Frederick W. Kaltenbach, Jane Anderson and Douglas Chandler, July 26, 1943. Francis Biddle Papers,

Georgetown University, Washington DC
United States District Court of the Central District of California indict-
    ment SA CR 05-254(A), United States v. Adam Gadahn, October
    2005, www.usdoj.gov/opa/documents

**The National Archives' "Notorious Offenders" files on Axis Sally
contain FBI interviews regarding the case as follows:**

FBI Interviews with former prisoners of war:
Carl Baker
Frank Beasley
Robert V. Begany,
James P. Caparell
Allan V. Clark
Andrew Coronato
Rudy Chestnut
Harvey M. Crosthwaite
Gunner D. Drangsholt
Robert Ehalt
Michael Evanick
Clarence Marion Gale
A.C. Gladson
Gilbert Lee Hansford
Paul G. Kestel
John T. Lynsky
Eugene McCarthy
Grover McKinley
Homer McNamara Jr.
Donald P. Rutter
Alan Tappenden
Seaborn Warren
Carl Zimmerman

FBI Interviews with former Reichsradio colleagues:
Kurt Altwein
Mario Balto
Werner Berger
Horst Cleinow

Benny de Weille
Adelbert Houben
Franz 'Teddy' Kleindin
Walter Leschetisky
Hans von Richter
Otto Tittmann
Gerd Wagner

Other Interviews:
Joseph Hewitson
Dr. Henry Kaufman
Thelma Homer
Catherine Samaha
Richard R. Shipley
United States Military Records (Counter-Intelligence Corps) regarding
    Axis Sally (Rita Luisa Zucca), US Military Records Collection,
    College Park: MD: NARA
United States Military Records (Counter-Intelligence Corps) regarding
    Axis Sally (Mildred Sisk Gillars), US Military Records Collection,
    College Park: MD: NARA

US Army Intelligence (Counter-Intelligence Corps) interviews with:
Erwin Christiani
Mildred Gillars
Rita Zucca

Primary sources: audio and transcripts

Audio: "Berlin Calling," National Public Radio produced by WUGA-
    FM, Athens, GA. Courtesy: John Carver Edwards.
Audio: "Medical Reports" broadcast, February 26, 1944, College Park,
    MD: National Archives and Records Administration.
Audio: "Midge at the Mike" broadcast, May 18, 1943, College Park
    MD: National Archives and Records Administration.
Audio: "Survivors of the Invasion Front" broadcast, August 22, 1944,
    College Park: National Archives and Records Administration.
Audio: "The Broadcasts of Lord Haw Haw" broadcast, c. May 1940.
    Courtesy: Earthstation One.

Written transcript of "Home Sweet Home" broadcast, July 27, 1944. Monitored and recorded by the Federal Communications Commission at Silver Hill, MD. Washington DC: Library of Congress Manuscript Division.

Written transcript of "Medical Reports" broadcast on October 6, 1944. Monitored and recorded by the Federal Communications Commission at Silver Hill, MD. Washington DC: Library of Congress Manuscript Division.

Secondary sources

Anonymous (2003) *A Woman in Berlin: Eight Weeks in the Conquered City*. New York: Metropolitan Books originally published 1953.

Bergmeier, Horst J. P. and Lotz, Rainer E. (1997) *Hitler's Airwaves*, New Haven and London: Yale University Press.

Beevor, Antony (2002) *The Fall of Berlin 1945*. New York: Penguin Books.

Boveri , Margret (1961) *Treason in the 20th Century*. New York: G.P. Putnam's Sons.

Dallas, Gregor (2005) *1945: The War That Never Ended*. New Haven: Yale University Press.

Davidson, Edward and Manning, Dale (1999) *Chronology of World War Two*, London: Cassell.

Diem, William Roy and Hunter, Rollin Clarence *The Story of Speech at Ohio Wesleyan*.

Dobb, Michael (2005) *Saboteurs: The Nazi Raid on America*. New York: Vintage.

Edwards, John Carver (1991) *Berlin Calling*, New York: Praeger.

Evans, Richard J. (2009) *The Third Reich at War*. New York: The Penguin Press.

Flynn, Elizabeth Gurley (1963) *My Life as a Political Prisoner*, New York: International Publishers.

Gabler, Neal. (1995) *Winchell: Gossip, Power and the Culture of Celebrity*. New York: Vintage Books.

Gilbert, Martin. (2006) *Kristallnacht* New York: HarperCollins

Hart, Russell and Hart, Stephen (2002) *Essential Histories: The Second World War (6): Northwest Europe 1944-1945*. Oxford: Osprey Publishing

Herf, Jeffrey (2006) *The Jewish Enemy: Nazi Propaganda During*

World War II and During the Holocaust, Cambridge, MA: Harvard Belknap

Herzstein, Robert Edwin (1978) *The War That Hitler Won: The Most Infamous Propaganda Campaign in History*, New York: Paragon House (1986 edition)

Hickman, Tom (1996) *What Did You Do in the War, Auntie? The BBC at War, 1939–1945.* London: BBC Publishing.

Howe, Russell Warren (1990) The *Hunt for "Tokyo Rose"*, Lanham MD: Madison Books.

Judt, Tony (2005) *Postwar: A History of Europe since 1945.* New York: Penguin Press.

Kantor, Michael and Maslon, Laurence (2004) *Broadway: The American Musical.* New York: Bulfinch Press,

Keiper, Gerhard & Kroger, Martin (eds.), (2005) *Biographisches Handbuch des deutschen äuswartigan Dienstes 1941–45*, Band 2

Koonz, Claudia (2003) *The Nazi Conscience.* Cambridge, MA: Belknap Press of Harvard University Press

Kreimeier, Klaus (1996) *The UFA Story: A History of Germany's Greatest Film Company 1918-1945* New York: Hill & Wang.

Large, David Clay (2000) *Berlin* New York: Basic Books

Liebovitz, Liel and Miller, Matthew (2009) *Lili Marlene; The Soldiers' Song of World War II* New York: W. W. Norton & Company

MacDonogh, Giles (2007) *After The Reich: The Brutal History of the Allied Occupation.* New York: Basic Books

Martland, Peter (2003) *Lord Haw Haw: The English Voice of Nazi Germany.* Latham, Maryland: Scarecrow Press.

Murphy, Sean (2003) *Letting the Side Down: British Traitors of the Second World War.* Stroud, Gloucestershire UK: Sutton Publishing Ltd.

Newcourt-Nowodworski, Stanley (2005) *Black Propaganda in the Second World War* Phoenix Mill, Gloucestershire UK: Sutton Publishing

Overy, Richard (2001) *Interrogations: The Nazi Elite in Allied Hands 1945.* New York: Penguin.

Powers, Thomas (2004) *Intelligence Wars: American Secret History from Hitler to Al-Qaeda.* New York: Random House.

Read, Anthony and Fisher, David (1992) *The Fall of Berlin.* New York:

W.W. Norton.

Reuth, Ralf Georg (1993) *Goebbels*, trans. Krishna Winston. Orlando: Harcourt.

Rousso, Henry (1991) *The Vichy Syndrome*, Cambridge: Harvard University Press

Russell, William (2003) *Berlin Embassy*, London: Elliott & Thompson, reprinted from 1940 edition

Schofield, William G. (William Greenough) (1964) *Treason Trail* Chicago: Rand McNally.

Shirer, William L. (2005 edition) *Berlin Diary: The Journal of a Foreign Correspondent 1934–41*. New York: Black Dog & Leventhal, 2005 edition.

Simpson, Christopher.(1988) *Blowback: The First Full Account of America's Recruitment of Nazis and its Disastrous Effects on the Cold War, our Domestic and Foreign Policy*. New York: Weidenfeld & Nicolson

Simpson, Christopher. (1995) *The Splendid Blond Beast: Money, Law and Genocide in the Twentieth Century*, Monroe, ME: Common Courage Press.

Sterling, Christopher H. editor (2004) *Museum of Broadcast Communication's Encyclopedia of Radio Volume 1*, New York: Fitzroy Dearborn.

Taylor, Paul Beekman. (2004) *Gurdjieff's America* Lighthouse Editions, Ltd

Taylor, Paul Beekman. (1998) *Shadows of Heaven: Gurdjieff and Toomer*. San Francisco: Samuel Weiser

Tegel, Susan (2007) *Nazis and the Cinema* New York: Hambledon Continuum

Weber, Ronald. (2006) *News of Paris*, Chicago: Ivan R. Dee

West, Rebecca (2000) *The Meaning of Treason*. London: Phoenix Press (originally published by Macmillan in 1949).

Wistrich, Robert (1984) *Who's Who in Nazi Germany* New York: Bonanza.

Yahil, Leni (1990) *The Holocaust: The Fate of European Jewry*. New York: Oxford University Press.

Yellin, Emily (2004) *Our Mothers' War: American Women at Home an at the Front in World War II*, New York: Free Press

Periodicals and journals
Anon., "Big Bad Bear," *Time,* January 11, 1932.
Anon., "Kiss Me No More," *Newsweek,* July 17, 1961.
Anon., "Koischwicz Broadcasts Nazi Propaganda to America," *The Hour,* July 20, 1940.
Anon., "New Part for Sally" *Newsweek,* February 7, 1949.
Anon., "No Sale," *Time,* September 22, 1947.
Anon, "Seltsamer Haufe," *Der Spiegel,* vol. 9, 1949
Anon., "Sally and Rose," *Time,* August 30, 1948.
Anon., "Shock for Sally," *Newsweek,* March 21, 1949.
Anon., "Trials End," *Time,* December 11, 1944.
Anon., "True to the Red, White and Blue," *Time,* March 7, 1949.
Anon., "Unhalting Nazis," *Time,* December 7, 1936
Martin, John Bartlow, "The Trials of Axis Sally," *McCall's,* June 1949
Rovere, Richard, "Letter from Washington," *New Yorker,* February 26, 1949.
Shirer, William L., "The American Radio Traitors," *Harper's,* vol. 87, October 1943
Van Dyne, Cpl. Edward. "No Other Gal Like Axis Sal," *Saturday Evening Post,* January 15, 1944. Young, James Carruthers "An Experiment at Fountainbleau: A Personal Reminiscence," *Gurdjieff International Review,* summer 1995.

Newspaper and Wire Services
Associated Press
Baltimore Sun, Baltimore MD
Boston Herald, Boston MA
Catholic University Bulletin, Cleveland OH
Charleston Daily Mail, Charleston WV
Chicago Daily Tribune, Chicago IL
Chronicle-Telegram, Elyria OH
Cleveland Plain-Dealer, Cleveland OH
Columbus Citizen, Columbus OH
Columbus Dispatch, Columbus OH
Conneaut Herald, Conneaut, OH
El Paso Herald Post, El Paso TX
Evening Courier, Camden NJ
Fresno Bee, Fresno CA

International News Service
Lima News, Lima OH
Lowell Sun, Lowell MA
Mansfield News-Journal, Mansfield OH
Oakland Tribune, Oakland CA
Portland Press-Herald, Portland ME
Rocky Mountain News, Denver, CO
Syracuse Herald, Syracuse NY
The New York Mirror, New York NY
The Daily News, New York NY
The Philadelphia Inquirer, Philadelphia PA
The New York Times, New York NY
The Washington Post, Washington DC
The Washington Times-Herald, Washington DC
The Evening Star, Washington DC
The Star-Beacon, Ashtabula OH
The Stars and Stripes, Darmstadt, Hesse, Germany
The Stars and Stripes, Rome, Italy
The Toronto Star, Toronto, Ontario
Times-Recorder, Zanesville, OH
United Press International

Index